Someth

Something to Declare

Selections from International Literature

Christine McClymont
Patrick O'Rourke
Julie Prest
Peter Prest
Glen Sorestad

OXFORD
UNIVERSITY PRESS

OXFORD
UNIVERSITY PRESS

70 Wynford Drive, Don Mills, Ontario M3C 1J9
www.oupcan.com

Oxford University Press is a department of the University of Oxford.
It furthers the University's objective of excellence in research, scholarship,
and education by publishing worldwide in

Oxford New York

Athens Auckland Bangkok Bogotá Buenos Aires Calcutta
Cape Town Chennai Dar es Salaam Delhi Florence Hong Kong Istanbul
Karachi Kuala Lumpur Madrid Melbourne Mexico City Mumbai
Nairobi Paris São Paulo Singapore Taipei Tokyo Toronto Warsaw

with associated companies in Berlin Ibadan

Oxford is a trade mark of Oxford University Press
in the UK and in certain other countries

Published in Canada
by Oxford University Press

Copyright © Oxford University Press Canada 1994

The moral rights of the author have been asserted

Database right Oxford University Press (maker)

First published 1994

Canadian Cataloguing in Publication Data

Main entry under title:
Something to declare: selections from international literature

1. Literature, Modern – 20th century. I. McClymont, Christine
PN6014.S65 1994   808.8'0045   C93-095248-0

ISBN 0-19-540998-1

Illustrator: Russ Willms
Design: Michael van Elsen Design Inc. / Marie Bartholomew

2 3 4 5 02 01 00 99

This book is printed on permanent (acid-free) paper ♾
Printed and bound in Canada by The Bryant Press

Table of Contents

Acknowledgements

Thanks to the following educators for their constructive comments in reviewing the manuscript:

Nora Allingham, City Adult Learning Centre, Toronto, Ontario

Lynn Archer, Surrey School District, Surrey, British Columbia

Vicky Armanios, Harbord Collegiate Institute, Toronto, Ontario

Elliott Beharrell, Dr. F.J. Donevan Collegiate Institute, Oshawa, Ontario

Bil Chinn, Edmonton Public Schools, Edmonton, Alberta

Jim O'Connell, Mount Douglas Secondary School, Victoria, British Columbia

Margaret Young, Halifax West High School, Halifax, Nova Scotia

Special thanks are due to students at the following schools for class-testing the selections:

Mount Douglas Secondary School, Victoria, B.C.

Dr. F.J. Donevan Collegiate Institute, Oshawa, Ontario

Harbord Collegiate Institute, Toronto, Ontario

City Adult Learning Centre, Toronto, Ontario

Preface

Something to Declare
The title of this anthology was inspired by the poem "Limbo Dancer at Immigration" by John Agard. We imagined writers crossing borders— like Agard's provocative limbo dancer—and wondered what they would reply to the question, "Anything to declare?" Surely the answer would be "Something, naturally. Read my books and get the message!" Of course, when it comes to literature, there should be no borders. All it takes for a successful crossing is a publisher, readers eager to explore new horizons, and enlightened customs officials.

Selections from International Literature
The fiction, poetry and non-fiction in this anthology come from all the world's continents and many of its countries. Many of the pieces originate in lands that were part of the British Empire, and are written in English. Others have hurdled the language barrier, thanks to the devotion of their translators. The term "international"—with its connotations of mingling and cooperating—seems particularly suitable. "Selections" recognizes the fact that we have only been able to scratch the surface of global literature.

The Writers Themselves
While their works represent the writers more than adequately, we couldn't help being fascinated by the details of their lives. Some writers have other jobs, like ranching in Saskatchewan or running a sugar company in Guyana. Some are famous Nobel Prize winners, whereas others are almost unknown. Some are happily rooted at home, others have been forced to live in exile, and a few have died. Writers are the human link in international literature, and their writings are testimony to the human spirit. Their biographies appear in the back of the book.

Conversations, Promises, Rumours, Roots, Clashes, Visions

We grouped the literature under these loose theme titles so that readers could easily compare treatments of similar subjects from different parts of the globe. In *Conversations*, for example, a Canadian story about a mother and her rebellious daughter appears side by side with a Japanese story about a father and son. In *Roots*, two cross-cultural encounters are contrasted, one from India, the other from Australia. "Passport to Themes," at the back of the book, takes a more detailed look at these and other thematic groupings.

A Footnote

Rather than printing footnotes to foreign terms, we have provided brief translations and definitions at the end of the story, poem, or non-fiction piece.

CONVERSATIONS

Eighteen,
and I know
no more of time

Growing up

SHUNTARŌ TANIKAWA

THREE, and
There is no past for me.

Five, and
My past reaches to yesterday.

Seven, and
My past reaches to my topknot.

Eleven, and
My past reaches to the dinosaur.

Fourteen, and
My past is as the textbooks say.

Sixteen, and
I stare timidly at the past's infinity.

Eighteen, and
I know no more of time.

Translated by Geoffrey Bownas
and Anthony Thwaite

The topknot, now outdated in Japan, survives as the hairstyle of Sumo wrestlers.

Half a Day

NAGUIB MAHFOUZ

Wearing his new tarboosh (a red felt cap with a silk tassel), a boy sets out for a very unusual first day at school.

I proceeded alongside my father, clutching his right hand, running to keep up with the long strides he was taking. All my clothes were new: the black shoes, the green school uniform, and the red tarboosh. My delight in my new clothes, however, was not altogether unmarred, for this was no feast day but the day on which I was to be cast into school for the first time.

My mother stood at the window watching our progress, and I would turn toward her from time to time, as though appealing for help. We walked along a street lined with gardens; on both sides were extensive fields planted with crops, prickly pears, henna trees, and a few date palms.

"Why school?" I challenged my father openly. "I shall never do anything to annoy you."

"I'm not punishing you," he said laughing. "School's not a punishment. It's the factory that makes useful men out of boys. Don't you want to be like your father and brothers?"

I was not convinced. I did not believe there was really any good to be had in tearing me away from the intimacy of my home and throwing me into this building that stood at the end of the road like some huge, high-walled fortress, exceedingly stern and grim.

When we arrived at the gate we could see the courtyard, vast and crammed full of boys and girls. "Go in by yourself," said my father, "and join them. Put a smile on your face and be a good example to others."

I hesitated and clung to his hand, but he gently pushed me from him. "Be a man," he said. "Today you truly begin life. You will find me waiting for you when it's time to leave."

I took a few steps, then stopped and looked but saw nothing. Then the faces of boys and girls came into view. I did not know a single one of them, and none of them knew me. I felt I was a stranger who had lost his way. But glances of curiosity were directed toward me, and one boy approached and asked, "Who brought you?"

"My father," I whispered.

"My father's dead," he said quite simply.

I did not know what to say. The gate was closed, letting out a pitiable screech. Some of the children burst into tears. The bell rang. A lady came along, followed by a group of men. The men began sorting us into ranks. We were formed into an intricate pattern in the great court-yard surrounded on three sides by high buildings of several floors; from each floor we were overlooked by a long balcony roofed in wood.

"This is your new home," said the woman. "Here too there are mothers and fathers. Here there is everything that is enjoyable and beneficial to knowledge and religion. Dry your tears and face life joyfully."

We submitted to the facts, and this submission brought a sort of contentment. Living beings were drawn to other living beings, and from the first moments my heart made friends with such boys as were to be my friends and fell in love with such girls as I was to be in love with, so that it seemed my misgivings had had no basis. I had never imagined school would have this rich variety. We played all sorts of different games: swings, the vaulting horse, ball games. In the music room we chanted our first songs. We also had our first introduction to language. We saw a globe of the Earth, which revolved and showed the various continents and countries. We started learning the numbers.

4

The story of the Creator of the universe was read to us, we were told of His present world and of His Hereafter, and we heard examples of what He said. We ate delicious food, took a little nap, and woke up to go on with friendship and love, play and learning.

As our path revealed itself to us, however, we did not find it as totally sweet and unclouded as we had presumed. Dust-laden winds and unexpected accidents came about suddenly, so we had to be watchful, at the ready, and very patient. It was not all a matter of playing and fooling around. Rivalries could bring about pain and hatred or give rise to fighting. And while the lady would sometimes smile, she would often scowl and scold. Even more frequently she would resort to physical punishment.

In addition, the time for changing one's mind was over and gone and there was no question of ever returning to the paradise of home. Nothing lay ahead of us but exertion, struggle, and perseverance. Those who were able took advantage of the opportunities for success and happiness that presented themselves amid the worries.

The bell rang announcing the passing of the day and the end of work. The throngs of children rushed toward the gate, which was opened again. I bade farewell to friends and sweethearts and passed through the gate. I peered around but found no trace of my father, who had promised to be there. I stepped aside to wait. When I had waited for a long time without avail, I decided to return home on my own. After I had taken a few steps, a middle-aged man passed by, and I realized at once that I knew him. He came toward me, smiling, and shook me by the hand, saying, "It's a long time since we last met—how are you?"

With a nod of my head, I agreed with him and in turn asked, "And you, how are you?"

"As you can see, not all that good, the Almighty be praised!"

Again he shook me by the hand and went off. I proceeded a few steps, then came to a startled halt. Good Lord! Where was the street lined with gardens? Where had it disappeared to? When did all these vehicles invade it? And when did all these hordes of humanity come to rest upon its surface? How did these hills of refuse come to cover its sides? And where were the fields that bordered it? High buildings had taken over, the street surged with children, and disturbing noises shook the air. At various points stood conjurers showing off their tricks and making snakes appear from baskets. Then there was a band announcing the opening of a circus, with clowns and weight lifters walking in front. A line of trucks carrying central security troops crawled majestically by. The siren of a fire engine shrieked, and it was not clear

5

how the vehicle would cleave its way to reach the blazing fire. A battle raged between a taxi driver and his passenger, while the passenger's wife called out for help and no one answered. Good God! I was in a daze. My head spun. I almost went crazy. How could all this have happened in half a day, between early morning and sunset? I would find the answer at home with my father. But where was my home? I could see only tall buildings and hordes of people. I hastened on to the crossroads between the gardens and Abu Khoda. I had to cross Abu Khoda to reach my house, but the stream of cars would not let up. The fire engine's siren was shrieking at full pitch as it moved at a snail's pace, and I said to myself, "Let the fire take its pleasure in what it consumes." Extremely irritated, I wondered when I would be able to cross. I stood there a long time, until the young lad employed at the ironing shop on the corner came up to me. He stretched out his arm and said gallantly, "Grandpa, let me take you across."

Translated by Denys Johnson-Davies

Evening Walk

GARY SOTO

My daughter runs outside to busy
Herself with tiny cakes of mud.
"It's important," she says,
Not wanting to hear my poor stories again.
Still I drag her to the car
And the short climb to the Berkeley
Hills, for gardens are in bloom,
Red thing and yellow this and that.
Trees with rootfuls of clouds
Line the walk. "They're older than me,"
I say, and she won't look at them
Or the grandma houses,
Quaint as tea cups.

The rich seem never to come out
Of their houses. They never sit on
Lawns, or bang a ball against
The garage door, or water the green strip
Along the street—hose in one hand,
Can of beer in the other.
At our place, the flowers fall
When we turn a hose on them
—even the pepper tree, rigged
With wire and rope, fell over
Like the neck of a sick giraffe.

I talk and talk. I say the poor
Rave about the color orange
And the rich yammer over egg-white.
I put this to Mariko, steps ahead,
A plucked branch dragging in her hand,
And begin again, a bore to the end.
When I was like you, I picked
Grapes like nobody's business . . .

She starts to skip. I walk faster,
Loud as a fool. When I was a kid,
I lugged oranges and shared plums with Okies . . .
But she's on the run, the branch
Fluttering like a green fire
Because the corner is up ahead
And an evening without me
Can't be far beyond.

"Okies" was the derogatory name given to migrant farm workers forced to leave
Oklahoma during the depression of the 1930s.

Anxiety

GRACE PALEY

Did you ever wish you could just lean out of your window and give a little advice to the passers-by?

The young fathers are waiting outside the school. What curly heads! Such graceful brown mustaches. They're sitting on their haunches eating pizza and exchanging information. They're waiting for the 3 p.m. bell. It's springtime, the season of first looking out the window. I have a window box of greenhouse marigolds. The young fathers can be seen through the ferny leaves.

The bell rings. The children fall out of school, tumbling through the open door. One of the fathers sees his child. A small girl. Is she Chinese? A little. Up u-u-p, he says, and hoists her to his shoulders. U-u-p, says the second father, and hoists his little boy. The little boy sits on top of his father's head for a couple of seconds before sliding to his shoulders. Very funny, says the father.

They start off down the street, right under and past my window. The two children are still laughing. They try to whisper a secret. The fathers haven't finished their conversation. The frailer father is uncomfortable; his little girl wiggles too much.

Stop it this minute, he says.

Oink oink, says the little girl.

What'd you say?

Oink oink, she says.

The young father says What! three times. Then he seizes the child, raises her high above his head, and sets her hard on her feet.

What'd I do so bad, she says, rubbing her ankle.

Just hold my hand, screams the frail and angry father.

I lean far out the window. Stop! Stop! I cry.

The young father turns, shading his eyes, but sees. What? he says.

9

His friend says, Hey? Who's that? He probably thinks I'm a family friend, a teacher maybe.

Who're you? he says.

I move the pots of marigolds aside. Then I'm able to lean on my elbow way out into unshadowed visibility. Once, not too long ago, the tenements were speckled with women like me in every third window up to the fifth story, calling the children from play to receive orders and instruction. This memory enables me to say strictly, Young man, I am an older person who feels free because of that to ask questions and give advice.

Oh? he says, laughs with a little embarrassment, says to his friend, Shoot if you will that old gray head. But he's joking, I know, because he has established himself, legs apart, hands behind his back, his neck arched to see and hear me out.

How old are you? I call. About thirty or so?

Thirty-three.

First I want to say you're about a generation ahead of your father in your attitude and behavior toward your child.

Really? Well? Anything else, ma'am.

Son, I said, leaning another two, three dangerous inches toward him. Son, I must tell you that madmen intend to destroy this beautifully made planet. That the murder of our children by these men has got to become a terror and a sorrow to you, and starting now, it had better interfere with any daily pleasure.

Speech speech, he called.

I waited a minute, but he continued to look up. So, I said, I can tell by your general appearance and loping walk that you agree with me.

I do, he said, winking at his friend; but turning a serious face to mine, he said again, Yes, yes, I do.

Well then, why did you become so angry at that little girl whose future is like a film which suddenly cuts to white. Why did you nearly slam this little doomed person to the ground in your uncontrollable anger.

Let's not go too far, said the young father. She *was* jumping around on my poor back and hollering oink oink.

When were you angriest—when she wiggled and jumped or when she said oink?

He scratched his wonderful head of dark well-cut hair. I guess when she said oink.

Have you ever said oink oink? Think carefully. Years ago, perhaps?

No. Well maybe. Maybe.

Whom did you refer to in this way?

He laughed. He called to his friend, Hey Ken, this old person's got something. The cops. In a demonstration. Oink oink, he said, remembering, laughing.

The little girl smiled and said, Oink oink.

Shut up, he said.

What do you deduce from this?

That I was angry at Rosie because she was dealing with me as though I was a figure of authority, and it's not my thing, never has been, never will be.

I could see his happiness, his nice grin, as he remembered this.

So, I continued, since those children are such lovely examples of what may well be the last generation of humankind, why don't you start all over again, right from the school door, as though none of this had ever happened.

Thank you, said the young father. Thank you. It would be nice to be a horse, he said, grabbing little Rosie's hand. Come on Rosie, let's go. I don't have all day.

U-up, says the first father. U-up, says the second.

Giddap, shout the children, and the fathers yell neigh neigh, as horses do. The children kick their fathers' horsechests, screaming giddap giddap, and they gallop wildly westward.

I lean way out to cry once more, Be careful! Stop! But they've gone too far. Oh, anyone would love to be a fierce fast horse carrying a beloved beautiful rider, but they are galloping toward one of the most dangerous street corners in the world. And they may live beyond that trisection across other dangerous avenues.

So I must shut the window after patting the April-cooled marigolds with their rusty smell of summer. Then I sit in the nice light and wonder how to make sure that they gallop safely home through the airy scary dreams of scientists and the bulky dreams of automakers. I wish I could see just how they sit down at their kitchen tables for a healthy snack (orange juice or milk and cookies) before going out into the new spring afternoon to play.

O What Venerable and Reverend Creatures

SHARON BUTALA

A discouraged mother and her rebellious daughter are locked in a painful tug-of-war—and it seems that neither can win.

He said it was a heart attack," Meredith said. She couldn't seem to fit the phone receiver onto the cradle. "He said she was bringing dessert to the table and she started to stagger. She sat down and then she said, 'oh,' and fell over." Meredith suddenly let go of the receiver and balled the napkin she had been holding, pressing it against her face, trying to stifle the noise she could hear herself making. She heard Bill move, felt his arm go around her, felt his hand smoothing her hair.

"Poor girl," he said. "Poor girl."

There was a rustling in the doorway. Stacey. Stacey would have to be told. Meredith wiped her eyes with the napkin and stood back from Bill who had turned to the door. Stacey leaned against the door frame, one hand raised to her shoulder, her thin, nicotine-stained fingers twisting a lock of thick, curly brown hair that hung uncombed in a mass around her shoulders. Her eyes glittered. The petulance of her expression made her look younger than eighteen.

"Who was that?" she asked, looking at the phone rather than them. Even when she was in a rage or coldly withdrawn from them, she could not change the startling depth and resonance of her voice. It was the voice of a great stage actress.

"Your Grandpa Robertson," Bill said. "Your grandmother is dead." Meredith put her hand on Bill's arm.

"About two hours ago," she said to her daughter and tried to think of something to add that might comfort Stacey, knowing at the same time the futility of this. Stacey's expression, held so carefully false for so long, wavered and she took a step into the room, staring at her mother, her eyes deepening to some infinite vision of horror.

"Oh," she said. "Oh."

Meredith put her hand out to Stacey, who, remembering herself, stiffened theatrically and made as though to back away.

Bill said suddenly, impatiently, "We can get the first flight to Regina in the morning. I'll start making arrangements." He patted Meredith's shoulder, then skirted the table, passed Stacey and paused in the doorway. "You'd better start packing, Stacey," he said. "You're coming too."

Meredith could see the abrupt shine of sweat on Stacey's neck as she lifted her chin. They watched her, Bill indifferent, no longer even amused; Meredith sadly, seeing how beautiful she was, like some spoiled decadent rich child in the movies, her lush hair, her fine, delicate nose, the dark shadows under her eyes, the hysteria prickling just beneath her skin.

"You must be out of your mind," Stacey said. She shoved her hands into her jeans pockets, lifted her chin, and turned toward the door. Bill didn't move, blocking it with his big, square body. He stood looking down at his daughter.

"I can't get away from school," she said finally, her voice rising, a tremor creeping in. "You were so damn anxious for me to go back and now . . ."

"I know it's semester break," he interrupted, his voice tight, his bitterness barely covered. "I know you failed all three courses. The school called my office. They can't see any point in your coming back for another semester. You're just wasting everybody's time." Standing behind her, Meredith saw beneath the sharp points of her shoulder blades the thin cloth of her shirt quivering minutely. She closed her eyes: Stacey, four, five, six years old, body arched, eyes rolled back, screaming in terror, smiling in the morning as if there were no blackness, no endless night. "Start packing," Bill said. "We're all going to your grandmother's funeral." Stacey twisted one shoulder and slid past him without speaking.

In the morning they boarded a plane, Bill in his three piece grey suit, Meredith in her aging but still smart blue Chanel suit, and Stacey, rumpled and sleepy, her hair uncombed, wearing fraying faded jeans and a stained brown suede windbreaker. They flew west with Stacey seated several rows behind them stilting their conversation, poisoning Meredith's grief with her hostility which they could feel boring through the rows of seats between them.

At Regina they rented a car and drove west for another four hours, soon leaving the wide paved highway for roads that grew narrower and more and more treacherous under their burden of ice and snow. Meredith had not been home in over a year. She was a rancher's daughter, but she had lived the last twenty years in Toronto, and for the last fifteen she had taught chemistry at the university. Each time she returned home she was grateful that she had escaped the hardship, the male chauvinism, the ignorance.

The small church was full even though outside a blizzard was blowing. Her father had begun to stoop and to move more slowly. After the service, stepping out of the church into the swirling snow, he hesitated and looked around in a bewildered way, blinking, as though he was surprised to find himself still in the town of his birth.

At the cemetery high on the hillside the wind whipped blasts of snow across the rectangular hole in the ground and made their heavy coats flap against their legs. Stacey had refused to get out of the car although Meredith did not notice this till later. The minister hurried through the ceremony, his words lost in the storm.

The next day before breakfast Bill went back east leaving Stacey and Meredith behind to look after Meredith's father for a week or two, "until he gets back on his feet." When Meredith served her father his bacon and eggs, he put his arm around her and said, "You're a good girl, Merry. Never gave us a moment's trouble. Who'd ever think I'd have a professor for a daughter." Meredith kissed his forehead and sat down across from him. "Your mother and me," he said carefully, as if he was trying out the sound of it, "your mother and me," he repeated, stronger this time, "we . . ." He seemed to have forgotten what he had started to say.

"Maybe now you'll think about retirement," Meredith said.

"Yeah," he said. He stirred his coffee. "You and Stacey could chase the cows around to the feed ground this morning," he said. "You know, like you used to. It's too damn cold for them to go without food."

"All right," Meredith said. "It'll be good for Stacey to have something to do."

After her father had gone out to the barn, Meredith knocked on Stacey's door. At home she had given up waking Stacey in the mornings. When she came home in the evening Stacey would be gone and Meredith would hear her coming in at three or four in the morning making noise so she and Bill would wake and know how late it was.

"Wake up Stacey," she called. "Your grandpa needs us. We have to give him a hand." Silence. "Stacey?" she said, opening the door. The curtains were closed but she could see Stacey lying on her back staring at the ceiling. Her clothes were strewn on the floor. The room had a musty, closed-in smell.

After a moment Stacey threw back the covers and sat on the side of the bed. Meredith went back to the kitchen. Soon Stacey came in wearing the same jeans and shirt she had worn since the funeral. Her hair needed washing and there was sleep in the corners of her eyes. Meredith noticed, but said nothing.

"What?" Stacey asked.

"We have to chase the cattle away from the riverbed up onto the feed grounds." Stacey was staring at the outdoor thermometer.

"It's twenty below out there!" she said. "You must be nuts!"

"I am not nuts," Meredith said, banging the coffee pot. "When it's very cold like this, they go down into all the nooks and crannies along the river bed looking for shelter." She poured Stacey a cup of coffee without looking at her. "Then they don't hear the tractor, or see the feed coming and they miss it." She put the coffee pot back on the stove. "And then they can't endure the cold without good feed and they die." She tried to smile at Stacey. "So it is essential that we go out and chase them up. It's only about a mile and a half."

"Christ!" Stacey said, but Meredith had seen the welling brightness in her eyes and knew nothing would stop her from going, from trying the bitter air in her lungs, from testing the feel of the thigh-deep snow, from challenging a twelve-hundred pound range cow or grovelling in panic in front of it.

On the third morning Stacey rose without being called. She came into the kitchen where Meredith, already wearing most of her outdoor clothing, was hurrying to get the dishes washed before she went out. Stacey poured herself a cup of coffee, not answering her mother's good morning, and stood looking out the window.

"You don't need to go out this morning," she said. Her voice was husky, as though she hadn't spoken for weeks. "I know what to do."

"I don't mind," Meredith said.

"I can do it!" Stacey said. "Meredith," she added, rolling the r. Meredith flushed but didn't speak. Stacey put on her parka and went outside. Meredith could hear her whistling for the dogs.

When the dishes were done, the beds made, and a pie in the oven, Stacey still had not returned. She might be romping with the dogs in the snow, Meredith thought, or maybe she's found those caves along the riverbank. The morning before Meredith had seen how they were overhung with ice and snow and remembered how, when she was a child, they had kept safe foxes and young coyotes all through the winter.

It surprised and pleased her to think that Stacey might be having fun. A creature of contradictions, paradoxes and extremes, Stacey possibly did not even know what fun was. Whenever the police brought her back after she had run away (and then seemed not to know what to do with herself, or even why she had gone), she always looked so pale and sickly that Meredith could only pity her for the demon that pursued her and would not give her peace.

She decided to clean Stacey's room as a way of thanking her for saving her from the long tiring walk through the deep snow on the riverbottom. She stripped her bed and put clean sheets on it and folded the discarded clothes. Stacey's suitcase was still lying on the floor. Meredith picked it up by the handle intending to set it upright in the closet, but as she lifted it, it fell open spilling the contents. She'll accuse me of snooping, Meredith thought. Quickly she bent over and began to replace the tangled underwear and cotton shirts. A plastic bag fell out on the floor. As she bent to pick it up she saw that it was plumped full of something that looked like dried grass. Marijuana.

I might have known, she thought. Stacey the troublemaker, the eternal embarrassment, the albatross she and Bill wore around their necks. How could she do such a thing? How could she bring this into her grandparents' house at a time like this? She went to the kitchen and looked out the window. Stacey was crossing the yard, snow clinging to her pants, to her thighs, the dogs jumping at her side.

She came into the house stamping the snow off her boots, and throwing back her hood. Meredith stood in the doorway of the kitchen facing her, holding the bag chest high in front of her. Stacey looked at it. For a moment she said nothing. Then she said, "Snooping again?" and grabbed for the bag. Meredith jerked it out of her reach and stepped back into the kitchen.

"How could you do this?" she asked.

"It's only grass, Meredith," Stacey said. "It's no big deal. How could you do this?" She mimicked her mother.

Meredith reached out, she did not know she was going to do this, and slapped Stacey across the face. They stared at each other. Stacey's face drained white; the red slap mark stood out like a birthmark. Meredith's palm stung.

The bag of marijuana had fallen to the floor. Neither of them bent to pick it up. Stacey's eyes began to fill with tears. Two large drops gathered at the bottom of each eye and as Meredith watched, they spilled over and began to run down Stacey's cheeks.

"You have caused me so much pain," Meredith said. She bent and picked up the bag, took it to the bathroom by the back door, emptied it into the toilet and flushed it. Stacey still had not moved. Meredith began to shake. She waited for the screams, the attack, the fainting.

There was a thumping on the step outside the door and then Meredith's father called, opening the door, "Somebody give me a hand here." Meredith quickly pulled the door back. He was struggling into the house, half-pushing, half-carrying a slick reddish creature ahead of him. Stacey gasped and put her hand over her mouth.

"It's a new calf, Sweetheart," her grandfather said, laughing. If he saw the red mark or the tears, he gave no sign.

"Is it alive?" Stacey asked. "Ugh!" she said. "It's all slimy!" Her grandfather put the calf down on the hall floor with a thump.

"Got to get it warmed up," he said. "Or it'll die."

"What are you doing, Dad, calving in January?" Meredith asked. She was surprised at how ordinary her voice sounded.

"Goddamn bulls must have got in with the heifers last spring. I found this one near the feed grounds, just born."

"Heifer okay?" Meredith asked, as if she had never left.

"Yeah, that one's all right, but I found another one dead up north. Calving too long. I didn't know they'd been bred. You can't tell with heifers. Now look at the mess. Its ears are frozen."

"The cord's frozen too," Meredith said. Behind her Stacey made a 'yuck' sound. Again Meredith was surprised that Stacey was still there.

"It'll be safe in the bathroom till it gets warm and dry," he said. "I didn't dare leave it for the mother to lick off." He turned to the door. "There's bound to be more," he said. "I have to go check the rest of the herd. Keep an eye on it, Merry," he said. "You too, Stacey." He went outside. Stacey knelt, ignoring Meredith, cooing to the calf.

In the late afternoon he came back to the house carrying another calf. Meredith was reading in the living room. When she went to the kitchen she saw Stacey on her hands and knees in the bathroom trying to dry the calf off with Meredith's blow dryer. Her grandfather was kneeling beside her and they were talking. Meredith left the room quickly before either of them saw her.

Every morning Stacey chased the cattle down the riverbed and when she finished that, she went up to the feed grounds and helped her grandfather and his hired man fork the hay off the flat deck to the waiting cows. After that, the three of them came in for the noon meal which Meredith had prepared, and then, leaving the dishes for Meredith, they went down to the barn to help the new calves nurse. Stacey did not answer when Meredith spoke to her. The days dragged by.

Late one afternoon Meredith's father came hurrying in.

"Jim and I have to take that steer with water belly to the vet," he said. "We should be back by seven. I got a heifer due to calve in the barn so I have to get back as soon as I can."

At eight o'clock Meredith's father still had not returned. The temperature had dropped to thirty below and the wind was rising. She supposed he was storm-stayed somewhere. After a lifetime in this country, she told herself, he won't take chances, he'll know how to take care of himself. Remembering the heifer, she put on her parka and went down to the barn. The heifer had begun to calve. She could see one tiny hoof protruding from beneath the upraised tail. She studied the small cow nervously. She couldn't tell if it had been trying to deliver for a long time or not. Oh lord, she thought. What will I do? She decided to wait an hour before she tried to help and, with luck, by then her father might be back.

At nine o'clock she went back to the barn. Now she could see both hooves. That's too slow, she said to herself. I'm pretty sure that's too slow. We'll have to help her. She struggled back to the house, the fur-trimmed hood of her parka pulled well around her face, her hands thrust up the opposite sleeves.

"Stacey," she said to her daughter who had not taken her eyes off the television.

"What?" Stacey said, still not looking at her.

"That heifer can't deliver on her own, and your grandfather's not back, and . . . we'll have to pull it."

"Pull it yourself," Stacey said.

"I can't, Stacey," Meredith said. "I'm not strong enough. You have to help me. I can't do it alone." To her amazement tears were running down her cheeks. She wiped them off and then stared at the wet streak on her hand. Stacey was watching her now, that brightness back in her eyes. "Please help me, Stacey," she said. "The heifer will die if we don't pull her calf. And the calf will die if we don't get it out of there."

Stacey's eyes, wide, bright and hard, had shifted away from Meredith to some invisible thing. Her mouth was open, she was almost smiling. She rose and went to the kitchen with Meredith following, and put on her parka, boots and mittens.

The weather had been getting steadily worse. When they opened the back door it blew out of their hands and banged against the wall. The wind, bitterly cold now, was blowing into their faces with such force they had to walk backwards to the barn.

"Well, where is she?" Stacey asked when they were inside the barn. Meredith pointed. The cow raised her head and mooed. Stacey went

to her and stared at the little pair of hooves. "How do we pull it?" she asked.

"This is all I know how to do," Meredith said. She picked up a rope hanging from a nail on the frosted barn wall. It had a loop on one end. She went to the heifer and set the loop over the two protruding hooves and tightened it. "Take the end." She held onto the rope in front of Stacey. "Pull," she said. Nothing happened. The heifer mooed again. "Pull!" Meredith grunted. "One, two, three!" They pulled so hard that when the calf came in one welcome whoosh, they fell backward into the straw on top of each other.

"We did it!" Stacey said, standing up and looking at the calf.

"I bet it weighs close to a hundred pounds," Meredith said. They took the rope off the calf and stood back, their white breaths fading in the air above them. "I don't know how we're going to get it to the house, especially in that wind."

"It'll freeze to death if we don't," Stacey said. She pushed open the barn door. They each took one end of the calf and, staggering with its weight, floundering in the drifts, falling, being pushed off course and blinded by the wind-driven snow, they got the calf to the house. It took them fifteen minutes to go a hundred yards. They put the calf in the bathroom and Meredith turned up the thermostat.

"It looks okay," Stacey said dubiously.

"At least not any worse than the others did," Meredith answered. "I'll put some coffee on. I hope Dad gets home soon." Stacey was rubbing her reddened hands together, blowing on her fingers and sniffing.

19

They turned on the television set and sat drinking coffee in the warm living room. Now and then the calf in the bathroom bleated and made a knocking noise with its hooves as it tried to stand on the slippery vinyl.

"I can just imagine the mess in there," Meredith said. Stacey laughed. Suddenly Meredith realized that she had not been watching Stacey, she had been only looking at her, as one person looks at another during a conversation. It had been years, years, since she had simply talked to Stacey, since she had been able to forget that this was her disturbed, delinquent child who couldn't be trusted, who had to be watched. Now she noticed that Stacey had put on a little weight, she was not quite so painfully thin and her skin was less yellowish. Stacey had lit a cigarette and was lounging in the chair laughing at something on the screen. Her socks were dirty, her jeans worn out and clumsily patched, her cotton shirt thin and faded and she wore no bra under it.

Meredith had a sense of the shadows around the edges of the room darkening, of Stacey's form taking on a depth, a richness of colour, another dimension that made her real and powerful, like the central figure in a Rembrandt.

Do I really love her, Meredith asked herself? She remembered what the school psychologist had said when Stacey was fourteen and had been caught in the boy's bathroom with five or six boys.

"I think, Mrs. Gilchrist, that some kids are already lost." Her hair was greying, she would soon retire. "I've been at this work a long time. I know I shouldn't say this to you. But I think some kids are already lost. From the moment they breathe on their own, they're lost. I don't know why it should be that way." She had looked very old. Meredith could hardly believe that this was the same woman who stood up at community meetings and gave speeches about you and your teenager. "Take her to a psychiatrist." That was all she would say.

When Meredith had asked the psychiatrist for some word, for some explanation, he had said only, "No one is responsible for what Ortega called, 'this terrible reality.'" Meredith did not know what he meant.

Do I really love her? she asked herself again.

She had been an ordinary baby, her brown eyes alert and intelligent, quick to smile, and when she could walk she had been into everything, like all babies. She was slightly underweight at birth, she cried a lot, Meredith had worked all through her childhood, but none of these things, not together, not singly, accounted for Stacey. Nothing accounted for Stacey.

They stayed up to watch the late movie and during it both Stacey and Meredith fell asleep. The next time Meredith looked at her watch, it was six o'clock. Her father, still wearing his snowmobile suit, was looking down at her.

"Had to sleep in the truck till it cleared," he said. He sat down heavily in a chair and unzipped his suit. "I'm getting too old for this," he said. "I'm going to have to cut back on my herd come spring. I don't know how I'd have managed without you two this last couple of weeks."

He had grown old since her last visit. He was an old man. He couldn't be left alone. She was his only relative, the only one to manage the burden of his life. But it would be impossible for him to live in the city. In the city, staying with them, he would die. She should stay here and look after him. He had leaned back. His eyes were closed and sadness wrapped around him like a cloak. I should stay, she thought. Snow was banked up around the picture window and the stars were still out.

"I hate to leave you, Dad," she said, her mouth was dry, "but I have to get back to my job, to Bill."

"I know, I know," her father said. He looked across to the window as though to hide his despair from her. One way or another, she thought, our children all break our hearts. It is the way things are.

Stacey, lying on the couch near them, stirred, and they both turned to her. She sat up and they saw that she had been awake through their talk.

"I'm staying," she said. Her face was lit with an internal light, her voice beautiful. Meredith and her father watched her, and Meredith opened her mouth to speak. "It's my life," Stacey said to her. She looked back to her grandfather. "I'm staying," she said.

Meredith's father drove her to town where she caught a bus to Regina, and from Regina, a plane to Toronto. It was a flight that had originated in Vancouver and the plane was full. A young mother and her four-year-old boy sat beside Meredith, the mother at the window, the child in the middle, and Meredith on the aisle. The child was active, sitting on his mother's knee at the window, asking for water, asking to go to the bathroom, whining for a toy.

"I don't know what to do with him," the young woman said apologetically to Meredith. Meredith thought, I could tell her that he's not bothering me, or that he will probably grow up to be Prime Minister, or at least, a decent, normal adult. Or I could tell her that there will come a time when she will wonder if she loves him. There will come a time when they will both have to realize that it is his life, that he will be what he is.

Instead, she said, "He's a handsome child, and he seems quite bright." After a while she said, "I have a daughter, she's grown up now. She was a beautiful baby, lots of dark hair and big brown eyes, and always asking questions too. She used to love to throw bread to the pigeons in the park. She wasn't at all afraid of them. They would come closer and closer and she would stand still, her little arm outstretched with the bread in her hand. They would take it out of her fingers and that delighted her. Once one perched on her shoulder and she smiled; there was such wonder in her smile and in her eyes."

But the little boy was squirming again; he had climbed from his seat and was banging against the window with a toy car. His mother held his arm to stop him and he began to wail. The young woman was not listening to Meredith. But Meredith hardly noticed. She leaned back in her seat, closed her eyes, and thought about Stacey in the park with the pigeons.

Swallowtails

SHIINA MAKOTO

With sometimes painful honesty, a father reveals the mistakes he makes—and the joys he experiences—trying to help his young son grow up.

Hey, Dad, am I bald?" Takashi suddenly asked me one day when we were in the bath, with a serious look on his face.

"No, Takashi, you're not bald," I said. I wanted to laugh, but the expression on his face was so serious that I felt a bit unnerved.

"Oh. But Yuji and those guys keep calling me a bald-headed monk."

"Well, it's true your head is shaved, but you're not bald. Bald means you don't have any hair on your head."

"Oh, really?" Takashi thought about this. "Then I guess it was OK," he said, evidently satisfied about something.

My son had always had his head shaved. At first I used to take him with me to a barbershop whenever his hair grew long, but it got to be a pain and I thought it was silly to spend ¥1,600 to cut a head of hair as small as that. So I bought an electric hair-clipper and did the job myself. I'd take him into the bath, strip him, and shave his head. In the beginning I didn't know how hard to press or how fast to move, and Takashi would scream a lot. After three years, though, it got to the point where just shaving Takashi's head wasn't quite enough for me. So I'd shave two or three other kids' heads as well.

"What was OK?" I asked, feeling a little nervous about Takashi's sudden calmness.

"Well, Yuji kept calling me a bald-headed monk, so today I hit him." Takashi looked straight at me without a smile and then began cleaning the back of his neck with a soapy towel. I'd already heard that, apparently, my son was the only one in his class with a shaved head.

"You hit him?"

23

"Yep."

"What happened then?"

"Yuji started crying."

"Are you and Yuji in the same class?"

"No."

"What class, then?"

"He's a third-grader. Yuji Yoshino, third grade, first class."

"I see."

I looked at Takashi's round, clean-shaven head, which was still about another two weeks from its next shave, and said nothing. Then I suddenly recalled the report card he brought home at the end of first grade. His grades were as bad as I thought they would be, but I wasn't prepared for what the teacher said about his behavior. Under the "Getting Along with Others" section was written this:

"For some reason, Takashi seems aggressive. When I asked his classmates if they had ever been hit by him, two thirds of them raised their hands."

My wife turned slightly pale and fell silent when she saw this. We'd never dreamed something like this was happening; it was hard to believe.

"Maybe we just didn't raise him right," she said later, whispering in the dark of a spring night so cold that it was spring in name only.

"No, I don't think it's that," I said, as cheerfully as I could. "I think what we did was fine."

The worried way in which she spoke sounded like the way people talk about how badly poor parents raise their children.

About a year before Takashi was to enter school, my wife and I talked it over and decided that we weren't going to send him to preschool.

Kodaira, an out-of-the-way town on the Musashino Plain where I live, is a classic Tokyo bedroom community. There seem to be a lot of households here with very pointed ideas on education, about which they are excessively clamorous. It is, in fact, the perfect nesting place for mothers with an obsessive concern about the education of their children. These are the mothers who in all seriousness ask kindergarten teachers such sickening questions as what they should have their children learn, absorb, understand, and otherwise master before entering school, imploring the teachers to advise them on the matter.

For better or worse, my son went to a noisy city-run nursery school locked in a battle over wages that left the staff with little time to attend to the children. From an odd sense of destiny engendered by this environment, we never gave Takashi the kind of bizarre schooling most of his peers got.

Takashi, for his part, thoroughly enjoyed himself at this nursery. He was happy to spend the entire day running wild with his friends, returning home at night to wrestle and box with his boring father.

Shortly after Takashi entered school, however, it became clear to us that children these days are thoroughly schooled in a variety of subjects at home, even before they enter school. Everyone in Takashi's class could easily read, and many could also write. Of the thirty-four pupils in my son's class, he alone could neither read or write.

One day, two or three months after he started school, I asked Takashi if he liked it. He did; his eyes sparkled with excitement. He thought the nursery school on the whole had been more fun because he didn't have to study, but characteristically he allowed that school was better because he could play soccer.

The second semester started while my wife and I were still trying to figure out what we could or should do about the first-semester reports of our son's lawless behaviour. For Takashi, as always, the best part about going to school was being able to play with his friends. But with the start of the second semester many of his friends started practising the piano or taking English conversation classes, and there were fewer and fewer opportunities for him to play every day with a dozen or more friends until dusk and exhaustion set in.

Sadly, too, the parks and open spaces in which children could play seemed to have suddenly disappeared.

The first school prohibited use of the playground after 3:40 in the afternoon, when the gates were closed and the children sent straight home. Students couldn't use the grounds on Sundays because they were taken over by city baseball teams and soccer clubs. The reason for this was that, supposedly, the school didn't want to be held responsible for injuries incurred by students using the playground.

Croquet became the craze with old people at about this time, and what little open space existed inside the city was, by city decree, quickly turned into croquet grounds. The grounds were surrounded by barbed-wire fences—to keep the children from ruining the grounds when they weren't in use.

That day Takashi, who was lying on his bed, called me. Ever since he could talk, he's addressed his parents without using the -*san* suffix—*otou* instead of *otousan*, for example. I asked him why he never did so. He said we weren't important enough for the -*san*. That time, too, he wore an unexpectedly serious expression on his face.

"*Otou*," he said again, "today I went to that park over there—Atchan-Yama Koen—and it'd been turned into another croquet ground.

The only place left where we can play baseball is Central Park, but the adults there get angry at us right away, and nobody wants to play there anymore."

"That park has gotten to be really terrible," I said.

Central Park used to be a large testing site full of big ginkgo trees and mulberry fields. At first the city got rid of the mulberry trees and turned the area into a large grass field, which was very nice. On Sundays I would take Takashi, who was still in nursery school, to that park. It was big enough to have four grass baseball fields, and even on Sundays teams would be engaged in fierce struggles from early in the morning. Children would play baseball and soccer in the small spaces around the fields. To the people in the neighborhood, the park was a good place to bring their dogs to play, and quite a few adults would gather to watch the baseball games.

But the park was suddenly closed just before the beginning of summer vacation, when schoolchildren would be out playing in this park in earnest. Legions of bulldozers and dumptrucks came in their place, constructing a city park. Construction went on for a year and a half after that. The grass fields were dug up, the sides of the fields were surrounded with concrete walls and the bleachers replaced, so that the place looked like a magnificent racetrack replete with grandstands. The small spaces off to the sides were replaced with brick-enclosed flower beds ("no admittance"), tennis courts, croquet grounds, and exercise grounds.

The city had spent some four billion yen on the park up to that point. It was planning to spend an additional six billion to turn the site into a major city park.

I went with Takashi one day to see a part of the new park that had been opened. At the entrance was a huge sign, almost as if the city fathers had erected it as a warning to the residents. NO CATS OR DOGS ALLOWED, it read, in big red and black letters.

"What does it say?" Takashi asked me.

"It says that dogs and cats are not allowed in this park."

"Oh," he said. He seemed to be thinking about something.

"But that's strange," he said, after a while.

"Why?"

"Because dogs and cats can't read!"

But of course! I thought. Most of the time dogs are taken for walks on a leash, so the owners, at least, will see this sign. Cats, however, usually come and go as they please. "You're right," I said with a laugh. "Cats can't read."

"What a stupid sign," said Takashi. He had recently learned how to write and not just print, and he laughed pleasantly, pleased with himself for being at least a little smarter than a cat.

Still, the city's usual display of abrupt discourtesy and a penchant for prohibiting admittance to anything and everything—as evidenced by this No Pets sign—struck me as ridiculous; at the same time, it made me boil with anger.

The bleachers had been turned into something like an all-purpose playing field. On the other side of the grass was a 300-meter track, at one end of which was something extraordinary—a shot-put circle like the ones usually found on practice fields at schools built long ago.

"Hey, Takashi, this is where they have the shot-put competitions."

He didn't seem very interested in it. On the other side of the park, a helicopter hovered over the forest of ginkgo trees where a gymnasium was going to be built. As I was walking past the shot-put circle, it dawned on me that, although this was supposed to be a city park, a park for all the people of the city, its planners appeared to have done their level best to ignore the wishes and needs of those people—of us. I felt disgusted. After all, how many shot-putters could there be in this city, anyway? Instead of taking all that space to accommodate at most one or maybe two competitions a year between a very limited number of people, wouldn't it have been better to make some space for children and pets to play and run around in at will? As I thought about these things while we walked, the thought of living in this town began to depress me.

Spring vacation ended, and Takashi started the second grade. I realized then that, in the end, I had never actually asked Takashi himself why he hit his classmates all during the time he was in first grade. I excused myself by saying that he'd done well enough in a year, considering that he was the only one in a class of thirty-four children who had been illiterate to begin with, that boys have their own problems to deal with when growing up, and so on.

Even in the second grade, for Takashi the best thing about going to school continued to be the chance to play with his friends. Every day, he and his friends seemed to find some new place to play and to do something different. At night, when I gave him his bath, he'd talk about what he'd done that day. It was at about this time that the name Takayama, a classmate of Takashi's of whom I'd not heard previously, began to crop up frequently. From what Takashi told me, I learned that Takayama had transferred into the second grade from another school; he and Takashi were in the same class. Takashi had mentioned Takayama when he told me about having hit Yuji.

"Takayama-kun knows a lot about fishing," Takashi said, as happy as if he had been talking about himself and with a funny kind of pride. "He has a brother in the fifth grade, and he says that his father takes them fishing a lot. There are a lot of really big fishing poles at his home." That's when he started going over to Takayama's house to play.

Takayama seemed to be a very generous boy. Every time Takashi came home from the Takayamas', he'd have some barbless fishhooks, or fishing line, or some outrageously big floats, or plastic models.

"You're always receiving a lot of different things from Takayama, but are you giving him anything in return?" I asked Takashi one day as we were walking through the woods near Central Park.

"Yeah, I gave him a metal erector set once," Takashi said. "But Takayama-kun seems to like giving me things more."

The park itself was closed off with ugly steel fencing of the kind used for construction sites, and the woods had been reduced to about half its former size. But the citron tree that Takashi and I were looking for that day was still there, covered with a thin layer of dust but otherwise standing aloof somewhat comically, as if at a loss for something to do.

"It's here! It's still here!" Takashi shouted as he swiftly circled its trunk. Bunches of caterpillars crawled about all but unseen on the undersides of the dark green leaves and between the stems, clustering there like lumps of salt and pepper scattered about.

We put about two dozen caterpillars in a paper bag, together with a bunch of citron leaves for food. Raising larvae and watching them change into butterflies was a big thing with kids just then.

"Is Takayama raising any butterflies?" I asked.

"No. He and his brother keep tropical fish. He's got a big aquarium full of them. He says his father buys them in foreign countries."

As we walked, I placed the bag close to Takashi's ear.

"I can hear them!" he cried. "I can hear them eating the leaves!"

I met Takayama for the first time the following Saturday. He had a sort of toy pistol in his right hand and a fishing rod—with reel and lure—in his left. He was only about half as big as Takashi and wore shorts with an apple design on them, which I thought was a little too young for a boy in the second grade. In complete contrast to Takashi, he wore his hair straight down in a bowl cut, which made him look like a little girl. The two of them standing together made an odd sight.

"You must be Takayama-kun," I said, sticking my head out from the living room. "Come inside."

"Excuse me," he said politely, in a high, slightly reedy voice. He took off his shoes.

"Did you make that pistol yourself?" I asked.

"Yes, I did," he answered.

I wanted to ask him to show me the gun so I could see how it was made, but he acted so adult for a second-grader that I decided against it. I found it hard to talk with him freely. If he had said "Yeah" or "Yeah, ya wanna see it?" things would have gone differently.

"Takashi's always getting some present from you, so I'll make you some *yakisoba* to eat later, OK?" I said. The boy had such an adult manner of answering me that I couldn't help talking to him in the same way.

"Thank you," he said, in his high-pitched voice. He followed Takashi upstairs. I couldn't help wondering if all second-graders said "Excuse me" when they went inside somebody else's home. Then I thought about my own son, my irreverent little Takashi, and I became very worried. I made a mental note to ask him about this after Takayama left, but that day I was distracted by other things and forgot about it.

"The incident" occurred about a month after the start of school, with a phone call from the school.

"I'm sorry to inconvenience you, but could you come over right away?" It was Yamagishi, the teacher. His voice was low and muffled, as if he had been talking through his hand into the receiver.

I relayed the message to my wife, who had gone to work early that day and had only just come home, also early. She became tense. "I wonder what it could be?"

"If it were an injury, the teacher would have spoken with more urgency, so I don't think it's something like that," I said.

About an hour later my wife came back with Takashi. She looked thoroughly exhausted, and the base of her nose was red. She waited for Takashi to go to his room upstairs.

"They said Takashi stole his friend's money." She spoke rapidly, in a whisper.

"What?" I said, incredulous. Though I'd been worried, I'd expected something no worse than Takashi's fighting with someone or having a trick he'd played exposed.

"Takayama's mother came in with this desperate look," my wife went on. "She said that, lately, the boy's brother's allowance had been disappearing quite often, and when she questioned Takayama about it yesterday, he said that Takashi had been stealing it."

"They said Takashi's been going into Takayama's house and stealing it?" I asked, still amazed. As I listened, for some reason I felt like laughing.

"That's what they said. His mother said her kids had no reason to steal, and she gave me a really threatening look!"

"I can't believe this."

"Neither can I, just suddenly being accused like that." I also thought we'd really have to ask Takashi himself.

"What did the teacher say?" I asked.

"He said we should all investigate the matter."

I even felt exasperated at how quickly I began to feel deeply unhappy inside.

"I wonder how Mrs. Takayama can be so sure Takashi stole the money," I said, realizing that it was this point that made me feel so uncomfortable.

"She says that's what Takayama-kun told her when she questioned him about it."

Takayama's bowl-cut head appeared briefly in my mind and then disappeared. The sum stolen was ¥500, a fresh new note that the boy's brother had been planning to put in the bank. Money wasn't the only thing to have disappeared, according to Mrs. Takayama. Artificial bait and floats that the elder Takayama prized had been missing frequently, and it looked as if Takashi had stolen these items, too. She wouldn't have felt so bad, she said, in a shrill voice heightened with agitation, if only these things had been involved. But stealing money at such an early age was a serious matter.

As I listened to my wife tell me all this, I felt a pain in the left side of my chest. I'd always heard that extraordinary apprehension or anger can cause chest pains, and the thought that this was apparently true remained vaguely in my mind like a monotonous soliloquy.

That night, in the bath, I suddenly asked: "Listen, Takashi, have you ever taken anything like fishhooks or money from the Takayamas' without asking anybody's permission?"

I tried to ask this question in as normal an intonation as possible, in a slightly clumsy, intentionally joking manner.

"Yep," he said with alacrity, making a big bubble out of his washcloth.

I felt my stomach sink.

"Without asking permission?" I said quickly.

"But I wasn't the one who took it. Takayama-kun just brings the stuff to me. He says it's all right. Then he gives it all to me."

"Money too?"

"Yep. Last time he brought five hundred and thirty yen."

"What did you do with it?"

"Four of us—Kei-chan, Imai's older brother, me and Takayama— hit the *gacha-gacha* at Medakaya."

"You spent the whole five hundred and thirty on that?"

"Yep. We had about three turns apiece. Imai's brother got mad when he got the same thing three times in a row, and he shook the machine, and a guy from the store came over and hollered at him. I'm pretty good at it, so I got what I wanted all three times."

Takashi was completely casual about it. This *gacha-gacha* is a kind of vending machine filled with toys in plastic containers that you can get by depositing twenty or thirty yen. The catch is that you don't always get the toy you want.

"That money and fishing tackle don't belong to Takayama, Takashi. They belong to his brother. So from now on don't take them, even if he gives them to you." This time I spoke a little severely.

"Why?" he asked.

"Because it's wrong. Especially money—you shouldn't take money from friends."

"O.K. I won't," he said right away.

"Have you ever had a fight with Takayama?"

"No, never."

"Did you ever hit him?"

"Nope. Why should I? He is my friend."

"I guess so. Are you the strongest in your class, Takashi?"

"Yep."

"Strongest in your grade?"

"Yeah, either me or Kyoichi in the second class. Kyoichi's pretty strong, too." He answered in an almost matter-of-fact tone. I hadn't taught him anything in the way of studies, I thought. Instead, I'd wrestled with him and boxed and played at karate with him, and nothing else. Now, he's training himself in these areas all by himself. This realization gave me a strange feeling.

My wife told me to meet with Takashi's teacher, so three days later I went to see him at his home. I thought I'd get the details of the various troubles my son's behavior was probably causing on a daily basis, and make some sort of general apology.

"Well, he's still just a child. Almost everybody does something like this once or twice in his life, as a kind of test," Yamagishi said, with all the calm confidence of a veteran teacher of fifty years or more.

I didn't clearly understand what exactly was supposed to be a test of what. As we talked, however, I realized that this Yamagishi had concluded that, as far as "the incident" was concerned, Takashi was thoroughly guilty of theft. What is going on here? I wondered, frankly amazed, as I listened to Yamagishi speak like a Sunday pastor delivering a sermon to a wayward disciple. I thought that this guy was really something else.

I felt as if my talk with Takashi in the bath three days earlier had confirmed my suspicions. As Takashi's father I couldn't say so, but I had thought all along that Takayama, that delicate-looking transfer-student with the bowl cut, had been currying favor with his new classmates by getting the strongest kid in the class into trouble.

The more I thought about what Takayama's mother had said—that my lackadaisical son had sneaked into her elder son's room like a professional thief and stolen a brand-new ¥500 note out of a desk drawer—the more absurd, even unreal, I found the scenario she'd described. Why would a boy who doesn't even use his monthly allowance of ¥150 but just leaves the coins scattered around on his desk go into someone else's home to steal money? The thought made me quake with anger inside.

"Well, as long as all the parents involved see to it that this sort of thing doesn't happen again, I see no need to pursue the matter any further," Yamagishi said, with an air of importance. His eyes gleamed behind his glasses. He finally lit the cigarette he'd been toying with for so long.

Later that night, I didn't even wait for my wife to change clothes after coming from work before telling her about my conversation with Yamagishi.

"It's terrible, making Takashi out to be a thief like that," I said to her. I felt indescribably empty inside.

As always, Takashi and I went into the bath before dinner, talking about nothing in particular.

"When I checked the box today, I found eighteen pupae," he said, pouring hot water over his shoulders and slowly shaking his head from side to side. "Three more are still larvae, so I guess they died."

"Oh? That was quick!"

"Yeah. That's because I gave them a lot of food every day. The ones that ate a lot turned into pupae first. Komatsu-kun and Maa-chan say theirs have turned into pupae, too, but I think mine'll turn into butterflies before anyone else's."

"I see."

"Then Takayama-kun wanted to give me some hairstreak pupae, but I told them I didn't want them. They're not worth it." At this he wrinkled his nose in a gesture so adult I just had to laugh.

"So they're not worth it?" I asked.

"Yeah, they're so small."

Exactly one week later all the pupae in Takashi's box metamorphosed into swallowtails.

"I did it, Dad!" Takashi came tumbling down the stairs waving his right hand in a circle. He seemed truly happy.

"Right now there are thirteen of them," he said. "At this rate they might all turn into butterflies."

I went upstairs to my son's room to find a commotion of black and yellow blurs that filled the interior of a small box on the desk. The tiny little box trembled and shook from side to side, and looked as if it might itself take flight at any moment.

"It's amazing how fast they turned into swallowtails," Takashi said, taking the box in his hands. He stood there, clearly but happily perplexed about what to do next.

All eighteen swallowtail pupae changed into butterflies overnight. The little box soon proved too small for them; they barely had room to spread their wings and move around. The next day at about noon, Takashi stood on the veranda of his room on the second floor and released them. At first, the newly metamorphosed swallowtails simply continued to flit about in vain inside the box, unable to find the entrance. Suddenly, two or three of the butterflies perched on the edge of the tiny square opening, stayed there a moment, then finally flew off into the hot, humid sunlight of an early summer day.

"Fly! Fly away!" Takashi shouted, pulling the swallowtails out into the air as he held the box on the far side of the railing.

Several more swallowtails appeared on the other side of the boy with the shaved head, beating their wings ceaselessly as they flew off into the midday summer sun.

Translated by Joseph Farrar

-chan: a suffix added to a girl's name to show affection

-kun: a suffix added to a boy's name to show affection

-san: a suffix added to someone's name to show respect

yakisoba: a Chinese-style noodle dish

Girl

JAMAICA KINCAID

A Caribbean girl recites all the advice her mother has taught her—but she must wonder whether or not to follow it.

Wash the white clothes on Monday and put them on the stone heap; wash the color clothes on Tuesday and put them on the clothesline to dry; don't walk barehead in the hot sun; cook pumpkin fritters in very hot sweet oil; soak your little cloths right after you take them off; when buying cotton to make yourself a nice blouse, be sure that it doesn't have gum on it, because that way it won't hold up well after a wash; soak salt fish overnight before you cook it; is it true that you sing benna in Sunday school?; always eat your food in such a way that it won't turn someone else's stomach; on Sundays try to walk like a lady and not like the slut you are so bent on becoming; don't sing benna in Sunday school; you mustn't speak to wharf-rat boys, not even to give directions; don't eat fruits on the street—flies will follow you; *but I don't sing benna on Sundays at all and never in Sunday school*; this is how to sew on a button; this is how to make a buttonhole for the button you have just sewed on; this is how to hem a dress when you see the hem coming down and so to prevent yourself from looking like the slut I know you are so bent on becoming; this is how you iron your father's khaki shirt so that it doesn't have a crease; this is how you iron your father's khaki pants so that they don't have a crease; this is how you grow okra—far from the house, because okra tree harbors red ants; when you are growing dasheen, make sure it gets plenty of water or else it makes your throat itch when you are eating it; this is how you sweep a corner; this is how you sweep a whole house; this is how you sweep a yard; this is how you smile to someone you don't like very much; this is how you smile to someone you don't like at all; this is how you smile to someone you like completely; this is how you set a table for tea; this is how you set a table for dinner; this is how you set a table for dinner with an important guest; this is how you set a table for lunch; this is how you set a table for breakfast; this is how to behave in the presence of men who don't know you very well, and this way they won't recognize immediately the slut I have warned you against becoming; be sure to wash every day, even if it is with your own spit; don't squat down to play marbles—you are not a boy, you know; don't pick people's flowers—you might catch something; don't throw stones at blackbirds, because it might not be a blackbird at all; this is how to make a bread pudding; this is how to make doukona; this is how to make pepper pot; this is how to make a good medicine for a cold; this is how to make a good medicine to throw away a child before it even becomes a child; this is how to catch a fish; this is how to throw back a fish you don't like, and that way something bad won't fall on you; this is how to bully a man; this is how a man bullies you; this is how to love a man, and if this doesn't work there are other ways, and if they don't work don't feel too bad about giving up; this is how to spit up in the air if you feel like it, and this is how to move quick so that it doesn't fall on you; this is how to make ends meet; always squeeze bread to make sure it's fresh; *but what if the baker won't let me feel the bread?*; you mean to say that after all you are really going to be the kind of woman who the baker won't let near the bread?

---

benna: folk music similar to Calypso

dasheen: a root vegetable

doukona: a sweet potato and coconut dish

Iguana Hunting

HERNÁN LARA ZAVALA

*Running wild in the beautiful Yucatan peninsula, three boys discover
something more exciting than iguanas.*

In those days we went into the wild to hunt. I had come from the
city to stay with my grandparents in Zitilchen for my holidays, and
I'd already made some friends. From the low hill that rises south
of town, Chidra, the half-breed Mayan, would first go to call for Crispin.
When he reached the house, he gave a long whistle and out Crispin
came: short, nervous, cunning. Then they came to fetch me. On their
way they collected the stones we were to use. They were special stones,
almost round, and they rattled in our pockets as we journeyed on.

When they got to our farm Chidra whistled again, and my grandfather would come to the door to let them in. Chidra lived in the wild
and had eaten no food. Not so Crispin. He lived a few streets away
and I knew he had had a good breakfast. Both, however, accepted the
hot chocolate and rolls my grandmother offered them. While we ate,
my grandfather, tall but stooping, joked gravely with us, as was his
manner. With Crispin particularly: the old man was very fond of Crispin.
He used to call him "don Crispin" and every now and then he'd suggest
jobs for him inspired by his diminutive stature and resilient character.
He asked him once: "How would you like to join the army when you
grow up? Your height would be greatly in your favor." Crispin responded
with a dutiful chuckle, revealing the dough between his teeth. In the
meantime, Chidra, his mind elsewhere, ate voraciously. My grandfather
seldom addressed him. I recall, however, one of his few observations
about Chidra. He was talking to Crispin about Padre Garcia's extrav-
agantly mystical sermons: "No," he said, "you're qualified for all sorts
of jobs but not that of a priest. You're too much of this world. I would

37

have to think of somebody else for that . . . Chidra, for instance." I don't remember Chidra's reaction.

Although we actually proposed iguana hunting, our expeditions were likely to involve anything. In our forays we spent our time looking for V-shaped branches to make catapults with, or stealing wedges of honeycomb from the hives left out in the fields. Often, as we were walking out of town, we would climb the wall of some orchard to steal oranges or to take a swim in the reservoir. On such occasions I arrived home for dinner clutching my damp underpants in my hand. As soon as my grandmother saw me she'd say: "Have you been swimming in Tomás's reservoir again? The day he finds out you'll be in big trouble and it'll be no use coming to me."

Many were the times we went out to hunt, but it has to be admitted that iguanas were not easy prey. We'd occasionally catch one—and then we'd sell it to a well-known iguana-eater in town—but their natural colors served them all too well. We hunted turtle-doves, lizards, and, on one occasion, even an armadillo that Chidra grabbed by the tail. As soon as we were on our own, shooting here and there at the slightest movement in the bushes, Chidra, who in the presence of adults was invariably silent and reserved, could restrain himself no longer. He would tell us the strange occurrences that, according to him, he experienced in his daily walk back home. These tales always provoked Crispin's anger and contempt. Chidra spoke, for instance, about the afternoon when, returning home from town, he had seen a herd of elephants.

"I yelled out for help but nobody came . . ."

"That was when you took coffee for the first time in your bloody life. I don't know how many coffees you had, but it drove you crazy," said Crispin, annoyed.

Chidra, however, would not be swayed. He told us that sometimes when he was on his way home toward midnight he could hear somebody hissing insistently: "pssst . . . pssst . . ." But he never dared turn around to see who it was because he was sure the noises were produced by Xtabay, the evil woman from Mayan mythology. He explained to us that those who turned to see her could not resist her summons since, apart from her feet, her beauty was irresistible. She hid behind the trunk of a ceybo tree and those who responded to her charms woke up next morning with their bodies covered with thorns.

We knew the legend of course. But when Chidra talked about it, he was charged with such conviction that almost every boy in town—Crispin excepted—listened to him enthralled. He told us about a cave

in the heart of the wild that led directly to hell. He told us about a wandering Indian, known as Tzintzinito, who was condemned to roam endlessly through the wild.

On one of those mornings Chidra told us that while returning from the camp where his father worked collecting gum, he had seen a naked woman with beautiful long hair bathing in a deep pool. Half joking, half serious, Crispin said:

"Of course you'll tell us she was Xtabay."

"I don't know," answered Chidra. "The woman I saw in the pool had the whitest feet I ever saw. She had long golden hair."

"He's a liar."

"No, I'm not," said Chidra, crossing himself and kissing his thumb.

"When was this?" I asked.

"Yesterday afternoon."

"That's hardly the time Xtabay would come out."

"We'll get him now," said Crispin. "Prove it."

"If you want. But I'd better tell you it's a long way."

"He's afraid," said Crispin.

"Let's go," answered Chidra. "If you're willing, let's go."

Chidra knew the area well. Not only because he lived in the wild but because of his father's work. Chidra was responsible for bringing him food and other necessities every so often. Once in the wild he was the official guide. We left town. We passed the orchards, we passed the hives, we penetrated the wild. We struggled through the undergrowth, parting bushes and trampling weeds. Chidra, confident of his capabilities, moved his head restlessly like a wild animal on a fresh scent.

There was something uncanny about the whole affair. In Zitilchen, days are usually hot and cloudless. That day, however, was humid and gray. When we were in the thickest and most tangled part of the wild we suddenly came across some ancient ruins. Crispin and I were stunned. It was a small abandoned Mayan village but so well kept that it seemed inhabited. We were silent, looking around in awe. After a while Chidra said, "This way. We're nearly there now." Crispin stared at me. I could sense that, like myself, he was afraid as well as fascinated.

Chidra moved forward again, parting the scrub that stood in our way. Nobody thought about the iguanas. Our sole concern was finding out the truth about Chidra's tale. Finally we came to the edge of a large pool. It was a transparent green and its waters were unusually quiet and still. There was nobody around. We found a clearing and hid behind some mangrove trees while we tried to agree what to do. Perhaps there never had been anyone around, except in Chidra's imagination. Crispin wanted to go back to town and repeated constantly that Chidra was a liar. A bloody liar. They had a long argument and were about to come to blows when I saw somebody moving on the other side of the pool. We quickly fell silent, curious to see who it was. A bearded man appeared. We could see him clearly: he was dressed for the bush. He wore glasses and was smoking a pipe. He had a saucepan and as he came to the edge of the pool, he put some soil in the pot and sank it in the water, emptying it some moments later. He was about to leave when a woman, dressed just like him, appeared, bringing a few more utensils to be washed. We couldn't hear what they were saying.

"There she is," said Chidra slowly.

And it was true, she was just as Chidra had described her: a tall, blonde woman. We saw them for just a few minutes; as soon as they finished their washing they left the pool. We stayed on, still waiting, when Crispin broke our silence. He stood up and said, "Shit! I've got a dreadful itching. What the hell is it?" He lifted up his shirt to show us his back.

"Ticks," said Chidra.

"Blast!" said Crispin as he took off his shirt.

"We must be covered in them too," Chidra said to me, looking at his ankles, scratching himself and standing up to take off his own shirt. I did the same. We undressed ourselves in order to shake off the ticks from our clothes. Chidra even had ticks in his armpits, entangled in the wispy hair. We were covered in them. We were still naked when Chidra began to talk about the woman we had briefly seen, full of the fact that this proved he was no liar. He told us again how, the day before, as he was wandering around the mangroves, he had seen a tall, blonde, white woman bathing in the pool. He described her meticulously. He had seen her in her entirety: feminine, naked, almost divine. He was enraptured. Carried away by Chidra's description, I noticed, at first with alarm and then with relief, that all three of us were experiencing the very same sensation.

Our bodies full of ticks, very tired, we got back to Zitilchen well after dark. We reached my grandfather's farm. I waved goodbye to Crispin and Chidra. My eyelids were heavy. My friends walked down the street. I thought about the blonde woman. I felt the ticks all over my body. Thorns. I was exhausted yet Chidra had a long way to go. Once in the house I went straight to my grandmother.

"I'm covered in ticks," I said. "Help me get rid of them."

"What's a few ticks," she answered, "They're not black widows. Come on then, off with your clothes and lie down in bed while I warm up some wax."

Feeling her press me all over with the hot wax, I heard her ask:

"For heaven's sake, there's thousands of them! Where on earth have you been?"

"Today we met Xtabay," I answered, satisfied.

Translated by the author in collaboration with Andrew C. Jefford

---

ceybo (ceibo): a tropical tree similar to silkwood

Trap Lines

THOMAS KING

for Christian

A seemingly innocent question—"Why do you sit in the bathroom, Dad?"—leads father and son to a deeper level of understanding.

W hen I was twelve, thirteen at the most, and we were still living on the reserve, I asked my grandmother and she told me my father sat in the bathroom in the dark because it was the only place he could go to get away from us kids. What does he do in the bathroom, I wanted to know. Sits, said my grandmother. That's it? Thinks, she said, he thinks. I asked her if he went to the bathroom, too, and she said that was adult conversation, and I would have to ask him. It seemed strange at the time, my father sitting in the dark, thinking, but rather than run the risk of asking him, I was willing to believe my grandmother's explanation.

At forty-six, I am sure it was true, though I have had some trouble convincing my son that sitting in the bathroom with the lights out is normal. He has, at eighteen, come upon language, much as a puppy comes upon a slipper. Unlike other teenagers his age who slouch in closets and basements, mute and desolate, Christopher likes to chew on conversation, toss it in the air, bang it off the walls. I was always shy around language. Christopher is fearless.

"Why do you sit in the bathroom, Dad?"

"My father used to sit in the bathroom."

"How many bathrooms did you have in the olden days?"

"We lived on the reserve then. We only had the one."

"I thought you guys lived in a teepee or something. Where was the bathroom?"

"That was your great grandfather. We lived in a house."

"It's a good thing we got two bathrooms," he told me.

The house on the reserve had been a government house, small and poorly made. When we left and came to the city, my father took a picture of it with me and my sisters standing in front. I have the picture in a box somewhere. I want to show it to Christopher, so he can see just how small the house was.

"You're always bragging about that shack."

"It wasn't a shack."

"The one with all the broken windows?"

"Some of them had cracks."

"And it was cold, right?"

"In the winter it was cold."

"And you didn't have television."

"That's right."

"Jerry says that every house built has cable built in. It's a law or something."

"We didn't have cable or television."

"Is that why you left?"

"My father got a job here. I've got a picture of the house. You want to see it?"

"No big deal."

"I can probably find it."

"No big deal."

Some of these conversations were easy. Others were hard. My conversations with my father were generally about the weather or trapping or about fishing. That was it.

"Jerry says his father has to sit in the bathroom, too."

"Shower curtain was bundled up again. You have to spread it out so it can dry."

"You want to know why?"

"Be nice if you cleaned up the water you leave on the floor."

"Jerry says it's because his father's constipated."

"Lawn has to be mowed. It's getting high."

"He says it's because his father eats too much junk food."

"Be nice if you cleaned the bottom of the mower this time. It's packed with grass."

"But that doesn't make any sense, does it? Jerry and I eat junk food all the time, and we're not constipated."

"Your mother wants me to fix the railing on the porch. I'm going to need your help with that."

"Are you constipated?"

Alberta wasn't much help. I could see her smiling to herself whenever Christopher starting chewing. "It's because we're in the city," she said. "If we had stayed on the reserve, Christopher would be out on a trapline with his mouth shut and you wouldn't be constipated."

"Nobody runs a trapline anymore."

"My grandfather said the outdoors was good for you."

"We could have lived on the reserve, but you didn't want to."

"And he was never constipated."

"My father ran a trapline. We didn't leave the reserve until I was sixteen. Your folks have always lived in the city."

"Your father was a mechanic."

"He ran a trapline, just like his father."

"Your grandfather was a mechanic."

"Not in the winter."

My father never remarried. After my mother died, he just looked after the four of us. He seldom talked about himself, and slowly, as my sisters and I got older, he became a mystery. He remained a mystery until his death.

"You hardly ever knew my father," I said. "He died two years after we were married."

Alberta nodded her head and stroked her hair behind her ears. "Your grandmother told me."

"She died before he did."

"My mother told me. She knew your grandmother."

"So, what did your mother tell you?"

"She told me not to marry you."

"She told me I was a damn good catch. Those were her exact words 'damn good'."

"She said that just to please you. She said you had a smart mouth. She wanted me to marry Sid."

"So, why didn't you marry Sid?"

"I didn't love Sid."

"What else did she say?"

"She said that constipation ran in your family."

After Christopher graduated from high school, he pulled up in front of the television and sat there for almost a month.

"You planning on going to university?" I asked him.

"I guess."

"You going to do it right away or you going to get a job?"

"I'm going to rest first."

"Seems to me, you got to make some decisions."

"Maybe I'll go in the bathroom later on and think about it."

"You can't just watch television."

"I know."

"You're an adult now."

"I know."

Alberta called these conversations father and son talks, and you could tell the way she sharpened her tongue on "father and son" that she didn't think much of them.

"You ever talk to him about important things?"

"Like what?"

"You know."

"Sure."

"Okay, what do you tell him?"

"I tell him what he needs to know."

"My mother talked to my sisters and me all the time. About everything."

"We have good conversations."

"Did he tell you he isn't going to college."

"He just wants some time to think."

"Not what he told me."

I was in a bookstore looking for the new Audrey Thomas novel. The Ts were on the third shelf down and I had to bend over and cock my head to one side in order to read the titles. As I stood there, bent over and twisted, I felt my face start to slide. It was a strange sensation. Everything that wasn't anchored to bone just slipped off the top half of my head, slopped into the lower half, and hung there like a bag of jello. When I arrived home, I got myself into the same position in front of the bathroom mirror. That evening, I went downstairs and sat on the couch with Christopher and waited for a commercial.

"How about turning off the sound?"

"We going to have another talk?"

"I thought we could talk about the things that you're good at doing."

"I'm not good at anything."

"That's not true. You're good at computers."

"I like games."

"You're good at talking to people. You could be a teacher."

"Teaching looks boring. Most of my teachers were boring."

"Times are tougher now," I said. "When your grandfather was a boy, he worked on a trapline up north. It was hard work, but you didn't need a university degree. Now you have to have one. Times are tougher."

"Mr. Johnson was the boringest of all."

"University is the key. Lot of kids go there not knowing what they want to do, and, after two or three years, they figure it out. Have you applied to any universities yet?"

"Commercial's over."

"No money in watching television."

"Commercial's over."

Alberta caught me bent over in front of the mirror. "You lose something?"

"Mirror's got a defect in it. You can see it just there."

"At least you're not going bald."

"I talked to Christopher about university."

"My father never looked a day over forty." Alberta grinned at herself in the mirror so she could see her teeth. "You know," she said, "When you stand like that, your face hangs funny."

I don't remember my father growing old. He was fifty-six when he died. We never had long talks about life or careers. When I was a kid—I forget how old—we drove into Medicine River to watch the astronauts land on the moon. We sat in the American Hotel and watched it on the old black and white that Morris Rough Dog kept in the lobby. Morris told my father that they were checking the moon to see if it had any timber, water, valuable minerals, or game, and, if it didn't, they planned to turn it into a reserve and move all the Cree up there. Hey, he said to my father, what's that boy of yours going to be when he grows up? Beats me, said my father. Well, said Morris, there's damn little money in the hotel business and sure as hell nothing but scratch and splinters in being an Indian.

For weeks after, my father told Morris' story about the moon and the astronauts. My father laughed when he told the story. Morris had told it straight-faced.

"What do you really do in the bathroom, Dad?"

"I think."

"That's all?"

"Just thinking."

"Didn't know thinking smelled so bad."

My father liked the idea of fishing. There were always fishing magazines around the house, and he would call me and my sisters over to show us a picture of a rainbow trout breaking water, or a northern pike rolled on its side or a tarpon sailing out of the blue sea like a silver missile. At the back of the magazines were advertisements for fishing tackle that my father would cut out and stick on the refrigerator door. When they got yellow and curled up, he would take them down and put up fresh ones.

I was in the downstairs' bathroom. Christopher and Jerry were in Christopher's room. I could hear them playing video games and talking.

"My father wants me to go into business with him," said Jerry.

"Yeah."

"Can you see it? Me, selling cars the rest of my life?"

"Good money?"

"Sure, but what a toady job. I'd rather go to university and see what comes up."

"I'm thinking about that, too."

"What's your dad want you to do," said Jerry.

It was dark in the bathroom and cool, and I sat there trying not to breathe.

"Take a guess."

"Doctor?" said Jerry. "Lawyer?"

"Nope."

"An accountant? My dad almost became an accountant."

"You'll never guess. You could live to be a million years old and you'd never guess."

"Sounds stupid."

"A trapper. He wants me to work a trapline."

"You got to be kidding."

"God's truth. Just like my grandfather."

"Your dad is really weird."

"You ought to live with him."

We only went fishing once. It was just before my mother died. We all got in the car and drove up to a lake just off the reserve. My dad rented a boat and took us kids out in pairs. My mother stayed on the docks and lay in the sun.

Towards the end of the day, my sisters stayed on the dock with my mother, and my father and I went out in the boat alone. He had a new green tackle box he had bought at the hardware store on Saturday. Inside was an assortment of hooks and spinners and lures and a couple of red things with long trailing red and white skirts. He snorted and showed me a clipping that had come with the box for a lure that could actually call the fish.

Used to be beaver all round here, he told me, but they've been trapped out. Do you know why the beavers were so easy to catch, he asked me. It's because they always do the same thing. You can count on beavers to be regular. They're not stupid. They're just predictable, so you always set the trap in the same place and you always use the same bait, and pretty soon, they're gone.

Trapping was good money when your grandfather was here, but

not now. No money in being a mechanic either. Better think of something else to do. Maybe I'll be an astronaut, I said. Have more luck trying to get pregnant, he said. Maybe I'll be a fisherman. No sir, he said. All the money's in making junk like this, and he squeezed the advertisement into a ball and set it afloat on the lake.

Christopher was in front of the television when I got home from work on Friday. There was a dirty plate under the coffee table and a box of crackers sitting on the cushions.

"What do you say we get out of the house this weekend and do something?"

"Like what?"

"I don't know. What would you like to do?"

"We could go to that new movie."

"I meant outdoors."

"What's to do outdoors besides work?"

"We could go fishing."

"Fishing?"

"Sure, I used to go fishing with my father all the time."

"This one of those father, son things?"

"We could go to the lake and rent a boat."

"I may have a job."

"Great. Where?"

"Let you know later."

"What's the secret?"

"No secret. I'll just tell you later."

"What about the fishing trip?"

"Better stick around the house in case someone calls."

Christopher slumped back into the cushions and turned up the sound on the television.

"What about the dirty plate?"

"It's not going anywhere."

"That box is going to spill if you leave it like that."

"It's empty."

My father caught four fish that day. I caught two. He sat in the stern with the motor. I sat in the bow with the anchor. When the sun dropped into the trees, he closed his tackle box and gave the starter rope a pull. The motor sputtered and died. He pulled it again. Nothing. He moved his tackle box out of the way, stood up, and put one foot on the motor and gave the rope a hard yank. It broke in his hand and he tumbled backwards, the boat tipping and slopping back and forth. Damn, he said, and he pulled himself back up on the seat. Well, son, he said, I've got a job for you, and he set the oars in the locks and leaned against the motor. He looked around the lake at the trees and the mountains and the sky. And he looked at me. Try not to get me wet, he said.

Alberta was in the kitchen peeling a piece of pizza away from the box. "Christopher got a job at that new fast food place. Did he tell you?"

"No. He doesn't tell me those things."

"You should talk with him more."

"I talk with him all the time."

"He needs to know you love him."

"He knows that."

"He just wants to be like you."

Once my sister and I were fighting, my father broke us up and sent us out in the woods to get four sticks apiece about as round as a finger. So we did. And when we brought them back, he took each one and broke it over his knee. Then he sent us out to get some more.

"Why don't you take him fishing?"

"I tried. He didn't want to go."

"What did you and your father do?"

"We didn't do much of anything."

"Okay, start there."

When we came home with the sticks, my father wrapped them all together with some cord. Try to break these, he said. We jumped on the sticks and we kicked them. We put the bundle between two rocks and hit it with a board. But the sticks didn't break. Finally, my father took the sticks and tried to break them across his knee. You kids get the idea, he said. After my father went back into the house, my youngest sister kicked the sticks around the yard some more and said it was okay but she'd rather have a ball.

Christopher's job at the fast food place lasted three weeks. After that he resumed his place in front of the television.

"What happened with the job?"

"It was boring."

"Lots of jobs are boring."

"Don't worry, I'll get another."

"I'm not worried," I said, and I told him about the sticks. "A stick by itself is easy to break, but it's impossible to break them when they stand together. You see what I mean."

"Chainsaw," said my son.

"What?"

"Use a chainsaw."

I began rowing for the docks, and my father began to sing. Then he stopped and leaned forward as though he wanted to tell me something. Son, he said, I've been thinking . . . And just then a gust of wind blew his hat off, and I had to swing the boat around so we could get it before it sank. The hat was waterlogged. My father wrung it out as best he could and then he settled in against the motor again and started singing.

My best memory of my father was that day on the lake. He lived alone, and after his funeral, my sisters and I went back to his apartment and began packing and dividing the things as we went. I found his tackle box in the closet at the back.

"Christopher got accepted to university."

"When did that happen?"

"Last week. He said he was going to tell you."

"Good."

"He and Jerry both got accepted. Jerry's father gave Jerry a car and they're going to drive over to Vancouver and see about getting jobs before school starts."

"Vancouver, huh?"

"Not many more chances."

"What?"

"For talking to your son."

Jerry came by on a Saturday, and Alberta and I helped Christopher pack his things in the station wagon.

"Nice car," said Alberta.

"It's a pig," said Jerry. "My father couldn't sell it because of the colour. But it'll get us there."

"Bet your father and mother are going to miss you."

"My father wanted me to stick around and help with the business. Gave me this big speech about traditions."

"Nothing wrong with traditions," Alberta said.

"Yeah, I guess. Look at this." Jerry held up a red metal tool box. "It's my grandfather's first tool box. My father gave it to me. You know, father to son and all that."

"That's nice," said Alberta.

"I guess."

"Come on," said Christopher. "Couple more things and we can get going."

Alberta put her arm around my waist and she began to poke me. Not so you could see. Just a sharp, annoying poke. "For Christ's sake," she whispered, "say something."

Christopher came out of the house carrying his boots and a green metal box. "All set," he said.

"Where'd you get the box?" I asked.

"It's an old fishing tackle box."

"I know."

"It's been sitting in the closet for years. Nobody uses it."

"It was my father's box."

"Yeah. It's got some really weird stuff in it. Jerry says that there's good fishing in B.C."

"That's right," said Jerry. "You should see some of those salmon."

"You don't fish."

"You never took me."

"My father gave me that box. It was his father's."

"You never use it."

"No, it's okay. I was going to give it to you anyway."

"No big deal. I can leave it here."

"No, it's yours."

"I'll take care of it."

"Maybe after you get settled out there, we can come out. Maybe you and I can do some fishing."

"Sure."

"Love you, honey," said Alberta and she put her arms around Christopher and held him. "I'm going to miss you. Call us if you need anything. And watch what you eat so you don't wind up like your father."

"Sure."

Alberta and I stood in the yard for a while after the boys drove off. "You could have told him you loved him," she said.

"I did. In my own way."

"Oh, he's supposed to figure that out because you gave him that old fishing box."

"That's the way my father did it."

"I thought you told me you found the box when you and your sisters were cleaning out his place."

After supper, Alberta went grocery shopping. I sat in the bathroom and imagined what my father had been going to say just before the wind took his hat, something important I guessed, something I could have shared with my son.

51

from Return to Frankfurt

MARIE LUISE KASCHNITZ

The girl thinks   if I can only manage
not to step on any of these
delicate hands of shadow
cast on the sidewalk by the chestnut trees

The boy thinks   if I reach the trolley
in time and if it doesn't have to wait
at the switch and the traffic policeman really
does his job and tries to clear the street

If   thinks the girl   before I reach that tree
the third on the left no nun comes out at me
and if not more than twice I pass small boys
crossing the street in groups, carrying toys
oh   then it's certain that we'll meet

Unless   the boy thinks   there's a power failure
unless forked lightning strikes the driver
unless the trolley-car gets smashed to bits
surely we'll meet   yes I can count on it

And many times the girl must shiver
And the boy think   will this last forever
until under the chestnut trees they meet,
wordless and smiling, in some quiet street.

Translated by Beatrice Cameron

P·R·O·M·I·S·E·S

water from
the feet
of lovers

You Walked Gently Towards Me

BEN OKRI

You walked gently towards me
In the evening light
And brought silence with you
Which fell off when
I touched your shoulder
And felt the rain on it.

We went through the city
Up the roaring streets
Full of many lights
And we sought a place
To be alone
And found none.

The evening was merciful
On your smile.
Your laughter touched
The hungry ghosts
Of passing years.

You moved smoothly
On the waters
Your shadow sounded of silk
You led me to places
Full of mellow darkness
Secret coves where they
Didn't let us in
And under the rain
You bid me kiss you with
Your silent and uncertain eyes.

We walked home
And the rain laughed around us
With its insistent benediction
And your hair was strung with
    Diadems
Your face with glittering dreams
And my eyes were wet
    With your luminous spirited joy.

Vanda

VASCO PRATOLINI

"You like the river better than me." Perhaps a strange thing for a man to say to the woman he loves. . .

Vanda had black eyes with a point of gold within; her hair was blond. I never managed to tell her I loved her. I didn't even know her name was Vanda. It was she who finally stopped one morning in the middle of the bridge; she waited until I had the courage to take two more steps toward her. "This is obsessive," she exclaimed. "You've been trailing behind me like a shadow for a month. Say what you have to say and then let's forget it."

"What?" I said, "What are you talking about?" Just then a woman holding a little girl by the hand and forcing her to repeat some lesson passed by; still half-asleep, the child was babbling conjugations of the verb to be: "*Sii, siate, siano.*" The two of us burst out laughing; it was a way to break the ice. Vanda placed a hand on the parapet and leaned over, and I did the same. I looked down at the river. It was green and the water was so high it nearly reached the large windows of the silver-smiths' workshops. I pointed towards the middle of the river: "Look at that man in a kayak." It seemed the most important thing I had to say to her.

"Obviously he has nothing better to do," she said. "I'm jealous." At the end of the bridge, the statues of the four seasons turned their backs.

We were eighteen years old; I was an apprentice at a newspaper; she was a salesgirl at a fashionable shop where she earned seven lire a day. She lived with her father and her grandmother, and her father was a marshall who collected unpaid bills. We met on the bridge, every day for a year. Her house was on the other side of the river, on the Spring and Summer side. We had coffee at the bar; they had brioches fresh out of the oven, and we would buy one and split it; she dunked her half and nibbled at it, sucking the coffee out before biting into it;

she scolded me for finishing my half all at once. I would walk her to the store; I lingered there a bit while she found some excuse to re-organize the window display so she could wave goodbye again. We would walk across the bridge at noon and then again in the evening. The days were reflected in the river as it flowed below us: yellow and turbid when the water was high, in January; it carried tree trunks and the overturned carcasses of boars, having flooded the countryside; the silversmiths would appear at the windows to check the water gauges. Then in the longer days of sun, islands emerged from the gravel, the weir dried out and naked children played there all day long. Right under the bridge the water quickened slightly and ran so clear that you could see to the bottom. But in spring the water was green; whenever we stopped there in the evenings, Vanda would sing, her elbows resting on the parapet, her face framed by her hands as she stared at the river, singing. "Love," I said to her, caressing her, but she never seemed to hear. "You like the river better than me," I said. Then summer came, people sat along the parapets, bands of mandolin players strolled up and down, the watermelon stand appeared in its spot just beyond the bridge.

It was 1938; the Spanish communists had lost Brunete, a husband had murdered his wife, the government had passed the race law, but these were all distant facts for us, mere newspaper headlines. What mattered to us were those hours on the bridge, our walks down the boulevards and her father's refusal to meet me.

"I'll convince him, you'll see," Vanda said. "Anyway, he has nothing against you, he just thinks we're too young." She grew more womanly every day, and taller. And as time passed and we learned to kiss, things changed. She became restless and began asking questions, even about the most insignificant things, anxiously, as if she lived in a continuous nightmare which would come back to her from time to time and overwhelm her. "This is obsessive," she would say then as she had that first day. "Why are the lights going on so late? Why did you have your hair cut today? Why has the moon been full for so many nights?"

I dreamed of our home, and of us married, and of a radio with headphones and a tuner, shiny as a toy. That June I gave her an amaranthine handkerchief; in the cool evenings, she would wear it around her neck on a white suit. "I didn't want to fall in love. I ran over to you that first night so that you would leave me alone."

"I know," I would answer foolishly and laugh. Then I would ask: "And when are you going to tell me the secret? Don't you know that you can't scare me any more, I love you too much for that," I asked her.

56

"Not yet." She looked at me gravely, and all I could do was kiss her.

She seemed paler, more and more distracted, uneasy. "Your responsibilities at home tire you out too much," I told her more than once.

"Do you really love me a lot?" she would ask, caressing me. Then one night she said: "But if you really love me so much why don't you try to see who I really am? I'm going to wait until you do to tell you the secret."

"I know everything about you, you're like the air I breathe. I can read you like an open book," I told her.

"Oh, you fool," she said, with a tone of affection and discomfort in her voice that I couldn't get out of my mind. We were leaning on the parapet; it was windy and the park was deep in fog; the parallel lines of lamps vanished in it. The river was a moving black mass that emerged from beneath the arches; you could hear it breaking continually against the pillars. Vanda said: "It's obsessive. You keep saying, 'I know, I know, I know.' But you don't. You don't know anything. Why am I blond? I shouldn't be. Do you know that?"

"You're blond because you are," I said.

"I shouldn't be blond. It's obsessive. And I love you too. Why do I love you? You must know why, so let's hear it. Why? I don't know. I only know that I love you and that I can't figure out why." There was a strange calm about her; the sense of her words was disordered, but not her voice; her voice was actually full of tenderness, the tenderness of someone who has been wronged and wants to forgive. "Sure, you know everything," she repeated. "You also know that the river ends up in the sea. But you can't know that I've never seen the sea. You see,

I'm twenty years old and I've never seen the sea, I've never even been on a train. Did you know that?"

"You dope," I said, "was that the secret?"

She had her elbows on the parapet and she leaned her head into her hands: "Oh, now you think that's the secret? It's obsessive."

I put my arms around her and turned her face toward me: then I realized that she was crying. I put my finger on a tear and wet her lips with it. "Listen," I told her, "the sea is salty like this." I kissed her cheek. "On Sunday we'll go to the sea. We'll even take the train. We'll go early enough to come back the same night. We'll find an excuse for your father."

"We don't have to," she answered slowly, looking out into the river. "My father's gone away for a while."

"Did he go to visit relatives?"

"Yes," she said.

As I was walking her home, she turned back toward the statues of the seasons on the bridge, then said: "What is spring doing here at this time of year? Can you tell me that? She punched my chest affectionately before she put her mouth to mine; but her eyes were wet with tears again. I dried them with the handkerchief.

That night my mother came into my room, waking me. "I just came to see whether you closed the window," she said. "Do you hear that storm?" It was a downpour and the rain, blown by the wind, beat in gusts against the glass. "Tomorrow the river will be high," my mother said as she left. The next morning the sun was shining on the bridge; and that new air that comes after a storm swept through the streets and across the facades of the houses.

The river had risen to the silversmiths' workshops, their large windows closed with iron shutters. I waited for Vanda and she didn't come; I wandered through the market without finding her; then I thought that she might have caught cold in the chill of the previous evening. I decided to go up to her house. When I knocked, a thin woman who was getting on in years answered the door; she wore glasses on a pince-nez and a faded, light blue housecoat. She was drying a food container with a towel. "Vanda's not home," she said discourteously in an irritated tone. "She must have gone out very early. A nurse has already been here twice looking for her, but she's nowhere to be seen."

"A nurse? Why?" I asked.

"Her father had a more violent episode . . . this time it seems . . ."

I was still standing in the doorway, and I was so bewildered that I only managed to say, "Why, is her father sick?"

The woman laid down the container and the towel on a nearby table and rearranged her housecoat. "You're not from the police, are you?" she asked.

"No," I said, "I'm a friend."

"Oh, please forgive me. Yes, they come nearly every day. You see, Vanda's father had a breakdown three months ago, after they fired him from his job because he's Jewish. It was the desperation that got him."

"And what about Vanda?" I asked.

"I have no idea where she could've gone," answered the woman. "Maybe she's gone to look for a loan. You know, we do our best to help out since she lost her job too, but we're not exactly swimming in money ourselves . . ."

Then two days later, way down near the mouth of the river, the water gave back Vanda's body.

Translated by Kathrine Jason

Sii, siate, siano: The child is using incorrect forms of the verb *to be*, which is why the couple laugh.

Siberian Wooing

YEVGENY YEVTUSHENKO

In Siberia there once was an old wedding custom: the bride had to wash the feet of the groom, then drink the water. Only then was she considered worthy to be his wife.

The bridegroom of forty-one,
     who tomorrow goes off to war
          in a heated van,
is planted by his Zima relatives
      on a creaky stool,
and new, still pale, bootstraps
      stick out of his smashing kid boots
where the wickedly elegant upper part
      is burned back
and where a golden
      kerosene light plays.
The bride of forty-one
     enters with a heavy washbowl
       painted with roses,
in which the softly steaming water
      shifts uneasily,
and pulling the groom's boots off,
      soiling both hands at once
       with shoeblack,
she unwinds his leg wrappings,
     all without shame.
Now she immerses
     his bare feet with their little-boy red spots
so that when he winces in reflex
     water spills over the rim
       onto the patterned floor mat,
and caresses his feet with water
     and the female tenderness
       of shaking girlish fingers,
diamond after diamond
     dropping from her eyes into the washbowl.

She stands on her knees
      before her future dead husband,
washing him in advance, so that if he is killed—
         he is cleansed,
and the tips of her fingers
      caress on his feet
        each tiny hair,
the way a peasant woman's fingers caress
        every tiny ear of corn in the field.
And her future husband sits there—
      neither alive
        nor dead.
She bathes his feet,
     but his cheeks and Cossack forelock are soaked.
He breaks into such a sweat
      that his eyes spend tears,
relatives
    and icons
      break into tears.
And when the bride bends over
       to drink the water of her beloved,
he jumps up,
    raises her up in a single motion,
        sits her down, as his wife,
falls on his own knees,
   and instantly pulls from her
     the garishly painted, combed felt boots,
and thrusts her feet into the washbowl,
       shaking as in a chill of fever.
How he washed her feet—
     each toe,
      each nail!
How he kneads
     her sweet-apple ankles
       in trembling palms!
How he washes her!
     As though she were his yet unborn daughter,
whose father,
    after his own future demise,
       he will become!

And then he raises the washbowl
>
> and presses his teeth—biting
>> until the enamel crunches

and his adam's apple dances on his neck—
> drinking that cup to the bottom,

and across his face,
> across his chest,
>> quivering, like a transparent flag
>>> of greatest purity,

flows the water from the feet of lovers,
> water from the feet of lovers . . .

Translated by Albert C. Todd and James Ragan

In Music

CZESLAW MILOSZ

Wailing of a flute, a little drum.
A small wedding cortege accompanies a couple
Going past clay houses on the street of a village.
In the dress of the bride much white satin.
How many pennies put away to sew it, once in a lifetime.
The dress of the groom black, festively stiff.
The flute tells something to the hills, parched, the color of deer.
Hens scratch in dry mounds of manure.

I have not seen it, I summoned it listening to music.
The instruments play for themselves, in their own eternity.
Lips glow, agile fingers work, so short a time.
Soon afterwards the pageant sinks into the earth.
But the sound endures, autonomous, triumphant,
For ever visited by, each time returning,
The warm touch of cheeks, interiors of houses,
And particular human lives
Of which the chronicles make no mention.

Translated by the author and Robert Hass

A Wedge of Shade

LOUISE ERDRICH

The heat was so intense that nobody wanted to think about anything other than ice—but some things, like love, just won't wait.

E very place that I could name you, in the whole world around us, has better things about it than Argus. I just happened to grow up there for eighteen years and the soil got to be part of me, the air has something in it that I breathed. Argus water, fluoridated by an order of the state, doesn't taste as good as water in the Cities. Still, the first thing I do, walking back into my mother's house, is stand at the kitchen sink and toss down glass after glass.

"Are you filled up?" My mother stands behind me. "Sit down if you are."

She's tall and board square, with long arms and big knuckles. Her face is rawboned, fierce and almost masculine in its edges and planes. Several months ago, a beauty operator convinced her that she should feminize her look with curls. Now the permanent, grown out in grizzled streaks, bristles like the coat of a terrier. I don't look like her. Not just the hair, since hers is pepper, mine is a reddish brown, but my build. I'm short, boxy, more like my Aunt Mary, although there's not much about me that corresponds even to her, except it's true that I can't seem to shake this town. I keep coming back here.

"There's jobs at the beet plant."

This rumor, probably false as the plant is in a slump, drops into the dim close air of the kitchen. We have the shades drawn because it's a hot June, over a hundred degrees, and we're trying to stay cool. Outside, the water has been sucked from everything. The veins in the leaves are hollow, the ditch grass is crackling. The sky has absorbed every drop. It's a thin whitish blue veil stretched from end to end over us, a flat gauze tarp. From the depot, I've walked here beneath it, dragging my suitcase.

We're sweating like we're in an oven, a big messy one. For a week, it's been too hot to move much or even clean, and the crops are stunted, failing. The farmer next to us just sold his field for a subdivision, but the workers aren't doing much. They're wearing wet rags on their heads, sitting near the house sites in the brilliance of noon. The studs of wood stand uselessly upright, over them. Nothing casts a shadow. The sun has dried them up too.

"The beet plant," my mother says again.

"Maybe so," I say, and then, because I've got something bigger on my mind, "maybe I'll go out there and apply."

"Oh?" She is intrigued now.

"God, this is terrible!" I take the glass of water in my hand and tip some on my head. I don't feel cooler though, I just feel the steam rising off me.

"The fan broke down," she states. "Both of them are kaput now. The motors or something. If Mary would get the damn tax refund we'd run out to Pamida, buy a couple more, set up a breeze. Then we'd be cool out here."

"Your garden must be dead," I say, lifting the edge of the pull shade.

"It's sick, but I watered. And I won't mulch, that draws the damn slugs."

"Nothing could live out there, no bug." My eyes smart from even looking at the yard, cleared on the north, almost incandescent.

"You'd be surprised."

I wish I could blurt it out, just tell her. Even now, the words swell in my mouth, the one sentence, but I'm scared and with good reason. There is this about my mother: it is awful to see her angry. Her lips press together and she stiffens herself within, growing wooden, silent. Her features become fixed and remote, she will not speak. It takes a long time, and until she does you are held in suspense. Nothing that she ever says, in the end, is as bad as that feeling of dread. So I wait, half believing that she'll figure out my secret for herself, or drag it out of me, not that she ever tries. If I'm silent, she hardly notices. She's not like Aunt Mary, who forces me to say more than I know is on my mind.

My mother sighs, "It's too hot to bake. It's too hot to cook. But it's too hot to eat, anyway." She's talking to herself, which makes me reckless. Perhaps she is so preoccupied by the heat that I can slip my announcement past her. I should just say it, but I lose nerve, make an introduction that alerts her.

"I have something to tell you."

I've cast my lot, there's no going back unless I think quickly. My thoughts hum.

But she waits, forgetting the heat for a moment.

"Ice," I say, "we have to have ice." I speak intensely, leaning toward her, almost glaring, but she is not fooled.

"Don't make me laugh," she says, "there's not a cube in town. The refrigerators can't keep cold enough."

She eyes me as if I'm an animal about to pop from its den and run.

"Okay." I break down. "I really do have something." I stand, turn my back. In this lightless warmth I'm dizzy, almost sick. Now I've gotten to her and she's frightened to hear, breathless.

"Tell me," she urges. "Go on, get it over with."

As so I say it. "I got married." There is a surge of relief, as if a wind blows through the room, but then it's gone. The curtain flaps and we're caught again, stunned in an even denser heat. It's now my turn to wait, and I whirl around and sit right across from her. But I can't bear the picture she makes, the shock that parts her lips, the stunned shade of hurt in her eyes. I have to convince her, somehow, that it's all right.

"You hate weddings! Just think, just picture it. Me, white net. On a day like this. You, stuffed in your summer wool, and Aunt Mary, God knows . . . and the tux, the rental, the groom . . ."

Her head lowered as my words fell on her, but now her forehead tips up and her eyes come into view, already hardening. My tongue flies back into my mouth.

She mimics, making it a question, "The groom . . ."

I'm caught, my lips half open, a stuttering noise in my throat. How to begin? I have rehearsed this but my lines melt away, my opening, my casual introductions. I can think of nothing that would, even in a small way, convey any part of who he is. There is no picture adequate, no representation that captures him. So I just put my hand across the table, and I touch her hand.

"Mother," I say, like we're in a staged drama, "he'll arrive here shortly."

There is something forming in her, some reaction. I am afraid to let it take complete shape.

"Let's go out and wait on the steps, Mom. Then you'll see him."

"I do not understand," she says in a frighteningly neutral voice. This is what I mean. Everything is suddenly forced, unnatural, as though we're reading lines.

"He'll approach from a distance." I can't help speaking like a bad

actor. "I told him to give me an hour. He'll wait, then he'll come walking down the road."

We rise and unstick our blouses from our stomachs, our skirts from the backs of our legs. Then we walk out front in single file, me behind, and settle ourselves on the middle step. A scrubby box elder tree on one side casts a light shade, and the dusty lilacs seem to catch a little breeze on the other. It's not so bad out here, still hot, but not so dim, contained. It is worse past the trees. The heat shimmers in a band, rising off the fields, out of the spars and bones of houses that will wreck our view. The horizon and the edge of town show through the spacing now, and as we sit we watch the workers move, slowly, almost in a practiced recital, back and forth. Their headcloths hang to their shoulders, their hard hats are dabs of yellow, their white T-shirts blend into the fierce air and sky. They don't seem to be doing anything, although we hear faint thuds from their hammers. Otherwise, except for the whistles of a few birds, there is silence. We certainly don't speak.

It is a longer wait than I anticipated, maybe because he wants to give me time. At last the shadows creep out, hard, hot, charred, and the heat begins to lengthen and settle. We are going into the worst of the afternoon, when a dot at the end of the road begins to form.

Mom and I are both watching. We have not moved our eyes around much, and we blink and squint to try and focus. The dot doesn't change, not for a long while. And then it suddenly springs clear in relief, a silhouette, lost a moment in the shimmer, reappearing. In that shining expanse he is a little wedge of moving shade. He continues, growing imperceptibly, until there are variations in the outline, and it can be seen that he is large. As he passes the construction workers, they turn and stop, all alike in their hats, stock-still.

Growing larger yet as if he has absorbed their stares, he nears us. Now we can see the details. He is dark, the first thing. I have not told my mother, but he's a Chippewa, from the same tribe as she. His arms are thick, his chest is huge and the features of his face are wide open. He carries nothing in his hands. He wears a black T-shirt, the opposite of the construction workers, and soft jogging shoes. His jeans are held under his stomach by a belt with a star beaded on the buckle. His hair is long, in a tail. I am the wrong woman for him. I am paler, shorter, unmagnificent. But I stand up. Mom joins me, and I answer proudly when she asks, "His name?"

"His name is Gerry."

We descend one step, and stop again. It is here we will receive him. Our hands are folded at our waists. We're balanced, composed. He continues to stroll toward us, his white smile widening, his eyes filling with the sight of me as mine are filling with him. At the end of the road, behind him, another dot has appeared. It is fast-moving and the sun flares off it twice, a vehicle. Now there are two figures. One approaching in a spume of dust from the rear, and Gerry, unmindful, not slackening or quickening his pace, continuing on. It is like a choreography design. They move at parallel speeds, in front of our eyes. At the same moment, at the end of our yard, as if we have concluded a performance now, both of them halt.

Gerry stands, looking toward us, his thumbs in his belt. He nods respectfully to Mom, looks calmly at me, and half smiles. He raises his brows, and we're suspended. Officer Lovchik emerges from the police car, stooped and tired. He walks up behind Gerry and I hear the snap of handcuffs, then I jump. I'm stopped by Gerry's gaze though, as he backs away from me, still smiling tenderly. I am paralyzed halfway down the walk. He kisses the air while Lovchik cautiously prods at him, fitting his prize into the car. And then the doors slam, the engine roars and they back out and turn around. As they move away there is no siren. I think I've heard Lovchik mention questioning. I'm sure it is lots of fuss for nothing, a mistake, but it cannot be denied, this is terrible timing.

I shake my shoulders, smooth my skirt and turn to Mother with a look of outrage.

"How do you like that?" I try.

She's got her purse in one hand, her car keys out.

"Let's go," she says.

"Okay," I answer. "Fine. Where?"

"Aunt Mary's."

"I'd rather go and bail him out, Mom."

"Bail," she says, "bail?"

She gives me such a look of cold and furious surprise that I sink immediately into the front seat, lean back against the vinyl. I almost welcome the sting of the heated plastic on my back, thighs, shoulders.

Aunt Mary's dogs are rugs in the dirt, flattened by the heat of the day. Not one of them barks at us to warn her. We step over them and get no more reaction than a whine, the slow beat of a tail. Inside, we get no answers either, although we call Aunt Mary up and down the hall. We enter the kitchen and sit at the table which contains a half-ruined watermelon. By the sink, in a tin box, are cigarettes. My mother takes one and carefully puts the match to it, frowning.

"I know what," she says. "Go check the lockers."

There are two, a big freezer full of labeled meats and rental space, and another, smaller one that is just a side cooler. I notice, walking past the display counter, that the red beacon beside the outside switch of the cooler is glowing. That tells you when the light is on inside.

I pull the long metal handle toward me and the thick door swishes open. I step into the cool, spicy air. She is there, too proud to ever register a hint of surprise. Aunt Mary simply nods and looks away, as though I've just gone out for a minute, although we've not seen one another in six months or more. She is relaxing, reading a scientific magazine article. I sit down on a barrel of alum labeled Zanzibar and drop my bomb with no warning. "I'm married." It doesn't matter how I tell it to Aunt Mary, because she won't be, refuses to be, surprised.

"What's he do?" she simply asks, putting aside the sheaf of paper. I thought the first thing she'd do is scold me for fooling my mother. But it's odd. For two women who have lived through boring times and disasters, how rarely one comes to the other's defense, and how often they are willing to take advantage of the other's absence. But I'm benefiting here. It seems that Aunt Mary is truly interested in Gerry. So I'm honest.

"He's something like a political activist. I mean he's been in jail and all. But not for any crime, you see, it's just because of his convictions."

She gives me a long, shrewd stare. Her skin is too tough to wrinkle, but she doesn't look young. All around us hang loops of sausages, every kind you can imagine, every color from the purple-black of blutwurst to the pale whitish links that my mother likes best. Blocks of butter and headcheese, a can of raw milk, wrapped parcels and cured bacons are stuffed onto the shelves around us. My heart has gone still and cool inside of me, and I can't stop talking.

"He's the kind of guy it's hard to describe, very different. People call him a free spirit, but that doesn't say it either because he's very disciplined in some ways. He learned to be neat in jail." I pause, she says nothing, so I go on. "I know it's sudden, but who likes weddings? I hate them, all that mess with the bridesmaid's gowns, getting material to match. I don't have girl friends, I mean, how embarrassing, right? Who would sing 'Oh Perfect Love?' Carry the ring?"

She isn't really listening.

"What's he do?" she asks again.

Maybe she won't let go of it until I discover the right answer, like a game with nouns and synonyms.

"He, well he agitates," I tell her.

"Is that some kind of factory work?"

"Not exactly, no, it's not a nine-to-five job or anything . . ."

She lets the pages fall, now cocks her head to the side and stares at me without blinking her cold yellow eyes. She has the look of a hawk, of a person who can see into the future but won't tell you about it. She's lost business for staring at customers, but she doesn't care.

"Are you telling me that he doesn't"—here she shakes her head twice, slowly, from one side to the other without removing me from her stare—"that he doesn't have regular work?"

"Oh, what's the matter anyway," I say roughly. "I'll work. This is the nineteen seventies."

She jumps to her feet, stands over me, a stocky woman with terse features and short, thin points of gray hair. Her earrings tremble and flash, small fiery opals. Her brown plastic glasses hang crooked on a cord around her neck. I have never seen her become quite so instantaneously furious, so disturbed.

"We're going to fix that," she says.

The cooler instantly feels smaller, the sausages knock at my shoulder and the harsh light makes me blink. I am as stubborn as Aunt Mary, however, and she knows that I can go head-to-head with her.

"We're married and that's final." I manage to stamp my foot.

Aunt Mary throws an arm back, blows air through her cheeks and waves away my statement vigorously.

"You're a little girl. How old is *he*?"

I frown at my lap, trace the threads in my blue cotton skirt and tell her that age is irrelevant.

"Big word," she says sarcastically. "Let me ask you this. He's old enough to get a job?"

"Of course he is, what do you think. Okay, he's older than me. He's in his thirties."

"Aha, I knew it."

"Geez! So what? I mean, haven't you ever been in love, hasn't someone ever gotten you *right here*?" I smash my fist on my chest. We lock our eyes, but she doesn't waste a second in feeling hurt.

"Sure, sure I've been in love. You think I haven't? I know what it feels like, you smartass. You'd be surprised. But he was no lazy sonofabitch. Now listen . . ." She stops, draws breath, and I let her. "Here's what I mean by 'fix'. I'll teach the sausage-making trade to him, you too, and the grocery business. I've about had it anyway, and so's your mother. We'll do the same as my aunt and uncle—leave the shop to you and move to Arizona. I like this place." She looks up at the burning safety bulb, down to me again. Her face drags in the light. "But what the hell. I always wanted to travel."

I'm kind of stunned, a little flattened out, maybe ashamed of myself.

"You hate going anywhere," I say, which is true.

The door swings open and Mom comes in with us. She finds a can and balances herself, sighing at the delicious feeling of the air, absorbing from the silence the fact we have talked. She hasn't anything to add, I guess, and as the coolness hits her eyes fall shut. Aunt Mary too. I can't help it either, and my eyelids drop although my brain is alert and conscious. From the darkness, I can see us in the brilliance. The light rains down on us. We sit the way we have been sitting, on our cans of milk and flour, upright and still. Our hands are curled loosely in our laps. Our faces are blank as the gods. We could be statues in a tomb sunk into the side of a mountain. We could be dreaming the world up in our brains.

It is later and the weather has no mercy. We are drained of everything but simple thoughts. It's too hot for feelings. Driving home, we see how field after field of beets has gone into shock, and even some of the soybeans. The plants splay, limp, burned into the ground. Only the sunflowers continue to struggle upright, bristling but small.

What drew me in the first place to Gerry was the unexpected. I went to hear him talk just after I enrolled at the U of M and then I demonstrated when they came and got him off the stage. He always went so willingly, accommodating everyone. I began to visit him. I sold lunar calendars and posters to raise his bail and eventually free him.

One thing led to another and one night we found ourselves alone in a Howard Johnson's where they put him up when his speech was finished. There were more beautiful women after him, he could have had his pick of Swedes or Yankton Sioux girls, who are the best-looking of all. But I was different, he says. He liked my slant on life. And then there was no going back once it started, no turning, as though it were meant. We had no choice.

I have this intuition as we near the house, in the fateful quality of light, as in the turn of the day the heat continues to press and the blackness, into which the warmth usually lifts, lowers steadily. We must come to the end of something. There must be a close to this day.

As we turn into the yard we see that Gerry is sitting on the stairs. Now it is our turn to be received. I throw the car door open and stumble out before the motor even cuts. I run to him and hold him, as my mother, pursuing the order of events, parks carefully. Then she walks over too, holding her purse by the strap. She stands before him and says no word but simply looks into his face, staring as if he's cardboard, a man behind glass who cannot see her. I think she's rude, but then I realize that he is staring back, that they are the same height. Their eyes are level. He puts his hand out.

"My name is Gerry."

"Gerry what?"

"Nanapush."

She nods, shifts her weight. "You're from that line, the old strain, the ones . . ." She does not finish.

"And my father," Gerry says, "was Old Man Pillager." He has said this before but I never heard any special meaning in it.

"Kashpaws," she says, "are my branch of course. We're probably related through my mother's brother." They do not move. They are like two opponents from the same divided country, staring across the border. They do not shift or blink and I see that they are more alike than I am like either of them, so tall, solid, dark-haired. She could be the mother, he the son.

"Well, I guess you should come in," she offers, "you are a distant relative after all." She looks at me. "Distant enough."

Whole swarms of mosquitoes are whining down, discovering us now, so there is no question of staying where we are. And so we walk into the house, much hotter than outside with the gathered heat. Instantly the sweat springs from our skin and I can think of nothing else but cooling off. I try to force the windows higher in their sashes, but there's no breeze anyway, nothing stirs, no air.

"Are you sure," I gasp, "about those fans?"

"Oh, they're broke," my mother says, distressed. I rarely hear this in her voice. She switches on the lights, which makes the room seem hotter, and we lower ourselves into the easy chairs. Our words echo, as though the walls have baked and dried hollow.

"Show me those fans," says Gerry.

My mother points toward the kitchen. "They're sitting on the table. I've already tinkered with them. See what you can do."

And so he does. After a while she hoists herself and walks out back with him. Their voices close together now, absorbed, and their tools clank frantically as if they are fighting a duel. But it is a race with the hell of darkness and their waning energy. I think of ice. I get ice on the brain.

"Be right back," I call out, taking the keys from my mother's purse, "do you need anything?"

There is no answer from the kitchen but a furious sputter of metal, the clatter of nuts and bolts spilling to the floor.

I drive out to the Super Pumper, a big new gas-station complex on the edge of town where my mother most likely has never been. She doesn't know about convenience stores, has no credit cards for groceries, gas, pays only with small bills and change. She never has used an ice machine. It would grate on her that a bag of frozen water costs eighty cents, but it doesn't bother me. I take the Styrofoam cooler and I fill it for a couple of dollars. I buy two six-packs of Shasta sodas and I plunge them into the uniform coins of ice. I drink two myself, on the way home, and I manage to lift the whole heavy cooler out of the trunk, carry it to the door.

The fans are shirring, beating the air.

I hear them going in the living room the minute I come in. The only light shines from the kitchen. Gerry and my mother have thrown the pillows from the couch onto the living room floor, and they are sitting in the rippling currents of air. I bring the cooler in and put it near us. I have chosen all dark flavors—black cherry, grape, black raspberry, so as we drink it almost seems the darkness swirls inside us with the night air, sweet and sharp, driven by small motors.

I drag more pillows down from the other rooms upstairs. There is no question of attempting the bedrooms, the stifling beds. And so, in the dark, I hold hands with Gerry as he settles down between my mother and me. He is huge as a hill between the two of us, solid in the beating wind.

The River-Merchant's Wife: A Letter

LI PO

*Married at fourteen, in love at fifteen, left alone at sixteen—
the pain of parting was as keen 1200 years ago as it is today.*

While my hair was still cut straight across my forehead
I played about the front gate, pulling flowers.
You came by on bamboo stilts, playing horse,
You walked about my seat, playing with blue plums.
And we went on living in the village of Chōkan:
Two small people, without dislike or suspicion.

At fourteen I married My Lord you.
I never laughed, being bashful.
Lowering my head, I looked at the wall.
Called to, a thousand times, I never looked back.

At fifteen I stopped scowling,
I desired my dust to be mingled with yours
Forever and forever and forever.
Why should I climb the lookout?

At sixteen you departed,
You went into far Ku-tō-en, by the river of swirling eddies,
And you have been gone five months.
The monkeys make sorrowful noise overhead.

You dragged your feet when you went out.
By the gate now, the moss is grown, the different mosses,
Too deep to clear them away!
The leaves fall early this autumn, in wind.
The paired butterflies are already yellow with August
Over the grass in the West garden;
They hurt me. I grow older.
If you are coming down through the narrows of the river Kiang,
Please let me know beforehand,
And I will come out to meet you
                    As far as Chō-fū-Sa.

Translated by Ezra Pound

The Winner

BARBARA KIMENYE

What would it be like to win the lottery? As old Pius Ndawula found out, first the relatives descend on your mud-and-wattle hut, then your old crony Salongo tries to get rid of them, and finally Cousin Sarah . . . well, let's just say that instant wealth does bring changes.

When Pius Ndawula won the football pools, overnight he seemed to become the most popular man in Buganda. Hosts of relatives converged upon him from the four corners of the kingdom: cousins and nephews, nieces and uncles, of whose existence he had never before been aware, turned up in Kalasanda by the busload, together with crowds of individuals who, despite their downtrodden appearance, assured Pius that they and they alone were capable of seeing that his money was properly invested—preferably in their own particular businesses!

Also lurking around Pius's unpretentious mud hut were newspaper reporters, slick young men weighed down with cameras and sporting loud checked caps or trilbies set at conspicuously jaunty angles, and serious young men from Radio Uganda who were anxious to record Pius's delight at his astonishing luck for the edification of the Uganda listening public.

The rest of Kalasanda were so taken by surprise that they could only call and briefly congratulate Pius before being elbowed out of the way by his more garrulous relations. All, that is to say, except Pius's greatest friend Salongo, the custodian of the Ssabalangira's tomb. He came and planted himself firmly in the house, and nobody attempted to move him. Almost blind, and very lame, he tottered out with the aid of a stout stick. Just to see him arrive had caused a minor sensation in the village, for he hadn't left the tomb for years. But recognizing at last a chance to house Ssabalangira's remains in a state befitting his former glory, made the slow tortuous journey worthwhile to Salongo.

Nantondo hung about long enough to have her picture taken with Pius. Or rather, she managed to slip beside him just as the cameras clicked, and so it was that every Uganda newspaper, on the following day, carried a front-page photograph of "Mr. Pius Ndawula and his happy wife," a caption that caused Pius to shake with rage and threaten legal proceedings, but over which Nantondo gloated as she proudly showed it to everybody who visited.

"Tell us, Mr. Ndawula, what do you intend to do with all the money you have won . . .?"

"Tell us, Mr. Ndawula, how often have you completed pools coupons . . .?"

"Tell us . . . Tell us . . . Tell us . . ."

Pius's head was reeling under this bombardment of questions, and he was even more confused by Salongo's constant nudging and muttered advice to "Say nothing!" Nor did the relatives make things easier. Their persistent clamouring for his attention, and the way they kept shoving their children under his nose, made it impossible for him to think, let alone talk.

It isn't at all easy, when you have lived for sixty-five years in complete obscurity, to adjust yourself in a matter of hours to the role of a celebrity, and the strain was beginning to tell.

Behind the hut—Pius had no proper kitchen—gallons of tea were being boiled, whilst several of the female cousins were employed in ruthlessly hacking down the bunches of *matoke* from his meagre plantains, to cook food for everybody. One woman—she had introduced herself as Cousin Sarah—discovered Pius's hidden store of banana beer, and dished it out to all and sundry as though it were her own. Pius had become very wary of Cousin Sarah. He didn't like the way in which she kept loudly remarking that he needed a woman about the place, and he was even more seriously alarmed when suddenly Salongo gave him a painful dig in the ribs and muttered, "You'll have to watch that one—she's a sticker!"

Everybody who came wanted to see the telegram that announced Pius's win. When it had arrived at the Ggombolola Headquarters—the postal address of everyone living within a radius of fifteen miles—Musisi had brought it out personally, delighted to be the bearer of such good tidings. At Pius's request he had gone straight away to tell Salongo, and then back to his office to send an acknowledgment on behalf of Pius to the pools firm, leaving the old man to dream rosy dreams.

76

An extension of his small coffee *shamba*, a new roof on his house—or maybe an entirely new house—concrete blocks this time, with a verandah perhaps. Then there were hens. Salongo and he had always said there was money in hens these days, now that the women ate eggs and chicken; not that either of them agreed with the practice. Say what you like, women who ate chicken and eggs were fairly asking to be infertile! That woman Welfare officer who came around snooping occasionally, tried to say it was all nonsense, that chicken meat and eggs made bigger and better babies. Well, they might look bigger and better, but nobody could deny that they were fewer! Which only goes to show.

But news spreads fast in Africa—perhaps the newspapers have contacts in the pools offices. Anyway, before the telegram had even reached Pius, announcements were appearing in the local newspapers, and Pius was still quietly lost in his private dreams when the first batch of visitors arrived. At first, he was at a loss to understand what was happening. People he hadn't seen for years and only recognized with difficulty fell upon him with cries of joy.

"Cousin Pius, the family are delighted!"

"Cousin Pius, why have you not visited us all this time?"

Pius was pleased to see his nearest and dearest gathered around him. It warmed his old heart once more to find himself in the bosom of his family, and he welcomed them effusively. The second crowd to arrive were no less well received, but there was a marked coolness on the part of their forerunners.

However, as time had gone by and the flood of strange faces had gained momentum, Pius's *shamba* had come to resemble a political meeting. All to be seen from the door of the house was a turbulent sea of white *kanzus* and brilliant *busutis*, and the house itself was full of people and tobacco smoke.

The precious telegram was passed from hand to hand until it was reduced to a limp fragment of paper with the lettering partly obliterated: not that it mattered very much, for only a few members of the company could read English.

"Now, Mr. Ndawula, we are ready to take the recording." The speaker was a slight young man wearing a checked shirt. "I shall ask you a few questions, and you simply answer me in your normal voice." Pius looked at the leather box with its two revolving spools, and licked his lips.

"Say nothing!" came a hoarse whisper from Salongo.

The young man steadfastly ignored him, and went ahead in his best BBC manner. "Well, first of all, Mr. Ndawula, let me congratulate you on your winning the pools. Would you like to tell our listeners what it feels like suddenly to find yourself rich?" There was an uncomfortable pause, during which Pius stared mesmerized at the racing spools and the young man tried frantically to span the gap by asking, "I mean, have you any plans for the future?"

Pius swallowed audibly, and opened his mouth to say something, but shut it again when Salongo growled, "Tell him nothing!"

The young man snapped off the machine, shaking his head in exasperation. "Look here, sir, all I want you to do is to say something—I'm not asking you to make a speech. Now, I'll tell you what. I shall ask you again what it feels like suddenly to come into money, and you say something like 'It was a wonderful surprise, and naturally I feel very pleased'—and will you ask your friend not to interrupt! Got it? Okay, off we go!"

The machine was again switched on, and the man brightly put the question, "Now, Mr. Ndawula, what does it feel like to win the pools?"

Pius swallowed, then quickly chanted in a voice all off key, "It was a wonderful surprise and naturally I feel very happy and will you ask your friend not to interrupt!" The young man nearly wept. This happened to be his first assignment as a radio interviewer, and it looked like being his last. He switched off the machine and mourned his lusterless future, groaning.

At that moment Cousin Sarah caught his eye. "Perhaps I can help you," she said. "I am Mr. Ndawula's cousin." She made this pronouncement in a manner that suggested Pius had no others. The young man brightened considerably. "Well, madam, if you could tell me something about Mr. Ndawula's plans, I would be most grateful."

Cousin Sarah folded her arms across her imposing bosom, and when the machine again started up, she was off. Yes, Mr. Ndawula was very happy about the money. No, she didn't think he had any definite plans on how to spend it—with all these people about he didn't have time to think. Yes, Mr. Ndawula lived completely alone, but she was prepared to stay and look after him for as long as he needed her. Here a significant glance passed between the other women in the room, who clicked their teeth and let out long "Eeeeeeehs!" of incredulity. Yes, she believed she was Mr. Ndawula's nearest living relative by marriage . . .

Pius listened to her confident aplomb with growing horror, whilst Salongo frantically nudged him and whispered, "There! What did I tell you? That woman's a sticker."

Around three in the afternoon, *matoke* and tea were served—the *matoke* on wide fresh plantain leaves, since Pius owned only three plates,

and the tea in anything handy—tin cans, old jars, etc.—because he was short of cups, too.

Pius ate very little, but he was glad of the tea. He had shaken hands with so many people that his arms ached, and he was tired of the chatter and the comings and goings in his house of all these strangers. Most of all he was tired of Cousin Sarah, who insisted on treating him like an idiot invalid. She kept everybody else at bay, as far as she possibly could, and when one woman plonked a sticky fat baby on his lap, Cousin Sarah dragged the child away as though it were infectious. Naturally, a few cross words were exchanged between Sarah and the fond mother, but by this time Pius was past caring.

Yosefu Mukasa and Kibuka called in the early evening, when some of the relatives were departing with effusive promises to come again tomorrow. They were both alarmed at the weariness they saw on Pius's face. The old man looked utterly worn out, his skin grey and sickly. Also, they were a bit taken aback by the presence of Cousin Sarah, who pressed them to take tea and behaved in every respect as though she was mistress of the house.

"I believe my late husband knew you very well, sir," she told Yosefu. "He used to be a Miruka chief in Buyaga County. His name was Kivumbi."

"Ah, yes," Yosefu replied. "I remember Kivumbi very well indeed. We often hunted together. I was sorry to hear of his death. He was a good man."

Cousin Sarah shrugged her shoulders. "Yes, he was a good man. But what the Lord giveth, He also taketh away." Thus was the late Kivumbi dismissed from the conversation.

Hearing all this enabled Pius to define the exact relationship between himself and Cousin Sarah, and even by Kiganda standards it was virtually nonexistent, for the late Kivumbi had been the stepson of one of Pius's cousins.

"Your stroke of luck seems to have exhausted you, Pius," Kibuka remarked, when he and Yosefu were seated on the rough wooden chairs brought forth by Cousin Sarah.

Salongo glared at the world in general and snarled, "Of course he is exhausted. Who wouldn't be with all these scavengers collected to pick his bones?" Pius hushed him as one would a child. "No, no, Salongo. It is quite natural that my family should gather round me at a time like this. Only I fear I am perhaps a little too old for all this excitement."

Salongo spat expertly through the open doorway, narrowly missing a group of guests who were preparing to bed down, and said, "That woman doesn't think he is too old. She's out to catch him. I've seen her type elsewhere."

Yosefu's mouth quirked with amusement at the thought that "elsewhere" could only mean the Ssabalangira's tomb, which Salongo had guarded for the better part of his adult life. "Well, she's a fine woman," he remarked. "But see here, Pius," he went on, "don't be offended by my proposal, but wouldn't it be better if you came and stayed with us at Mutunda for tonight? Miriamu would love to have you, and you look as though you need a good night's rest, which you wouldn't get here—those relatives of yours outside are preparing a fire and are ready to dance the night away!"

"I think that's a wonderful idea!" said Cousin Sarah, bouncing in to remove the tea cups. "You go with Mr. Mukasa, Cousin Pius. The change will do you as much good as the rest. And don't worry about your home—I shall stay here and look after things."

Pius hesitated. "Well, I think I shall be all right here—I don't like to give Miriamu any extra work . . ."

Salongo muttered, "Go to Yosefu's. You don't want to be left alone in the house with that woman—there's no knowing what she might get up to . . ."

"I'll pack a few things for you, Pius," announced Cousin Sarah and bustled off before anything more could be said, pausing only long enough to give Salongo a look that was meant to wither him on the spot.

So Pius found himself being driven away to Mutunda in Yosefu's car, enjoying the pleasant sensation of not having to bother about a thing. Salongo too had been given a lift to as near the tomb as the car could travel, and his wizened old face was contorted into an irregular smile, for Pius had promised to help him build a new house for the Ssabalangira. For him the day had been well spent, despite Cousin Sarah.

Pius spent an enjoyable evening with the Mukasas. They had a well-cooked supper, followed by a glass of cool beer as they sat back and listened to the local news on the radio. Pius had so far relaxed as to tell the Mukasas modestly that he had been interviewed by Radio Uganda that morning, and when Radio Newsreel was announced they waited breathlessly to hear his voice. But instead of Pius, Cousin Sarah came booming over the air. Until that moment, the old man had completely forgotten the incident of the tape-recording. In fact, he had almost forgotten Cousin Sarah. Now it all came back to him with a shiver of apprehension. Salongo was right. That woman did mean business! It was a chilling thought. However, it didn't cause him to lose any sleep. He slept like a cherub, as if he didn't have a care in the world.

Because he looked so refreshed in the morning, Miriamu insisted on keeping him at Mutunda for another day. "I know you feel better, but after seeing you yesterday, I think a little holiday with us will do you good. Go home tomorrow, when the excitement has died down a bit," she advised.

Soon after lunch, as Pius was taking a nap in a chair on the verandah, Musisi drove up in the landrover, with Cousin Sarah by his side. Miriamu came out to greet them, barely disguising her curiosity about the formidable woman about whom she had heard so much. The two women sized each other up and decided to be friends.

Meanwhile, Musisi approached the old man. "Sit down, son," Pius waved him to a chair at his side. "Miriamu feeds me so well it's all I can do to keep awake."

"I am glad you are having a rest, sir." Musisi fumbled in the pocket of his jacket. "There is another telegram for you. Shall I read it?" The old man sat up expectantly and said, "If you'll be so kind."

Musisi first read the telegram in silence, then he looked at Pius and commented, "Well, sir, I'm afraid it isn't good news."

"Not good news? Has somebody died?"

Musisi smiled. "Well, no. It isn't really as bad as that. The thing is, the pools firm say that owing to an unfortunate oversight they omitted to add, in the first telegram, that the prize money is to be shared among three hundred other people."

Pius was stunned. Eventually he murmured, "Tell me, how much does that mean I shall get?"

"Three hundred into seventeen thousand pounds won't give you much over a thousand shillings."

To Musisi's astonishment, Pius sat back and chuckled. "More than a thousand shillings!" he said. "Why, that's a lot of money!"

"But it's not, when you expected so much more."

"I agree. And yet, son, what would I have done with all those thousands of pounds? I am getting past the age when I need a lot."

Miriamu brought a mat onto the verandah and she and Cousin Sarah made themselves comfortable near the men. "What a disappointment!" cried Miriamu, but Cousin Sarah sniffed and said, "I agree with Cousin Pius. He wouldn't know what to do with seventeen thousand pounds, and the family would be hanging round his neck forevermore."

At the mention of Pius's family, Musisi frowned. "I should warn you, sir, those relatives of yours have made a terrific mess of your *shamba*—your plantains have been stripped—and Mrs. Kivumbi here," nodding at Sarah, "was only just in time to prevent them digging up your sweet potatoes."

"Yes, Cousin Pius," added Sarah. "It will take us some time to put the *shamba* back in order. They've trodden down a whole bed of young beans."

"Oh, dear," said Pius weakly. "This is dreadful news."

"Don't worry. They will soon disappear when I tell them there is no money, and then I shall send for a couple of my grandsons to come and help us do some replanting." Pius could not help but admire the way Sarah took things in her stride.

Musisi rose from his chair. "I'm afraid I can't stay any longer, so I will go now and help Cousin Sarah clear the crowd, and see you tomorrow to take you home." He and Sarah climbed back into the landrover and Sarah waved energetically until the vehicle was out of sight.

"Your cousin is a fine woman," Miriamu told Pius, before going indoors. Pius merely grunted, but for some odd reason he felt the remark to be a compliment to himself.

All was quiet at Pius's home when Musisi brought him home next day. He saw at once that his shamba was well-nigh wrecked, but his drooping spirits quickly revived when Sarah placed a mug of steaming tea before him, and sat on a mat at his feet, explaining optimistically how matters could be remedied. Bit by bit he began telling her what he planned to do with the prize money, ending with, "Of course, I shan't be able to do everything now, especially since I promised Salongo something for the tomb."

Sarah poured some more tea and said, "Well, I think the roof should have priority. I noticed last night that there are several leaks. And whilst we're about it, it would be a good idea to build another room on and a small outside kitchen. Mud and wattle is cheap enough, and then the whole place can be plastered. You can still go ahead and extend your coffee. And as for hens, well, I have six good layers at home, as well as a fine cockerel. I'll bring them over!"

Pius looked at her in silence for a long time. She is a fine-looking woman, he thought, and that blue *busuti* suits her. Nobody would ever take her for a grandmother—but why is she so anxious to throw herself at me?

"You sound as if you are planning to come and live here," he said at last, trying hard to sound casual.

Sarah turned to face him and replied, "Cousin Pius, I shall be very frank with you. Six months ago my youngest son got married and brought his wife to live with me. She's a very nice girl, but somehow I can't get used to having another woman in the house. My other son is in Kampala, and although I know I would be welcome there, he too has a wife, and three children, so if I went there I wouldn't be any better off.

"When I saw that bit about you in the paper, I suddenly remembered—although I don't expect you to—how you were at my wedding and so helpful to everybody. Well, I thought to myself, here is somebody who needs a good housekeeper, who needs somebody to keep the leeches off, now that he has come into money. I came along right away to take a look at you, and I can see I did the right thing. You do need me." She hesitated for a moment, and then said, "Only you might prefer to stay alone . . . I'm so used to having my own way, I never thought of that before."

Pius cleared his throat. "You're a very impetuous woman," was all he could find to say.

A week later, Pius wandered over to the tomb and found Salongo busily polishing the Ssabalangira's weapons. "I thought you were dead," growled the custodian, "it is so long since you came here—but then, this tomb thrives on neglect. Nobody cares that one of Buganda's greatest men lies here."

"I have been rather busy," murmured Pius. "But I didn't forget my promise to you. Here! I've brought you a hundred shillings, and I only wish it could have been more. At least it will buy a few cement blocks."

Salongo took the money and looked at it as if it were crawling with lice. Grudgingly he thanked Pius and then remarked, "Of course, you will find life more expensive now that you are keeping a woman in the house."

"I suppose Nantondo told you," Pius smiled sheepishly.

"Does it matter who told me?" the custodian replied. "Anyway, never say I didn't warn you. Next thing she'll want will be ring marriage!"

Pius gave an uncertain laugh. "As a matter of fact, one of the reasons I came up here was to invite you to the wedding—it's next month."

Salongo carefully laid down the spear he was rubbing upon a piece of clean barkcloth and stared at his friend as if he had suddenly grown another head. "What a fool you are! And all this stems from your scribbling noughts and crosses on a bit of squared paper. I knew it would bring no good! At your age you ought to have more sense. Well, all I can advise is that you run while you still have a chance."

For a moment Pius was full of misgivings. Was he, after all, behaving like a fool? Then he thought of Sarah, and the wonders she had worked with his house and his *shamba* in the short time they had been together. He felt reassured.

"Well, I'm getting married, and I expect to see you at both the church and the reception, and if you don't appear, I shall want to know the reason why!" He was secretly delighted at the note of authority in his voice, and Salongo's face was the picture of astonishment.

"All right," he mumbled, "I shall try and come. Before you go, cut a bunch of bananas to take back to your good lady, and there might be some cabbage ready at the back. I suppose I've got to hand it to her. She's the real winner!"

Buganda: A state in southern Uganda; capital city is Kampala

busuti: a long cloak decorated with gold threadwork

kanzu: a long white robe worn by African men

matoke: a Ugandan dish

shamba: a fruit and vegetable garden

Ssabalangira: a great man of Uganda, now dead

How to Be Old

MAY SWENSON

It is easy to be young. (Everybody is,
at first.) It is not easy
to be old. It takes time.
Youth is given; age is achieved.
One must work a magic to mix with time
in order to become old.

Youth is given. One must put it away
like a doll in a closet,
take it out and play with it only
on holidays. One must have many dresses
and dress the doll impeccably
(but not to show the doll, to keep it hidden.)

It is necessary to adore the doll,
to remember it in the dark on the ordinary
days, and every day congratulate
one's ageing face in the mirror.

In time one will be very old.
In time, one's life will be accomplished.
And in time, in time, the doll—
like new, though ancient—will be found.

Mr. and Mrs. Martins

EDLA VAN STEEN

Mr. and Mrs. Martins could have been a comfort to each other in their old age. Why did they choose loneliness instead?

It rained all week long and Mrs. Martins didn't leave the house even to do her bit of shopping. Often she checked on the weather, looking down at the street crowded with gleaming cars and open umbrellas, feeling no trace of boredom, but merely affirming: what rain! And she would go back to the television.

Despite her polite and smiling manner when greeting the neighbors, she seemed not to have friends, for no one ever visited her. Even so, she neatly combed her short gray hair and applied her lipstick discreetly, ready for any eventuality. No one wrote her letters and she paid her bills on time.

On Sunday she woke up happy—the sun was coming in through the half-open blinds. She dusted the furniture lightly, fried two eggs, and, as usual, put on her best black silk dress and remembered the pearl necklace. Then she bought a bunch of flowers at the corner and headed for the taxi stop, empty at that hour of the morning.

She was one of the first people to enter the cemetery. She walked slowly, reading the familiar inscriptions, for she was afraid of slipping on the stone pavement, which was still wet. Something new caught her by surprise: "At last your wife's come to keep you company, eh, Mr. Mario?" She read aloud: "Claire Heller de Alencar 1908-1974. We feel your absence." She counted mentally: eight from fourteen, six; zero from six, six. Eight years older than she. Now the sun burned her back and brightened the plants and flowers in the damp beds. It's strange, she thought, men die before women; there are more widows in the world than widowers. Sighing gently, she started up the hill leading to her

sepulchre, an austere marble rectangle that rose several centimeters above the ground. The names were written in gilded letters: Abel Martins 1910 space Laura Martins 1916 space. I'm making a point of leaving everything settled, her husband insisted; we have no children, who would bother with us? We must even prepare for living alone.

She climbed the step to the tomb, took a bundle from her handbag, and put it down on the slab. From the package she removed a tool, one of those with a spade on one end and two teeth for mixing the earth on the other, and she calmly began to tend the bed.

"What beautiful flowers." The man approached, hat and newspaper in hand.

Mrs. Martins greeted him without interrupting her task.

"I didn't think this was the season for immortelles," he went on, politely.

"That's true, I was astonished too."

"They're my favorites. They last longer than any others."

"All right then, as long as they have them at the florist's I'll keep on bringing them." She examined the arrangement.

"And you? Which do you prefer?"

"Violets, but they're difficult . . ."

"Next Sunday it's my turn. I'll try to find a few bunches."

Mrs. Martins gathered the withered plants, threw them into the garbage bin, and, using a handkerchief, wiped off the remnants of earth. The rose and purple hues of the immortelles blended harmoniously. She exhaled a sweet and ecstatic expression for both of them and sat on the step next to her husband.

"Do you want part of the paper? I hear that the rains have destroyed some cities in the south. Here's the article. Look at this picture."

"Oh my, and the people?"

"Whole families were found in the branches of trees where they'd tried to escape from the floods. They'd miscalculated the height of the water."

"How horrible."

When they finished reading, they chatted about details of their week until they ran out of subjects.

At noon they ate crackers and apples.

"Is it awful being a widow?"

"I thought it would be worse. But the apartment is what bothers me. It's too big. If I could rent a smaller one, the size of yours . . . I couldn't go out on account of the rain and I felt really alone."

"That's impossible. Everything's all set. Can't you get used to it?"

Mrs. Martins, submissive, didn't argue. She would wait for another opportunity.

"Doesn't the television help?" he inquired, concerned, without turning his head: he knew that entreating look.

"More or less, and for you?" She looked at him curiously: clean collar and suit, polished shoes. A shame he was losing his former posture, his back bending.

He noted her gaze.

"Remember at what loose ends I was at the beginning? But you, you look wonderful, you even seem to have grown younger."

Dozens of people were visiting their dead—movable colors on the landscape. Soon solitude would resume its post there and in those people capable of hearing its very reverberations—as if their souls had found a refuge in the sound they could still emit. Mrs. Martins swallowed a deep sob.

"How many installments are left?"

"None."

"What will happen now?"

"We'll just go on waiting."

"Do you think I'll go first?" Mrs. Martins at once regretted the question, so unguarded.

"Would you like to?"

"No, but I feel prepared. If it happens . . ."

"That's why we're practising." He wanted to embrace his wife, but he refrained.

She thought the moment opportune for her much rehearsed question: "What if I bought a cat?"

"And who'll take care of it if . . .?"

88

"You're right, it's a silly idea. The poor little thing might suffer." She was embarrassed.

An employee sweeps the ground. He wears patched gray overalls. He's of the type that seems to have sprung up from the very ground, so much a part of the surroundings is he.

Mr. Martins hands him an envelope.

"It's so you'll always come take care of this . . . well, we're old, and even if one of us lingers more than the other, this way your dedication will have been rewarded."

"Really, sir, you needn't worry."

"Please, take it."

The employee shifted his shoulders in a rude gesture: why do these two come here every Sunday? The thought was cut off by someone asking for information.

Mr. and Mrs. Martins proceeded to pass the day conversing and simply enjoying one another's presence. Perhaps fragments of their life in common peopled the ample silences.

"Are you really sure about changing apartments?"

"One bedroom and a living room would be enough."

"We'll take care of it tomorrow," he promised.

She smiled, grateful.

"Do you suppose there's one in this neighborhood?" He consulted his watch. "Let's go, it's almost six."

The cool wind caused him to turn up his coat collar before lending his support to Mrs. Martins for the descent.

"We won't have more rain. The weather's calming down."

Slow shadows appear along the cemetery lanes, swelling the line going back.

Mr. and Mrs. Martins part with a kiss, each taking a separate path: Abel misses the feel of an arm on him; Laura must take care not to stumble.

Translated by Daphne Patai

Mother

JOHN BERGER

for Katya

"Truly we writers are the secretaries of death," writes John Berger, in this memoir about the death of his own mother.

From the age of five or six I was worried about the death of my parents. The inevitability of death was one of the first things I learnt about the world on my own. Nobody else spoke of it yet the signs were so clear.

Every time I went to bed—and in this I am sure I was like millions of other children—the fear that one or both my parents might die in the night touched the nape of my neck with its finger. Such a fear has, I believe, little to do with a particular psychological climate and a great deal to do with nightfall. Yet since it was impossible to say: You won't die in the night, will you? (when Grandmother died, I was told she had gone to have a rest, or—this was from my uncle who was more outspoken—that she had passed over), since I couldn't ask the real question and I sought a reassurance, I invented—like millions before me—the euphemism: See you in the morning! To which either my father or mother, who had come to turn out the light in my bedroom, would reply: See you in the morning, John.

After their footsteps had died away, I would try for as long as possible not to lift my head from the pillow so that the last words spoken remained, trapped like fish in a rock-pool at low tide, between my pillow and ear. The implicit promise of the words was also a protection against the dark. The words promised that I would not (yet) be alone.

Now I'm no longer usually frightened by the dark and my father died ten years ago and my mother a month ago at the age of ninety-three. It would be a natural moment to write an autobiography. My version of my life can no longer hurt either of them. And the book, when finished, would be there, a little like a parent. Autobiography begins with a sense of being alone. It is an orphan form. Yet I have no wish to do so. All that interests me about my past life are the common moments. The moments—which if I relate them well enough—will join countless others lived by people I do not personally know.

Six weeks ago my mother asked me to come and see her; it would be the last time, she said. A few days later, on the morning of my birthday, she believed she was dying. Open the curtains, she asked my brother, so I can see the trees. In fact, she died the following week.

On my birthdays as a child, it was my father rather than she who gave me memorable presents. She was too thrifty. Her moments of generosity were at the table, offering what she had bought and prepared and cooked and served to whoever came into the house. Otherwise she was thrifty. Nor did she ever explain. She was secretive, she kept things to herself. Not for her own pleasure, but because the world would not forgive spontaneity, the world was mean. I must make that clearer. She didn't believe life was mean—it was generous—but she had learnt from her own childhood that survival was hard. She was the opposite of quixotic—for she was not born a knight and her father was a warehouse foreman in Lambeth. She pursed her lips together, knitted her brows as she calculated and thought things out and carried on with an unspoken determination. She never asked favours of anyone. Nothing shocked her. From whatever she saw, she just drew the necessary conclusions so as to survive and to be dependent on nobody. If I were Aesop, I would say that in her prudence and persistence my mother resembled the agouti. (I once wrote about an agouti in the London zoo, but I did not then realize why the animal so touched me.) In my adult life, the only occasions on which we shouted at each other were when she estimated I was being quixotic.

When I was in my thirties she told me for the first time that, ever since I was born, she had hoped I would be a writer. The writers she admired when young were Bernard Shaw, J.M. Barrie, Compton Mackenzie, Warwick Deeping, E.M. Dell. The only painter she really admired was Turner—perhaps because of her childhood on the banks of the Thames.

Most of my books she didn't read. Either because they dealt with subjects which were alien to her or because—under the protective influence of my father—she believed they might upset her. Why suffer surprise from something which, left unopened, gives you pleasure? My being a writer was unqualified for her by what I wrote. To be a writer was to be able to see to the horizon where, anyway, nothing is ever very distinct and all questions are open. Literature had little to do with the writer's vocation as she saw it. It was only a by-product. A writer was a person familiar with the secrets. Perhaps in the end she didn't read my books so that they should remain more secret.

If her hopes of my becoming a writer—and she said they began on the night after I was delivered—were eventually realized, it was not because there were many books in our house (there were few) but because there was so much that was unsaid, so much that I had to discover the existence of on my own at an early age: death, poverty, pain (in others), sexuality . . .

These things were there to be discovered within the house or from its windows—until I left for good, more or less prepared for the outside world, at the age of eight. My mother never spoke of these things. She didn't hide the fact that she was aware of them. For her, however, they were wrapped secrets, to be lived with, but never to be mentioned or opened. Superficially this was a question of gentility, but profoundly, of a respect, a secret loyalty to the enigmatic. My rough and ready preparation for the world did not include a single explanation—it simply consisted of the principle that events carried more weight than the self.

Thus, she taught me very little—at least in the usual sense of the term: she a teacher about life, I a learner. By imitating her gestures I learnt how to roast meat in the oven, how to clean celery, how to cook rice, how to chose vegetables in a market. As a young woman she had been a vegetarian. Then she gave it up because she did not want to influence us children. Why were you a vegetarian? I once asked her, eating my Sunday roast, much later when I was first working as a journalist. Because I'm against killing. She would say no more. Either I understood or I didn't. There was nothing more to be said.

In time—and I understand this only now writing these pages—I chose to visit abattoirs in different cities of the world and to become something of an expert concerning the subject. The unspoken, the unfaceable beckoned me. I followed. Into the abattoirs and, differently, into many other places and situations.

The last, the largest, and the most personally prepared wrapped secret was her own death. Of course I was not the only witness. Of those close to her, I was maybe the most removed, the most remote. But she knew, I think, with confidence that I would pursue the matter. She knew that if anybody can be at home with what is kept a secret, it was me, because I was her son whom she hoped would become a writer.

The clinical history of her illness is a different story about which she herself was totally uncurious. Sufficient to say that with the help of drugs she was not in pain, and that, thanks to my brother and sister-in-law who arranged everything for her, she was not subjected to all the mechanical ingenuity of aids for the artificial prolongation of life.

Of how many deaths—though never till now of my own mother's—have I written? Truly we writers are the secretaries of death.

She lay in bed, propped up by pillows, her head fallen forward, as if asleep.

I shut my eyes, she said, I like to shut my eyes and think. I don't sleep though. If I slept now, I wouldn't sleep at night.

What do you think about?

She screwed up her eyes which were gimlet sharp and looked at me, twinkling, as if I'd never, not even as a small child, asked such a stupid question.

Are you working hard? What are you writing?

A play, I answered.

The last time I went to the theatre I didn't understand a thing, she said. It's not my hearing that's bad though.

Perhaps the play was obscure, I suggested.

She opened her eyes again. The body has closed shop, she announced. Nothing, nothing at all from here down. She placed a hand on her neck. It's a good thing, make no mistake about it, John, it makes the waiting easier.

On her bedside table was a tin of handcream. I started to massage her left hand.

Do you remember a photograph I once took of your hands? Working hands, you said.

No, I don't.

Would you like some more photos on your table? Katya, her granddaughter, asked her.

She smiled at Katya and shook her head, her voice very slightly broken by a laugh. It would be *so* difficult, so difficult, wouldn't it, to choose.

She turned towards me. What exactly are you doing?

I'm massaging your hand. It's meant to be pleasurable.

To tell you the truth, dear, it doesn't make much difference. What plane are you taking back?

I mumbled, took her other hand.

You are all worried, she said, especially when there are several of you. I'm not. Maureen asked me the other day whether I wanted to be cremated or buried. Doesn't make one iota of difference to me. How could it?" She shut her eyes to think.

For the first time in her life and in mine, she could openly place the wrapped enigma between us. She didn't watch me watching it, for we had the habits of a lifetime. Openly she knew that at that moment her faith in a secret was bound to be stronger than any faith of mine in facts. With her eyes still shut, she fingered the Arab necklace I'd attached round her neck with a charm against the evil eye. I'd given her the necklace a few hours before. Perhaps for the first time I had offered her a secret and now her hand kept looking for it.

She opened her eyes. What time is it?

Quarter to four.

It's not very interesting talking to me, you know. I don't have any ideas any more. I've had a good life. Why don't you take a walk.

Katya stayed with her.

When you are very old, she told Katya confidentially, there's one thing that's very very difficult—it's very difficult to persuade other people that you're happy.

She let her head go back onto the pillow. As I came back in, she smiled. In her right hand she held a crumpled paper handkerchief. With it she dabbed from time to time the corner of her mouth when she felt there was the slightest excess of spittle there. The gesture was reminiscent of one with which, many years before, she used to wipe her mouth after drinking Earl Grey tea and eating watercress sandwiches. Meanwhile with her left hand she fingered the necklace, cushioned on her forgotten bosom.

Love, my mother had the habit of saying, is the only thing that counts in this world. Real love, she would add, to avoid any factitious misunderstanding. But apart from that simple adjective, she never added anything more.

---

agouti: a South American rodent similar to a guinea pig

Secrets

BERNARD MACLAVERTY

"You are dirt, and always will be dirt." What kind of secret could a young boy have discovered about his aunt to make her lash out at him this way?

He had been called to be there at the end. His great-aunt Mary had been dying for some days now and the house was full of relatives. He had just left his girlfriend's home—they had been studying for 'A' levels together—and had come back to the house to find all the lights spilling on to the lawn and a sense of purpose which had been absent from the last few days.

He knelt at the bedroom door to join in the prayers. His knees were on the wooden threshold and he edged them forward on to the carpet. They had tried to wrap her fingers around a crucifix but they kept loosening. She lay low on the pillow and her face seemed to have shrunk by half since he had gone out earlier in the night. Her white hair was damped and pushed back from her forehead. She twisted her head from side to side, her eyes closed. The prayers chorused on, trying to cover the sound she was making deep in her throat. Someone said about her teeth and his mother leaned over her and said, "That's the pet," and took her dentures from her mouth. The lower half of her face seemed to collapse. She half opened her eyes but could not raise her eyelids enough and showed only crescents of white.

"Hail Mary full of grace . . ." the prayers went on. He closed his hands over his face so that he would not have to look but smelt the trace of his girlfriend's handcream from his hands. The noise, deep and guttural, that this aunt was making became intolerable to him. It was as if she were drowning. She had lost all the dignity he knew her to have. He got up from the floor and stepped between the others who were kneeling and went into her sitting-room off the same landing.

He was trembling with anger or sorrow, he didn't know which. He sat in the brightness of her big sitting-room at the oval table and waited for something to happen. On the table was a cut-glass vase of irises, dying because she had been in bed for over a week. He sat staring at them. They were withering from the tips inward, scrolling themselves delicately, brown and neat. Clearing up after themselves. He stared at them for a long time until he heard the sounds of women weeping from the next room.

His aunt had been small—her head on a level with his when she sat at her table—and she seemed to get smaller each year. Her skin fresh, her hair white and waved and always well washed. She wore no jewelry except a cameo ring on the third finger of her right hand and, around her neck, a gold locket on a chain. The white classical profile on the ring was almost worn through and had become translucent and indistinct. The boy had noticed the ring when she had read to him as a child. In the beginning fairy tales, then as he got older extracts from famous novels, *Lorna Doone*, *Persuasion*, *Wuthering Heights* and her favourite extract, because she read it so often, Pip's meeting with Miss Havisham from *Great Expectations*. She would sit with him on her knee, her arms around him and holding the page flat with her hand. When he was bored he would interrupt her and ask about the ring. He loved hearing her tell of how her grandmother had given it to her as a brooch and she had had a ring made from it. He would try to count back to see how old it was. Had her grandmother got it from *her* grandmother? And if so, what had she turned it into? She would nod her head from side to side and say, "How would I know a thing like that?" keeping her place in the closed book with her finger.

"Don't be so inquisitive," she'd say. "Let's see what happens next in the story."

One day she was sitting copying figures into a long narrow book with a dip pen when he came into her room. She didn't look up, but when he asked her a question she just said, "Mm?" and went on writing. The vase of irises on the oval table vibrated slightly as she wrote.

"What is it?" She wiped the nib on blotting-paper and looked up at him over her reading glasses.

"I've started collecting stamps and Mamma says you might have some."

"Does she now—?"

She got up from the table and went to the tall walnut bureau-bookcase standing in the alcove. From a shelf of the bookcase she took a small wallet of keys and selected one for the lock. There was a harsh metal shearing sound as she pulled the desk flap down. The writing area was covered with green leather which had dog-eared at the corners. The inner part was divided into pigeon-holes, all bulging with papers. Some of them, envelopes, were gathered in batches nipped at the waist with elastic bands. There were postcards and bills and cash-books. She pointed to the postcards.

"You may have the stamps on those," she said. "But don't tear them. Steam them off."

She went back to the oval table and continued writing. He sat on the arm of the chair, looking through the picture postcards—torchlight processions at Lourdes, brown photographs of town centres, dull black and whites of beaches backed by faded hotels. Then he turned them over and began to sort the stamps. Spanish with a bald man, French with a rooster, German with funny jerky print, some Italian with what looked like a chimney-sweep's bundle and a hatchet.

"These are great," he said. "I haven't got any of them."

"Just be careful how you take them off."

"Can I take them downstairs?"

"Is your mother there?"

"Yes."

"Then perhaps it's best if you bring the kettle up here."

He went down to the kitchen. His mother was in the morning-room polishing silver. He took the kettle and the flex upstairs. Except for the dipping and scratching of his aunt's pen the room was silent. It was at the back of the house overlooking the orchard, and the sound of traffic from the main road was distant and muted. A tiny rattle began as the kettle warmed up, then it bubbled and steam gushed quietly from its spout. The cards began to curl slightly in the jet of steam, but she didn't seem to be watching. The stamps peeled moistly off and he put them in a saucer of water to flatten them.

"Who is Brother Benignus?" he asked. She seemed not to hear. He asked again and she looked over her glasses.

"He was a friend."

His flourishing signature appeared again and again. Sometimes Bro. Benignus, sometimes Benignus and once Iggy.

"Is he alive?"

"No, he's dead now. Watch the kettle doesn't run dry."

When he had all the stamps off, he put the postcards together and replaced them in the pigeon-hole. He reached over towards the letters but before his hand touched them his aunt's voice, harsh for once, warned.

"A-a-a," she moved her pen from side to side. "Do-not-touch," she said and smiled. "Anything else, yes! That section, no!" She resumed her writing.

The boy went through some other papers and found some photographs. One was a beautiful girl. It was very old-fashioned but he could see that she was beautiful. The picture was a pale brown oval set on a white square of card. The edges of the oval were misty. The girl in the photograph was young and had dark, dark hair scraped severely back and tied like a knotted rope on the top of her head—high, arched eyebrows, her nose straight and thin; her mouth slightly smiling, yet not smiling, the way a mouth is after smiling. Her eyes looked out at him, dark and knowing and beautiful.

"Who is that?" he asked.

"Why? What do you think of her?"

"She's all right."

"Do you think she is beautiful?" The boy nodded.

"That's me," she said. The boy was glad he had pleased her in return for the stamps.

Other photographs were there, not posed ones like Aunt Mary's but Brownie snaps of laughing groups of girls in bucket hats like German helmets and coats to their ankles. They seemed tiny faces covered in clothes. There was a photograph of a young man smoking a cigarette, his hair combed one way by the wind against a background of sea.

"Who is that in the uniform?" the boy asked.

"He's a soldier," she answered without looking up.

"Oh," said the boy. "But who is he?"

"He was a friend of mine before you were born," she said; then added, "Do I smell something cooking? Take your stamps and off you go. That's the boy."

The boy looked at the back of the picture of the man and saw in black spidery ink "John, Aug '15 Ballintoye."

"I thought maybe it was Brother Benignus," he said. She looked at him not answering.

"Was your friend killed in the war?"

At first she said no, then she changed her mind.

"Perhaps he was," she said, then smiled. "You are far too inquisitive. Put it to use and go and see what is for tea. Your mother will need the kettle." She came over to the bureau and helped tidy the photographs away. Then she locked it and put the keys on the shelf.

"Will you bring me up my tray?"

The boy nodded and left.

It was Sunday evening, bright and summery. He was doing his homework and his mother was sitting on the carpet in one of her periodic fits of tidying out the drawers of the mahogany sideboard. On one side of her was a heap of paper scraps torn in quarters and bits of rubbish, on the other the useful items that had to be kept. The boy heard the bottom stair creak under Aunt Mary's light footstep. She knocked and put her head round the door and said that she was walking to Devotions. She was dressed in her good coat and hat and was just easing her fingers into her second glove. The boy saw her stop and pat her hair into place before the mirror in the hallway. His mother stretched over and slammed the door shut. It vibrated, then he heard the deeper sound of the outside door closing and her first few steps on the gravelled drive-way. He sat for a long time wondering if he would have time or not. Devotions could take anything from twenty minutes to three quarters of an hour, depending on who was saying it.

Ten minutes must have passed, then the boy left his homework and went upstairs and into his aunt's sitting room. He stood in front of the bureau wondering, then he reached for the keys. He tried several before he got the right one. The desk flap screeched as he pulled it down. He pretended to look at the postcards again in case there were any stamps he had missed. Then he put them away and reached for the bundle of letters. The elastic band was thick and old, brittle almost, and when he took it off its track remained on the wad of letters. He carefully opened one and took out the letter and unfolded it, frail, khaki-coloured.

> My dearest Mary [it began] I am so tired I can hardly write to you. I have spent what seems like all day censoring letters (there is a how-itzer about 100 yds away firing every 2 minutes). The letters are heart-rending in their attempt to express what they cannot. Some of the men are illiterate, others almost so. I know that they feel as much as we do, yet they do not have the words to express it. That is your job in the schoolroom, to give us generations who can read and write well. They have . . .

The boy's eye skipped down the page and over the next. He read the last paragraph.

> Mary, I love you as much as ever—more so that we cannot be to-gether. I do not know which is worse, the hurt of this war or being separated from you. Give all my love to Brendan and all at home.

It was signed, scribbled with what he took to be John. He folded the paper carefully into its original creases and put it in the envelope.

He opened another.

> My love, it is thinking of you that keeps me sane. When I get a moment I open my memories of you as if I were reading. Your long dark hair—I always imagine you wearing the blouse with the tiny roses, the white one that opened down the back—your eyes that said so much without words, the way you lowered your head when I said anything that embarrassed you, and the clean nape of your neck.
>
> The day I think about most was the day we climbed the head at Ballycastle. In a hollow, out of the wind, the air full of pollen at the sound of insects, the grass warm and dry and you lying beside me, your hair undone, between me and the sun. You remember that that was where I first kissed you and the look of disbelief in your eyes that made me laugh afterwards.
>
> It makes me laugh now to see myself savouring these memories standing alone up to my thighs in muck. It is everywhere, two, three feet deep. To walk ten yards leaves you quite breathless.
>
> I haven't time to write more today, so I leave you with my feet in the clay and my head in the clouds. I love you, John.

He did not bother to put the letter back into the envelope but opened another.

> My dearest, I am so cold that I find it difficult to keep my hand steady enough to write. You remember when we swam, the last two fingers of your hand went the colour and texture of candles with the cold. Well that is how I am all over. It is almost four days since I had any real sensation in my feet or legs. Everything is frozen. The ground is like steel.
>
> Forgive me telling you this but I feel I have to say it to someone. The worst thing is the dead. They sit or lie frozen in the position they died. You can distinguish them from the living because their faces are the colour of slate. God help us when the thaw comes . . . This war is beginning to have an effect on me. I have lost all sense of feeling. The only emotion I have experienced lately is one of anger. Sheer white trembling anger. I have no pity or sorrow for the dead and injured. I thank God it is not me but I am enraged that it had to be them. If I live through this experience I will be a different person.
>
> The only thing that remains constant is my love for you.
>
> Today a man died beside me. A piece of shrapnel had pierced his neck as we were moving under fire. I pulled him into a crater and

stayed with him until he died. I watched him choke and then drown in his blood.

I am full of anger which has no direction.

He sorted through the pile and read half of some, all of others. The sun had fallen low in the sky and shone directly into the room on to the pages he was reading, making the paper glare. He selected a letter from the back of the pile and shaded it with his hand as he read.

Dearest Mary, I am writing this to you from my hospital bed. I hope that you were not too worried about not hearing from me. I have been here, so they tell me, for two weeks, and it took another two weeks before I could bring myself to write this letter.

I have been thinking a lot as I lie here about the war and about myself and about you. I do not know how to say this but I feel deeply that I must do something, must sacrifice something to make up for the horror of the past year. In some strange way Christ has spoken to me through the carnage . . .

Suddenly the boy heard the creak of the stair and he frantically tried to slip the letter back into its envelope but it crumpled and would not fit. He bundled them all together. He could hear his aunt's familiar puffing on the short stairs to her room. He spread the elastic band wide with his fingers. It snapped and the letters scattered. He pushed them into their pigeon hole and quietly closed the desk flap. The brass screeched loudly and clicked shut. At that moment his aunt came into the room.

"What are you doing boy?" she snapped.

"Nothing." He stood with the keys in his hand. She walked to the bureau and opened it. The letters sprung out in an untidy heap.

"You have been reading my letters," she said quietly. Her mouth was tight with the words and her eyes blazed. The boy could say nothing. She struck him across the side of the face.

"Get out," she said. "Get out of my room."

The boy, the side of his face stinging and red, put the keys on the table on his way out. When he reached the door she called to him. He stopped, his hand on the handle.

"You are dirt," she hissed, "and always will be dirt. I shall remember this till the day I die."

Even though it was a warm evening, there was a fire in the large fireplace. His mother had asked him to light it so that she could clear out Aunt Mary's stuff. The room could then be his study, she said. She came in seeing him at the table said, "I hope I'm not disturbing you."

"No."

She took the keys from her pocket, opened the bureau and began burning papers and cards. She glanced quickly at each one before she flicked it on to the fire.

"Who was Brother Benignus?" he asked.

His mother stopped sorting and said, "I don't know. Your aunt kept herself very much to herself. She got books from him through the post occasionally. That much I do know."

She went on burning the cards. They built into strata, glowing red and black. Now and again she broke up the pile with the poker, sending showers of sparks up the chimney. He saw her come to the letters. She took off the elastic band and put it to one side with the useful things and began dealing the envelopes into the fire. She opened one and read quickly through it, then threw it on top of the burning pile.

"Mama," he said.

"Yes?"

"Did Aunt Mary say anything about me?"

"What do you mean?"

"Before she died—did she say anything?"

"Not that I know of—the poor thing was too far gone to speak, God rest her." She went on burning, lifting the corners of the letters with the poker to let the flames underneath them.

When he felt a hardness in his throat, he put his head down on his books. Tears came into his eyes for the first time since she had died, and he cried silently into the crook of his arm for the woman who had been his maiden aunt, his teller of tales, that she might forgive him.

The Duel in Mercy Ward

IAN McDONALD

Rowing (rhymes with vowing) means quarreling—and Benjie and Beepat are good at it. So good that their fierce competition soon involves everyone in the chronic care ward.

Benjie and Beepat arrived in the ward at Mercy about the same time. This ward was for chronic, not exactly terminal, cases. One or two used to make a kind of recovery and totter out into the land of the living. But generally when you went in there you only came out on the long journey. Benjie was wheeled in one morning, Beepat the same afternoon, and ever afterwards Benjie made his seniority a point to emphasize and exaggerate.

"I was here long, long before you come in making trouble," Benjie would say.

"You old fool," Beepat would respond. "We come in the exact same time."

And that would be good for an hour or two of satisfying, acrimonious debate.

But that was just a very small bone in the huge pot of contention that Benjie and Beepat soon began to cook up. They argued about everything. They drove the nurses to distraction. They were in next-door beds at first but they soon had to be separated. They still found ample ways to meet and quarrel and suck teeth at each other's views.

They made as many as possible in the ward take sides, which added to the confusion. The halt and the lame and the nearly blind, not to mention the dying and the nearly dead, were summoned to make a choice. It was World Cup Final every day, Benjie's team against Beepat's team, and you better have helmets because bouncers bound to fly.

Everything was a case of competition between Benjie and Beepat.

They had some big rows about politics—how the other one's party was full of vagabonds and fools. They had some big rows about religion—how Hindus have so many thousands and thousands of Gods they even have a God for water-snake and carrion-crow and how Christians like cannibals, wanting to drink the blood of Jesus Christ. And they had some big rows about race—how Indians are mean and sly and can't take their liquor and how black people only like to fête and play with women. But somehow in these rows you had the feeling they were rowing for rowing's sake. It was Beepat so Benjie had to say one thing and it was Benjie so Beepat had to say the other thing. But they didn't seem to want to put their heart in it. Politics, religion, and race really were not worth getting worked up about. Life was too short.

Cricket was the cause of more important rowing. Right at the beginning they made a mistake and in one argument both said, while the other was also saying, how Kanhai was the greatest batsman in the world. So from then on they had to forget Kanhai in the rowing and row instead about who the second best was. And if Benjie selected a team not one man could be the same as in the team Beepat selected. And if a man had a good cover-drive for Benjie, no, he only had a good hook-shot for Beepat. And when they were listening to Test Match cricket there were always three commentaries—Benjie's commentary which was giving one view, Beepat's commentary which was giving a view as if it was a different game, and the real commentator's commentary which, to tell the truth, wasn't half so interesting or quarter so scandalous as Benjie's and Beepat's commentaries.

But even cricket wasn't all that much. What Benjie and Beepat really put their hearts into were rivalries that could be decided definitely and specifically right there in the ward on a daily basis.

Like the rivalry to see who was the most popular patient in the ward. This amounted to seeing who could get the most visitors to come at visiting hour. The story started when one of Beepat's cousins and five nieces and nephews happened to come and visit at the same time when his old brother and sister-in-law were there. That made eight people around Beepat's bed. And Benjie only had two people visiting him. So Beepat made a big thing about how some people so bad-natured they don't have any family or friends left to visit them while some other people at least could say a lot of friends and family still think highly of them and show their devotion.

Well, you can imagine Benjie's response. It only took about three days before ten people turned up around Benjie's bed at visiting hour and only four by Beepat's bed that same day. Benjie didn't forget to rub the salt in the wound, and what could Beepat say? He stayed quiet and planned his own counter-attack. He sent word out by his cousins and by his cousin's cousins. I am sure I don't have to describe all what happened then: more and more people coming in to visit Benjie and Beepat. Benjie drew from all over town and up the East Bank; Beepat drew from the East Coast mostly but as far away as Crabwood Creek too. Benjie even sent out and hired a bus to bring visitors in one day after competition was going about a month. By this time only a few of the visitors were actually getting in to see Benjie and Beepat, but that didn't prevent both of them getting a count of how many had turned up to visit and then each announcing, like an election official, the total number that had tried to pay a visit to their beloved Benjie/Beepat. It was a hard battle and visiting hour was an exciting time for the whole ward until a stop had to be put to all the nonsense, the authorities cracked down, and Benjie and Beepat had to find another contest in which to test wits and belligerence.

That ward is more often than not a place of anguish and despair where people at best lose their grip on life and quietly fade away and at worst die in a hopeless, lonely agony which shakes the soul to think about too long. But in the era of Benjie and Beepat a little more of something like a last vital spark was preserved a little longer in all those hopeless, discarded cases. It wasn't much and it wasn't for long but it was something and it was for a while and in life can you be sure that in the end there is much more than that? I don't know.

And that leads directly to by far the intensest rivalry between these two obscure but determined representatives of the life-force, Benjie and Beepat. Neither of them was going to be the one to die first. That was the ultimate competition. Benjie, you could say, would rather have died than pass away before Beepat. And Beepat felt exactly the same way. They put their last surge of will-power into this battle to the last breath not to be first to go.

They kept an eager eye on each other to see what signs of wear and tear might be appearing—further wear and tear, I should say, because you can imagine that Benjie and Beepat were both worn and torn a good bit already by the time they were brought in to the ward at Mercy. If one of them coughed an extra amount in the night the other started up at once and the next morning was sure to make a comment. They kept an eye on each other's bowel movements. Nothing they would have liked better than to get a sight of each other's urine samples to see if they were clear or cloudy. They each had ancient village remedies to supplement the despised hospital medicine and they both made sure the other knew a new and extra-potent cure was being smuggled in which would give the recipient an edge in the struggle to survive.

Twice they had to take Beepat down to the operating theatre.

"He gone now," Benjie said. "Old Beepat gone. I don't know how he last so long, he was so sickly-looking. But now he gone."

But Beepat returned both times and continued the fight to the death. Once Benjie in his turn had to be given blood and saline, right there in his bed. A doctor and some nurses bustled about setting up the apparatus and plastic bottles and Benjie in truth looked gone, lying with his eyes closed and a deadly waxen look in his face. It was Beepat's turn to intone the last rites.

"Benjie could never make it now. When you see those bottles hook up like that in a man, that is the end. The end. He can't make it any more. It was only mouth when he said he was feeling so good yesterday. Now look at that face, it could be in a coffin already."

But Benjie pulled through.

One morning at crack of dawn Beepat was amazed to see Benjie trying to do what appeared to be push-ups on the floor by the side of the bed. The word went round that Benjie was feeling so good that he had decided to begin a regime of light exercises every morning and evening. It was good psychology, and had the effect of shaking up Beepat and putting him on the defensive for a while. But it turned out to be counter-productive. After a couple of mornings Benjie couldn't make the grade and had to put the get-fit regime in cold storage. In fact he had a bad relapse and couldn't even get out of bed for a few days, which gave Beepat the chance to make a special effort to walk around the whole place and show how strong he was.

It would be good to tell how the story ended with Benjie and Beepat walking out one fine day, good for a few more years rowing. But, in truth, life isn't like that, not for you, not for me, and not for Benjie and Beepat. The day came when Benjie began to go down. It was Diwali and Beepat had got some clay *diyas* and put them glimmering around his bed. It looked beautiful. Beepat was very proud. Normally Benjie would have had some comment to make, but he was silent and still. Beepat was surprised. From that time Benjie couldn't get out of bed anymore. He tried hard one or two more times but he couldn't raise himself to take the bait. Beepat began to get silent.

Benjie had a bad case of sugar and it had got to the time when the doctors couldn't even slow down the ravages of the disease. The legs were going bad. They had to operate and cut and try to keep the rest of Benjie whole. But the sickness was too far gone and Benjie was

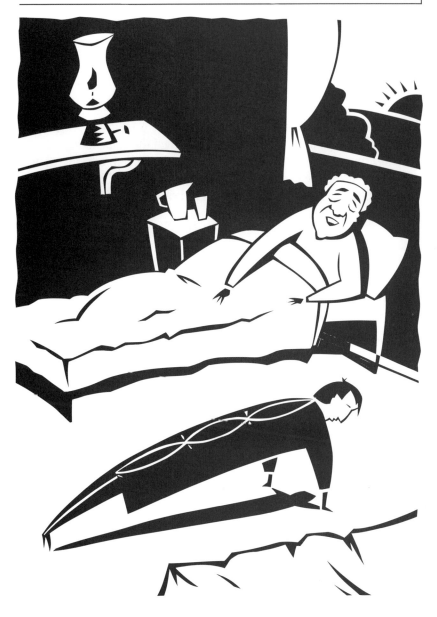

too old. You can't only live on strong will. In the last month they cut him down four times, but he still hung on. The first time Beepat made a joke at Benjie's expense, but after that he didn't make any more jokes. Every time they cut Benjie, Beepat grew more quiet. The whole ward grew silent: no more Benjie and Beepat rowing. The time for that was over.

When they cut Benjie for the fourth time they brought him back up to the ward with his legs cut off just above the knees. He was hardly living any more but he was still alive. Beepat lit a *diya* in front of the greatest of his Gods before he lay down for the night. During the night you could hear Benjie's breathing across the ward. The *diya* by Beepat's bed flickered out and he fed it with oil a few times. Beepat lay awake late and then he composed himself to sleep. It was strange. When the nurses made their second morning round, when the birds had just begun to sing, they found that Beepat's sleep had eased into dying. It was recorded that his heart gave out, after respiratory troubles, and he died at 9.02 a.m. Benjie lasted until noon that day.

---

diya: a small clay oil lamp often lighted at Hindu festivals

At the River

PATRICIA GRACE

The morepork *is the native owl of New Zealand, whose night call sounds like "more pork."*

Sad I wait, and see them come back from the river. The torches move slow.

To the tent to rest after they had gone to the river, and while asleep the dream came. A dream of death. He came to me in the dream, not sadly but smiling, with hand on heart and said, I go but do not weep. No weeping, it is my time.

Woke then and out into the night to watch for them with sadness on me, sadness from the dream. And waiting, there came a morepork with soft wingbeat and rested above my head. "Go," I said to the bird. "He comes not with you tonight. He is well and strong. His time is not here."

But it cried, the morepork. Its call went out. Out and out until the tears were on my face. And now I wait and I see the torches come, they move slow back from the river. Slow and sad they move and I think of him. Many times have we come to this place for eels. Every year we come at this time. Our children come and now our grandchildren, his and mine. This is the river for eels and this the time of year.

A long way we have travelled with our tents and food stores, our lamps and bedding and our big eel drums. Much work for us today preparing our camp. But now our camp is ready and they have gone with the torches downriver to the best eel place. And this old lady stays behind with her old kerosene lamp and the campfire dying, and the little ones sleeping in their beds. Too tired for the river tonight, too old for the work of catching eels. But not he. He is well and strong. No aching back or tired arms he. No bending, no sadness on him or thought of death like this old one.

His wish but not mine to come here this year. "Too old," I said to him. "Let the young ones go. Stay back we two and tend our sweet potatoes and corn."

"This old body," he said. "It hungers for the taste of eel."

"The drums will be full when they return," I said. "Let them bring the eels to us, as they would wish to do."

"Ah no," he said. "Always these hands have fetched the food for the stomach. The eels taste sweeter when the body has worked in fetching."

"Go then," I said, and we prepared.

I think of him now as I await their return. "My time is here," he said in the dream, and now the bird calls out. And I think too of the young ones who spoke to him today in a new way, a way I did not like.

Before the night came they worked, all of them, to make their torches for the river. Long sticks from the tea-tree, long and straight. Tins tied at the tops of the sticks, and in the tins rags soaked in oil. A good light they made as they left tonight for the river. Happy and singing they went with their torches. But I see the lights return now, dim. Dim and slow they come and sadly I await them.

And the young ones, they made their eel hooks. Straight sticks with strong hooks tied for catching eels. He smiled to see the eel hooks, the straight sticks with the strong hooks tied.

"Your hooks," he said. "They work for the hands?" But the young ones did not speak, instead bent heads to the work of tying hooks.

Then off, the young ones, to the hills for hare bait as the sun went down. Happy they went with the gun. Two shots went out and we awaited their return. The young ones, they came back laughing. Happy they came with the hare. "Good bait this," they said. "Good bait and good hooks. Lots of eels for us tonight."

But their nanny said to them, "A hook is good for the eel but bad for the leg. Many will be there at the river tonight, your uncles, aunties, big cousins, your nanny too. Your hooks may take a leg in place of an eel. The old way, with the stick, and the bait tied is a safe way and a good way. You waste your hooks."

But the young ones rolled on the ground. "Ho, Grandpa," they called, "You better watch your leg tonight. The hook might get your leg, Grandpa."

"And watch your hand, Grandpa, the eel might get your hand."

"Bite your hand off, Grandpa. You better watch out."

Did not like their way of talking to their nanny but he has patience with the young.

"You'll see," he said. "You want to know how to get eels then you watch your grandpa."

They did not keep quiet, the young ones after that. Called out to him in a way I did not like, but he is patient.

"Ah, Grandpa, that old way of yours is not good. That way is old like you, Grandpa."

"You might end up in the river with your old way of catching eels."

Spoke sharply to them then in our own language.

"Not for you to speak in this manner. Not our way to speak like this. It is a new thing you are doing. It is a bad thing you have learned."

No more talk from these two then, but laughing still, and he spoke up for them.

"They make their torches, the boys, and they make the hooks, and then they go to the hills for hare. They think of the river and the eels in the river, and then they punch each other and roll on the ground. Shout and laugh waiting for the night to come. The funny talk it means nothing."

"Enough to shout and fight," I said. "Enough to roll on the ground and punch each other, but the talk needs to stay in the mouth."

Put my head down then not pleased, and worked at my task of kneading the bread for morning.

Now I wait and stir the ashes round the oven while the morning bread cooks, and on the ashes I see my tears fall. The babies sleep behind me in the tent, and above me the bird cries.

Much to do after a night of eeling when the drum is full. From the fire we scrape away the dead ashes to put into the drum of eels. All night our eels stay there in the drum of ashes to make easier the task of scraping. Scrape off the ashes and with it comes the sticky eel slime.

Cut the eels, and open them out then ready for smoking. The men collect green wood from the tea-tree for our smoke drum. Best wood this, to make a good smoke. Good and clear. All day our smoke house goes. Then wrap our smoked eel carefully and pack away before night comes and time for the river again.

But no eels for us this night. No scraping and smoking and packing this time. Tonight our camp comes down and we return. The dim lights come and they bring him back from the river. Slow they bring him.

Now I see two lights come near. The two have come to bring me sad news of him. But before them the bird came, and before the bird the dream—he in the dream with hand on heart.

And now they stand before me, the boys, heads down. By the dim torchlight I see the tears on their faces, they do not speak.

"They bring your nanny back," I say. "Back from the river." But they do not speak.

"Hear the morepork," I say to them. "It calls from the trees. Out and out it cries. They bring him back from the river, I see your tears."

"We saw him standing by the river," they say. "Saw him bend, looking into the water, and then we saw him fall."

They stand, the young ones in the dim torchlight with tears on their faces, the tears fall. And now they come to me, kneeling by me, weeping.

"We spoke bad to him," they say. "They were bad things we said. Now he has fallen and we have said bad things to him."

So I speak to them to comfort them. "He came to me tonight with hand on heart. 'Do not weep,' he said. 'It is my time.' Not your words that made him fall. His hand was on his heart. Hear the morepork cry. His time is here."

And now we weep together, this old lady and these two young ones by her. No weeping he said. But we will weep a little while for him and for ourselves. He was our strength.

We weep and they return. His children and mine return from the river bearing him. Sad they come in the dim light of torches. The young ones help me to my feet, weeping still, and I go toward them as they come.

And in my throat I feel a cry well up. Lonely it sounds across the night. Lonely it sounds, the cry that comes from in me.

R·U·M·O·U·R·S

riding
through
bratislava

The Kiss

ALICE WALKER

i was kissed once
by a beautiful man
all blond and
        czech
riding through bratislava
on a motor bike
screeching "don't yew let me fall off heah naow!"

the funny part was
he spoke english
and setting me gallantly
on my feet
kissed me for
not anyhow *looking*
like aunt jemima.

Aunt Jemima, a cheerful African-American woman wearing a bandana, was dreamed up by advertisers to sell pancake mix. Her image is now viewed as a negative stereotype.

Limbo Dancer at Immigration

JOHN AGARD

It was always the same
at every border/at every frontier/
at every port/at every airport/
                              of every metropolis

The same hassle
from authorities

the same battle
with bureaucrats

a bunch of official cats
ready to scratch

looking limbo dancer up & down
scrutinizing passport with a frown

COUNTRY OF ORIGIN: SLAVESHIP

Never heard of that one
the authorities sniggered

Suppose you got here on a banana boat
the authorities sniggered

More likely a spaceship
the authorities sniggered

Slaveship/spaceship/Pan Am/British Airways/Air France
It's all the same
smiled limbo dancer

Now don't give us any of your lip
the authorities sniggered

ANY IDENTIFYING MARKS?

And when limbo dancer showed them sparks
of vision in eyes that held rivers
                        it meant nothing to them

And when limbo dancer held up hands
that told a tale of nails
                        it meant nothing to them

And when limbo dancer offered a neck
that bore the brunt of countless lynchings
                        it meant nothing to them

And when limbo dancer revealed ankles
bruised with the memory of chains
                        it meant nothing to them

So limbo dancer bent over backwards
                        & danced
                        & danced
                        & danced

until from every limb
flowed a trail of red

& what the authorities thought
was a trail of blood

was only spilt duty-free wine

so limbo dancer smiled
saying I have nothing to declare

& to the sound of drum disappeared

Notes of a Native Son

JAMES BALDWIN

*James Baldwin was nineteen when his father died in July, 1943.
Returning for the funeral, he remembers what a difficult man his
father was. But he also recalls recent experiences in his own life that
have forced him to understand his father's bitterness.*

The only white people who came to our house were welfare workers
and bill collectors. It was almost always my mother who dealt
with them, for my father's temper, which was at the mercy of his
pride, was never to be trusted. It was clear that he felt their very presence
in his home to be a violation: this was conveyed by his carriage, almost
ludicrously stiff, and by his voice, harsh and vindictively polite. When
I was around nine or ten I wrote a play which was directed by a young,
white schoolteacher, a woman, who then took an interest in me, and
gave me books to read and, in order to corroborate my theatrical bent,
decided to take me to see what she somewhat tactlessly referred to as
"real" plays. Theatergoing was forbidden in our house, but, with the
really cruel intuitiveness of a child, I suspected that the color of this
woman's skin would carry the day for me. When, at school, she suggested
taking me to the theater, I did not, as I might have done if she had
been a Negro, find a way of discouraging her, but agreed that she should
pick me up at my house one evening. I then, very cleverly, left all the
rest to my mother, who suggested to my father, as I knew she would,
that it would not be very nice to let such a kind woman make the trip
for nothing. Also, since it was a schoolteacher, I imagine that my mother
countered the idea of sin with the idea of "education," which word, even
with my father, carried a kind of bitter weight.

Before the teacher came my father took me aside to ask *why* she
was coming, what *interest* she could possibly have in our house, in a
boy like me. I said I didn't know but I, too, suggested that it had something
to do with education. And I understood that my father was waiting
for me to say something—I didn't quite know what; perhaps that I

117

wanted his protection against this teacher and her "education." I said none of these things and the teacher came and we went out. It was clear, during the brief interview in our living room, that my father was agreeing very much against his will and that he would have refused permission if he had dared. The fact that he did not dare caused me to despise him: I had no way of knowing that he was facing in that living room a wholly unprecedented and frightening situation.

Later, when my father had been laid off from his job, this woman became very important to us. She was really a very sweet and generous woman and went to a great deal of trouble to be of help to us, particularly during one awful winter. My mother called her by the highest name she knew: she said she was a "christian." My father could scarcely disagree but during the four or five years of our relatively close association he never trusted her and was always trying to surprise in her open, Midwestern face the genuine, cunningly hidden, and hideous motivation. In later years, particularly when it began to be clear that this "education" of mine was going to lead me to perdition, he became more explicit and warned me that my white friends in high school were not really my friends and that I would see, when I was older, how white people would do anything to keep a Negro down. Some of them could be nice, he admitted, but none of them were to be trusted and most of them were not even nice. The best thing was to have as little to do with them as possible. I did not feel this way and I was certain, in my innocence, that I never would.

But the year which preceded my father's death had made a great change in my life. I had been living in New Jersey, working in defense plants, working and living among southerners, white and black. I knew about the South, of course, and about how southerners treated Negroes and how they expected them to behave, but it had never entered my mind that anyone would look at me and expect *me* to behave that way. I learned in New Jersey that to be a Negro meant, precisely, that one was never looked at but was simply at the mercy of the reflexes the color of one's skin caused in other people. I acted in New Jersey as I had always acted, that is as though I thought a great deal of myself— I had to *act* that way—with results that were, simply, unbelievable. I had scarcely arrived before I had earned the enmity, which was extraordinarily ingenious, of all my superiors and nearly all of my co-workers. In the beginning, to make matters worse, I simply did not know what was happening. I did not know what I had done, and I shortly began to wonder what *anyone* could possibly do, to bring about such unanimous, active, and unbearably vocal hostility. I knew about jim-crow but

I had never experienced it. I went to the same self-service restaurant three times and stood with all the Princeton boys before the counter, waiting for a hamburger and coffee; it was always an extraordinarily long time before anything was set before me; but it was not until the fourth visit that I learned that, in fact, nothing had ever been set before me: I had simply picked something up. Negroes were not served there, I was told, and they had been waiting for me to realize that I was always the only Negro present. Once I was told this, I determined to go there all the time. But now they were ready for me and, though some dreadful scenes were subsequently enacted in that restaurant, I never ate there again.

It was the same story all over New Jersey, in bars, bowling alleys, diners, places to live. I was always being forced to leave, silently, or with mutual imprecations. I very shortly became notorious and children giggled behind me when I passed and their elders whispered or shouted— they really believed that I was mad. And it did begin to work on my mind, of course; I began to be afraid to go anywhere and to compensate for this I went places to which I really should not have gone and where, God knows, I had no desire to be. My reputation in town naturally enhanced my reputation at work and my working day became one long series of acrobatics designed to keep me out of trouble. I cannot say that these acrobatics succeeded. It began to seem that the machinery of the organization I worked for was turning over, day and night, with but one aim: to eject me. I was fired once, and contrived, with the aid of a friend from New York, to get back on the payroll; was fired again, and bounced back again. It took a while to fire me for the third time, but the third time took. There were no loopholes anywhere. There was not even a way of getting back inside the gates.

That year in New Jersey lives in my mind as though it were the year during which, having an unsuspected predilection for it, I first contracted some dread, chronic disease, the unfailing symptom of which is a kind of blind fever, a pounding in the skull and fire in the bowels. Once this disease is contracted, one can never be really carefree again, for the fever, without an instant's warning, can recur at any moment. It can wreck more important things than race relations. There is not a Negro alive who does not have this rage in his blood—one has the choice, merely, of living with it consciously or surrendering to it. As for me, this fever has recurred in me, and does, and will until the day I die.

My last night in New Jersey, a white friend from New York took me to the nearest big town, Trenton, to go to the movies and have a few drinks. As it turned out, he also saved me from, at the very least, a violent whipping. Almost every detail of that night stands out very clearly in my memory. I even remember the name of the movie we saw because its title impressed me as being so patly ironical. It was a movie about the German occupation of France, starring Maureen O'Hara and Charles Laughton and called *This Land Is Mine*. I remember the name of the diner we walked into when the movie ended: it was the "American Diner." When we walked in the counterman asked what we wanted and I remember answering with the casual sharpness which had become my habit: "We want a hamburger and a cup of coffee, what do you think we want?" I do not know why, after a year of such rebuffs, I so completely failed to anticipate his answer, which was, of course, "We don't serve Negroes here." This reply failed to discompose me, at least for a moment. I made some sardonic comment about the name of the diner and we walked out into the streets.

This was the time of what was called the "brown-out," when the lights in all American cities were very dim. When we reentered the streets something happened to me which had the force of an optical illusion, or a nightmare. The streets were very crowded and I was facing north. People were moving in every direction but it seemed to me, in that instant, that all of the people I could see, and many more than that, were moving toward me, against me, and that everyone was white. I remember how their faces gleamed. And I felt, like a physical sensation, a *click* at the nape of my neck as though some interior string connecting my head to my body had been cut. I began to walk. I heard my friend call after me, but I ignored him. Heaven only knows what was going on in my mind, but he had the good sense not to touch me—I don't know what would have happened it he had—and to keep me in sight. I don't know what was going on in my mind, either; I certainly had no conscious plan. I wanted to do something to crush these white faces, which were crushing me. I walked for perhaps a block or two until I came to an enormous, glittering, and fashionable restaurant in which I knew not even the intercession of the Virgin would cause me to be served. I pushed through the doors and took the first vacant seat I saw, at a table for two, and waited.

I do not know how long I waited and I rather wonder, until today, what I could possibly have looked like. Whatever I looked like, I frightened the waitress who shortly appeared, and the moment she appeared all of my fury flowed toward her. I hated her for her white face, and for her great, astounded, frightened eyes. I felt that if she found a black man so frightening, I would make her fright worthwhile.

She did not ask me what I wanted, but repeated, as though she had learned it somewhere, "We don't serve Negroes here." She did not say it with the blunt, derisive hostility to which I had grown accustomed, but, rather, with a note of apology in her voice, and fear. This made me colder and more murderous than ever. I felt I had to do something with my hands. I wanted her to come close enough for me to get her neck between my hands.

So I pretended not to have understood her, hoping to draw her closer. And she did step a very short step closer, with her pencil poised incongruously over her pad, and repeated the formula: ". . . don't serve Negroes here."

Somehow, with the repetition of that phrase, which was already ringing in my head like a thousand bells of a nightmare, I realized that she would never come any closer and that I would have to strike from a distance. There was nothing on the table but an ordinary water-mug half full of water, and I picked this up and hurled it with all my strength at her. She ducked and it missed her and shattered against the mirror behind the bar. And, with that sound, my frozen blood abruptly thawed, I returned from wherever I had been, I *saw*, for the first time, the restaurant, the people with their mouths open, already, as it seemed to me, rising as one man, and I realized what I had done, and where I was, and I was frightened. I rose and began running for the door. A round, potbellied man grabbed me by the nape of the neck just as I reached the doors and began to beat me about the face. I kicked him and got loose and ran into the streets. My friend whispered, *"Run!"* and I ran.

My friend stayed outside the restaurant long enough to misdirect my pursuers and the police, who arrived, he told me, at once. I do not know what I said to him when he came to my room that night. I could not have said much. I felt, in the oddest, most awful way, that I had somehow betrayed him. I lived it over and over and over again, the way one relives an automobile accident after it has happened and one finds oneself alone and safe. I could not get over two facts, both equally difficult for the imagination to grasp, and one was that I could have been murdered. But the other was that I had been ready to commit murder. I saw nothing very clearly but I did see this: that my life, my *real* life, was in danger, and not from anything other people might do but from the hatred I carried in my own heart.

---

jim-crow: segregation of or discrimination against blacks (from the name of a song in a minstrel show)

Obasan

JOY KOGAWA

*A niece's visit to Obasan, "honoured aunt," stirs painful memories of
the injustices done to her uncle and aunt during the Second World War.*

She is sitting at the kitchen table when I come in. She is so deaf
now that my knocking does not rouse her and when she sees
me she is startled.

"O," she says, and the sound is short and dry as if there is no energy
left to put any inflection into her voice. She begins to rise but falters
and her hands, outstretched in greeting, fall to the table. She says my
name as a question.

I put my shoulder bag down, remove the mud-caked boots and stand
before her.

"Obasan," I say loudly and take her hands. My aunt is not one for
hugs and kisses.

She peers into my face. "O," she says again.

I nod in reply. We stand for a long time in silence. I open my mouth
to ask, "Did he suffer very much?" but the question feels pornographic.

"Everyone dies some day," she says eventually. She tilts her head
to the side as if it's all too heavy inside.

I hang my jacket on a coat peg and sit beside her.

The house is familiar but has shrunk over the years and is even
more cluttered than I remember. The wooden table is covered with a
plastic table cloth over a blue and white cloth. Along one edge are African
violets in profuse bloom, salt and pepper shakers, a soya sauce bottle,
an old radio, a non-automatic toaster, a small bottle full of toothpicks.
She goes to the stove and turns on the gas flame under the kettle.

"Everyone dies some day," she says again and looks in my direction,
her eyes unclear and sticky with a gum-like mucous. She pours the
tea. Tiny twigs and bits of popcorn circle in the cup.

When I last saw her nine years ago, she told me her tear ducts were clogged. I have never seen her cry. Her mouth is filled with a gummy saliva as well. She drinks warm water often because her tongue sticks to the roof of her false plate.

"Thank you," I say, taking the cup in both hands.

Uncle was disoriented for weeks, my cousin's letter told me. Towards the end he got dizzier and dizzier and couldn't move without clutching things. By the time they got him to the hospital, his eyes were rolling.

"I think he was beginning to see everything upside down again," she wrote, "the way we see when we are born." Perhaps for Uncle, everything had started reversing and he was growing top to bottom, his mind rooted in an upstairs attic of humus and memory, groping backwards through cracks and walls to a moist cellar. Down to water. Down to the underground sea.

Back to the fishing boat, the ocean, the skiff moored off Vancouver Island where he was born. Like Moses, he was an infant of the waves, rocked to sleep by the lap lap and *"Nen, nen, korori"*, his mother's voice singing the ancient Japanese lullaby. His father, Japanese craftsman, was also a son of the sea which had tossed and coddled his boatbuilding ancestors for centuries. And though he had crossed the ocean from one island as a stranger coming to an island of strangers, it was the sea who was his constant landlord. His fellow tenants, the Songhee Indians of Esquimalt, and the fishermen, came from up and down the BC coast to his workshop in Victoria, to watch, to barter and to buy.

In the framed family photograph hanging above the sideboard, Grandfather sits on a chair with his short legs not quite square on the floor. A long black cape hangs from his shoulders. His left hand clutches a pair of gloves and the top of a cane. On a pedestal beside him is a top hat, open end up. Uncle stands slightly to his right, and behind, with his hand like Napoleon's in his vest. Sitting to their left is Grandmother in a lace and velvet suit with my mother in her arms. They all look in different directions, carved and rigid with their expressionless Japanese faces and their bodies pasted over with Rule Britannia. There's not a ripple out of place.

And then there is the picture, not framed, not on display, showing Uncle as a young man smiling and proud in front of an exquisitely detailed craft. Not a fishing boat, not an ordinary yacht—a creation of many years and many winter evenings—a work of art. Uncle stands, happy enough for the attention of the camera, eager to pass on the message that all is well. That forever and ever all is well.

But many things happen. There is the voice of the RCMP officer saying "I'll keep that one," and laughing as he cuts through the water. "Don't worry, I'll make good use of her." The other boats are towed away and left to rot. Hundreds of Grandfather's boats belonging to hundreds of fishermen.

The memories are drowned in a whirlpool of protective silence. "For the sake of the children," it is whispered over and over. *"Kodomo no tame."*

And several years later, sitting in a shack on the edge of a sugar beet field in southern Alberta, Obasan is watching her two young daughters with their school books doing homework in the light of a coral lamp. Her words are the same. *"Kodomo no tame."* For their sakes, they will survive the dust and the wind, the gumbo, the summer oven sun. For their sakes, they will work in the fields, hoeing, thinning acres of sugar beets, irrigating, topping, harvesting.

"We must go back," Uncle would say on winter evenings, the ice thick on the windows. But later, he became more silent.

"Nen nen." Rest, my dead uncle. The sea is severed from your veins. You have been cut loose.

They were feeding him intravenously for two days, the tubes sticking into him like grafting on a tree. But Death won against the medical artistry.

"Obasan, will you be all right?" I ask.

She clears her throat and wipes dry skin off her lips but does not speak. She rolls a bit of dried up jam off the table cloth. She isn't going to answer.

The language of grief is silence. She knows it well, its idioms, its nuances. She's had some of the best tutors available. Grief inside her body is fat and powerful. An almighty tapeworm.

Over the years, Grief has roamed like a highwayman down the channels of her body with its dynamite and its weapons blowing up every moment of relief that tried to make its way down the road. It grew rich off the unburied corpses inside her body.

Grief acted in mysterious ways, its melancholy wonders to perform. When it had claimed her kingdom fully, it admitted no enemies and no vengeance. Enemies belonged in a corridor of experience with sense and meaning, with justice and reason. Her Grief knew nothing of these and whipped her body to resignation until the kingdom was secure. But inside the fortress, Obasan's silence was that of a child bewildered.

"What will you do now?" I ask.

What choices does she have? Her daughters, unable to rescue her or bear the silent rebuke of her suffering have long since fled to the ends of the earth. Each has lived a life in perpetual flight from the density of her inner retreat—from the rays of her inverted sun sucking in their lives with the voracious appetite of a dwarf star. Approaching her, they become balls of liquid metal—mercurial—unpredictable in their moods and sudden departures. Especially for the younger daughter, departure is as necessary as breath. What metallic spider is it in her night that hammers a constant transformation, lacing open doors and windows with iron bars?

"What will you do?" I repeat.

She folds her hands together. I pour her some more tea and she bows her thanks. I take her hands in mine, feeling the silky wax texture.

"Will you come and stay with us?" Are there any other words to say? Her hands move under mine and I release them. Her face is motionless. "We could leave in a few days and come back next month."

"The plants . . ."

"Neighbours can water them."

"There is trouble with the house," she says. "This is an old house. If I leave . . ."

"Obasan," I say nodding, "it is your house."

She is an old woman. Every homemade piece of furniture, each pot holder and child's paper doily, is a link in her lifeline. She has preserved in shelves and in cupboards, under layers of clothing in closets—a daughter's rubber ball, colouring books, old hats, children's dresses. The items are endless. Every short stub pencil, every cornflake box stuffed with paper bags and old letters is of her ordering. They rest in the corners of the house like parts of her body, hair cells, skin tissue, food particles, tiny specks of memory. This house is now her blood and bones.

She is all old women in every hamlet in the world. You see her on a street corner in a village in southern France, in her black dress and her black stockings. She is squatting on stone steps in a Mexican mountain village. Everywhere she stands as the true and rightful owner of the earth, the bearer of love's keys to unknown doorways, to a network of astonishing tunnels, the possessor of life's infinite personal details.

"I am old," she says.

These are the words my grandmother spoke that last night in the house in Victoria. Grandmother was too old then to understand political expediency, race riots, the yellow peril. I was too young.

She stands up slowly. "Something in the attic for you," she says.

We climb the narrow stairs one step at a time carrying a flashlight with us. Its dull beam reveals mounds of cardboard boxes, newspapers, magazines, a trunk. A dead sparrow lies in the nearest corner by the eaves.

She attempts to lift the lid of the trunk. Black fly corpses fall to the floor. Between the wooden planks, more flies fill the cracks. Old spider webs hang like blood clots, thick and black from the rough angled ceiling.

Our past is as clotted as old webs hung in dark attics, still sticky and hovering, waiting for us to adhere and submit or depart. Or like a spider with its skinny hairy legs, the past skitters out of the dark, spinning and netting the air, ready to snap us up and ensnare our thoughts in old and complex perceptions. And when its feasting is complete, it leaves its victims locked up forever, dangling like hollowed out insect skins, a fearful calligraphy, dry reminders that once there was life flitting about in the weather.

But occasionally a memory that refuses to be hollowed out, to be categorized, to be identified, to be explained away, comes thudding into the web like a giant moth. And in the daylight, what's left hanging there, ragged and shredded, is a demolished fly trap, and beside it a bewildered eight-legged spinning animal.

My dead refuse to bury themselves. Each story from the past is changed and distorted, altered as much by the present as the present is shaped by the past. But potent and pervasive as a prairie dust storm, memory and dream seep and mingle through cracks, settling on furniture, into upholstery. The attic and the living room encroach onto each other, deep into their invisible places.

I sneeze and dust specks pummel across the flashlight beam. Will we all be dust in the end—a jumble of faces and lives compressed and powdered into a few lines of statistics—fading photographs in family albums, the faces no longer familiar, the clothing quaint, the anecdotes lost?

I use the flashlight to break off a web and lift the lid of the trunk. A strong whiff of mothballs assaults us. The odour of preservation. Inside, there are bits of lace and fur, a 1920s nightgown, a shoe box, red and white striped socks. She sifts through the contents, one by one.

"That's strange," she says several times.

"What are you looking for?" I ask.

"Not here. It isn't here."

She turns to face me in the darkness. "That's strange," she says and leaves her questions enclosed in silence.

I pry open the folds of a cardboard box. The thick dust slides off like chocolate icing sugar—antique pollen. Grandfather's boat building tools are wrapped in heavy cloth. These are all he brought when he came to this country wearing a western suit, western shoes, a round black hat. Here is the plane with a wooden handle which he worked by pulling it towards him. A fundamental difference in workmanship—to pull rather than push. Chisels, hammer, a mallet, a thin pointed saw, the handle extending from the blade like that of a kitchen knife.

"What will you do with these?" I ask.

"The junk in the attic," my cousins's letter said, "should be burned. When I come there this summer, I'll have a big bonfire. It's a fire trap. I've taken the only things that are worth keeping."

Beneath the box of tools is a pile of *Life* magazines dated in the 1950s. A subscription maintained while the two daughters were home. Beside the pile is another box containing shoe boxes, a metal box with a disintegrating elastic band, several chocolate boxes. Inside the metal box are pictures, duplicates of some I have seen in our family albums. Obasan's wedding photo—her midcalf dress hanging straight down from her shoulders, her smile glued on. In the next picture, Uncle is wearing a sailor suit.

The shoe box is full of documents.

Royal Canadian Mounted Police, Vancouver, BC, March 4, 1942. A folded mimeographed paper authorizes Uncle as the holder of a numbered Registration Card to leave a Registered Area by truck for Vernon where he is required to report to the local Registrar of Enemy Aliens, not later than the following day. It is signed by the RCMP superintendent.

Uncle's face, young and unsmiling, looks up at me from the bottom right hand corner of a wallet size ID card. "The bearer whose photograph and specimen of signature appear hereon, has been duly registered in compliance with the provisions of Order-in-Council PC 117." A purple stamp underneath states "Canadian Born". His thumb print appears on the back with marks of identification specified—scar on right hand.

There is a letter from the Department of the Secretary of State. Office of the Custodian. Japanese Evacuation Section. 506 Royal Bank Bldg. Hastings and Granville. Vancouver, BC.

Dear Sir.

Dear Uncle. With whom were you corresponding and for what did you hope? That the enmity would cease? That you could return to your boats? I have grown tired, Uncle, of seeking the face of the enemy hiding in the thick forests of the past. You were not the enemy. The police who came to your door were not the enemy. The men who rioted against you were not the enemy. The Vancouver alderman who said "Keep BC

White" was not the enemy. The men who drafted the Order-in-Council were not the enemy. He does not wear a uniform or sit at a long meeting table. The man who read your timid letter, read your polite request, skimmed over your impossible plea, was not your enemy. He had an urgent report to complete. His wife was ill. The phone rang all the time. The senior staff was meeting in two hours. The secretary was spending too much time over coffee breaks. There were a billion problems to attend to. Injustice was the only constant in a world of flux. There were moments when expedience demanded decisions which would later be judged unjust. Uncle, he did not always know what he was doing. You too did not have an all-compassionate imagination. He was just doing his job. I am just doing my work, Uncle. We are all just doing our jobs.

My dear dead Uncle. Am I come to unearth our bitterness that our buried love too may revive?

"Obasan, what shall we do with these?"

She has been waiting at the top of the stairs, holding the railing with both hands. I close the shoe box and replace the four interlocking flaps of the cardboard box. With one hand I shine the flashlight and with the other, guide her as I precede her slowly down the stairs. Near the bottom she stumbles and I hold her small body upright.

"Thank you, thank you," she says. This is the first time my arms have held her. We walk slowly through the living room and back to the kitchen. Her lips are trembling as she sits on the wooden stool.

Outside, the sky of the prairie spring is painfully blue. The trees are shooting out their leaves in the fierce wind, the new branches elastic as whips. The sharp-edged clarity is insistent as trumpets.

But inside, the rooms are muted. Our inner trees, our veins, are involuted, cocooned, webbed. The blood cells in the trunks of our bodies, like tiny specks of light, move in a sluggish river. It is more a potential than an actual river—an electric liquid—the current flowing in and between us, between our generations. Not circular, as in a whirlpool, or climactic and tidal as in fountains or spray—but brooding. Bubbling. You expect to hear barely audible pip-pip electronic tones, a pre-concert tuning up behind the curtains in the darkness. Towards the ends of our branches and fingertips, tiny human-shaped flames or leaves break off and leap towards the shadows. My arms are suffused with a suppressed urge to hold.

At the edges of our flesh is a hint of a spiritual osmosis, an eagerness within matter, waiting to brighten our dormant neurons, to entrust our stagnant cells with movement and dance.

Obasan drinks her tea and makes a shallow scratching sound in her throat. She shuffles to the door and squats beside the boot tray. With a putty knife, she begins to scrape off the thick clay like mud that sticks to my boots.

Essay

NAWAL EL SAADAWI

Either a veiled woman or a belly dancer—these are the only images many people have of Arab women.

The first time I visited the United States, an American woman asked me my nationality. I told her that I am from Egypt. She said, "You are Arab?" I said, "Yes, I'm an Arab woman." And she said, "You're sure you are an Arab woman?" I said, "Yes, I'm sure I am an Arab woman." Then I realized that the image of Arab women here in the United States is limited to either the veiled woman or the belly dancer. There is nothing in between. Now, several years later, I am still astonished by Americans who question my nationality. "Are you sure you're an Arab woman?" Today, they are likely to follow up with the question, "Then why aren't you veiled?"

There are many misconceptions about the identity, character, and diversity of Arab women, most certainly about the diversity of the culture of Arab women. Feminism is a part of our culture, our history. In the Arab Women Solidarity Association, we call ourselves historical socialist feminists. We insist on these three words. Historical, because we have a long history of struggle and because we must know our past before we can conceive a nonpatriachal future. Socialist, because we cannot separate patriarchy and class; we are oppressed because we are women and because we are poor. Finally, feminist, because we have formulated a powerful critique of patriarchy.

As a writer, I am often invited to international conferences, and I must say that I hate this division between Eastern and Western feminists. Because, in fact, many women in the West are quite backward and many women in the East are very progressive, and vice versa, so the division between East and West is ambiguous and misleading. And when I attend such international meetings I am frequently asked a question by Western women that I know is well intentioned but, even so, is grounded in assumptions that are quite racist: "You have come from an impoverished, backward country. How can we help you?" It is always assumed that we women of color need assistance and that so-called First World women must help us. And so we often hear, "How can we help you?" We usually respond by saying, "Well, you can help us by fighting here in your country against the same system that is oppressing us all."

Here's another example of this misapprehension of our common problems. Many Western women know very little about African/Arab cultures (although this is changing, particularly over the past decade). Consequently, upon meeting a woman from Sudan or Egypt, many Western women respond with the cursory "Oh, you are the women who are circumcised. This is very barbaric." Now, this circumcision is a terrifying and horrible business, but it also has its sensationalist side, and to know nothing but this about another woman's culture borders on racism. After all, there are other kinds of circumcision under patriarchy—psychological, for instance. My point is that we must recognize the similarities in our oppression and fight oppression together.

Patriarchy exists everywhere, it differs only by degree. In the Middle East and North Africa, we are experiencing a revival of Islamic fundamentalism—oppressive to women, of course. But here, in the United States, under Reagan and now Bush, you are experiencing a revival of Christian fundamentalism, equally oppressive to women. Westerners refuse to see or acknowledge these similarities. But the point is that women are oppressed under Christianity, Islam, Judaism, Hinduism—under all religions—because all religions are class-patriarchal structures.

Arab women live in a formerly colonized area of the world. The colonial repression continues, but it is more subtle now—not a colonization through military means, but through economic means and through systems of representation. Representation is quite important, because, as in your country, the media are very powerful in Egypt. The problem of representations of our culture in the media is a problem that women writers must contend with. What are the best means of struggle against this misinformation? The problem is acute in my country, because printed material is censored in Egypt. In fact, two days before I left for the United States, while I was still in Cairo, the government censored the only feminist magazine (of which I am an editor) in Egypt, which deals with class, patriarchy, and sexuality.

In 1972, all of my books—novels and nonfiction—were censored. I went to jail under President Sadat because of the content of my work, because I am a writer—not because I am a member of any particular political party or group, but simply because I expressed myself in written form on a variety of subjects having to do with Arab women. My arrest proved for me the tremendous power of the pen. It was actually ex-hilarating to know that Sadat was afraid of one woman with a pen! And the state's fear was demonstrated to me every morning when the jailer would search my cell and say to me, "If I find a pen or paper in your cell, it is much more dangerous to you than if I find a gun." I understood then the power of the word.

The Prisoner

WILLIAM McILVANNEY

McQueen, the burglar just out of solitary, inhabits a different world from the governor of the prison. But who has the better life?

All right, Rafferty," the governor said. "Good luck. And let's hope we won't be seeing you again."

The next one he certainly would be seeing again.

McQueen: over the past twenty years more time in prison than out of it. Recidivist. Always the same crime: burglary without violence but also burglary without the slightest indication of ever stopping. Show McQueen a big house and he wanted to screw it. The Don Juan of burglary. His only saving grace as a burglar was his inefficiency. But at least inside he had tended to behave. And now this.

The governor closed the file. He prepared himself for McQueen's presence, the rumpled hair, the heavy shoulders, the puzzling introverted eyes. The feeling that you might never get through to him. Conversations with a totem pole.

Without looking up, the governor knew that the assistant governor was watching him. He also knew, irritatedly, the way he was watching him: that look of those who wait for someone else to see the light. The governor hated that look, smugness like bell metal. The assistant governor was like a Jehovah's Witness of the hard line, always ready to canvass for his cause, always patient before the benightedness of others, always convinced that phoney liberals would eventually see the error of their ways.

The governor looked up and saw the expression that was pointed towards him like a Bible tract. Let us be righteous and burn the other bastards in hellfire.

"Okay," the governor said. "Let's have him in."

"This is a bad one, chief."

The governor wondered where the assistant governor got his dialogue.

"Uh-huh," he said. "Let's have him in."

"You want me in with you on this one?"

"No, Frank."

"After what he's done?"

"I know McQueen."

"We all thought we knew McQueen."

"Frank. If I shout for help, you come in with the machine-gun."

Levity was the best defence against the assistant governor. Humour was a foreign language to him. If you wanted him to laugh, you had to tell him it was a joke. He had his customary reaction of mild affront and went out and officiously ushered in McQueen, giving the governor a last significant look: help is at hand.

McQueen came in pleasantly and stood in front of the governor's desk. The governor decided not to tell him to sit down. This was a stand-up problem. McQueen returned the governor's look and almost smiled and gazed out of the window. The governor tried not to like that crumpled face that looked as if it might have come out of the womb asking for directions and still not received an answer.

"McQueen."

"Sur!"

The governor felt that McQueen's respect was subtly disrespectful. He invariably addressed the governor as "Sir" but he invariably used the inflection of his West of Scotland dialect, as if reminding him that they didn't quite speak the same language. "Sur" was the fifth-column in the standard English McQueen affected when speaking to the governor.

"You know what this is about."

"Yes, sur."

"Why?"

McQueen shrugged.

"Sur?"

"McQueen. You were obviously unhappy throughout the Christmas meal. Officer Roberts warned you three times. Christmas is a bad time for the men. The slightest bit of trouble could cause a riot. And what did you do? At the end of the meal you smashed your plate on the floor. You jumped on to the table and danced through all the other empty plates. You broke three chairs. And it took four warders to get you out of there. Is that a fair report?"

"Two chairs, sur. One of them wouldny brek."

The governor decided to let the pedantry pass.

"Just tell me why, McQueen."

He looked off into the distance that lay outside the window and the governor was aware again of the opaque quality of McQueen's eyes. They were the eyes—the governor had to admit it—of a visionary. A private, bizarre, non-conformist visionary. You could never be sure what was going on in McQueen's head but you could always be sure it was something. If only he would keep it in there, whatever it was, the governor thought. McQueen looked back at the governor and the governor briefly felt their roles reversed. He knew that McQueen was going to tell him, but with something that felt like condescension. It was as if McQueen had set the governor a simple problem and he was saddened that the governor couldn't solve it. He would tell him but in the manner of a disappointed teacher reluctantly admitting that his pupil hadn't made much progress.

"The turkey, sur," he said.

"The turkey?"

"The turkey, sur."

"What was wrong with the turkey?"

"Did you see the turkey, sur?"

"I saw the turkey. McQueen. I *ate* the turkey. McQueen. It may interest you to know that during any working day I eat the same food as the inmates. I don't have lunches sent up from the Ritz. I *care* about this establishment. I think every inmate in here deserves to be punished. But punished in specific ways. And spoiling the food isn't one of them. I check the kitchen every single day. That was a very special Christmas meal we made. The turkey was of high quality. I *tasted* it!"

"It wasn't the taste."

"I beg your pardon?"

"Sur. It wasn't the taste. Sur."

"No, no. That's not what I mean. You thought the turkey tasted all right?"

"I've tasted better, sur. But it was all right."

The governor looked down at the impeccable order of his desk. There was the matching set of marled fountain-pen and propelling pencil which his wife had given him years ago on his first senior appointment. There was the photograph of Catriona and Kim and Jason, looking laundered. There were the books of reference, sandbags between him and procedural error. There was the correspondence waiting to be signed, not an edge of a sheet out of place. The only thing that hinted at the invading chaos of a life like McQueen's was the big desk blotter. It was covered in hieroglyphics, countless comments and signatures that had come out backwards, overlaying one another and creating a complex palimpsest as difficult to decipher as an ancient manuscript. He would have to renew it soon.

Looking at the blotter, he felt the familiar feeling that came from taking to McQueen. He was trying to define the feeling. About three years ago, Catriona and he had gone to a play. It was the last time they had been to the theatre. They had sat through an hour-and-three-quarters during which people did things that had no connection with anything they had done before and made remarks to one another that seemed to come out of thin air. One character spoke for ten minutes at one point without interruption and then the play went on as if she hadn't opened her mouth. As far as Catriona and he were concerned, she might as well not have. They stayed for the whole performance out of a kind of baffled guilt, exchanging looks. Were they the only ones who hadn't read the guide-book? At the interval, an ageing man who had two attractive girls with him had said, "Surrealist," into a gin and tonic. Perhaps McQueen was a surrealist.

"So the turkey tasted all right," the governor said. "So what was the problem? The presentation? Did the waiter serve you from the wrong side?"

Something resembling relaxed enjoyment surfaced in McQueen's eyes and sank again, like a fish in a polluted pool. McQueen had liked the remark. The governor had a moving glimpse of what it might have been like to talk to McQueen outside the walls.

"Well?"

"You ate it, sur?"

"I've told you that."

"Ye didn't notice anything, sur?"

"I noticed it tasted very good. And so did the roast potatoes. And the other vegetable. What was it again? And the stuffing. And the cranberry sauce. We even gave you cranberry sauce!"

"And that's all, sur?"

"What more did you want?"

"Naw, sur. I meant that's all you noticed? The taste, like."

"What else is there, man?"

McQueen looked at the governor as if he had only just realised what a wag he was. He shook his head: I may look simple but you don't catch me out as easily as that.

"McQueen! For heaven's sake! If you don't tell me *now* what was wrong with the turkey . . . "

McQueen pursed his lips. His expression suggested he was being asked to tell a watch the time.

"It was round," he said.

The governor stared at him. He was back watching that incomprehensible play.

"It was round?" he asked with the involuntary tone of someone being admitted to a deep secret.

"The turkey was round, sur," McQueen confirmed.

The governor recovered quickly.

"Of course the turkey was round. I saw the bloody thing. The turkey was bloody round." The governor paused. He had used a swear-word. The governor never swore in front of the men. He looked sternly at McQueen as though trying to convince McQueen that he was the one who had sworn. "So what?"

"Turkeys aren't round, sur."

"I know turkeys aren't round, McQueen. You don't have to tell me that. That was *part* of a turkey. What you ate was *part* of a turkey."

"Which part was that, sur?"

"What do you mean?"

"What part of a turkey's round?"

"There's no part of a turkey that's round." The governor hesitated. "Or if there is, I wouldn't know. That's not the point. You ate turkey. You had turkey for your Christmas dinner. I'm telling you that. You ate turkey, McQueen."

McQueen looked at the floor stubbornly, unconvinced. A small dawn rose in the governor's eyes. McQueen had been in for six years this time. Before that, he had been outside only for brief spells over a period of twelve years. Other inmates referred to McQueen's time outside as taking his holidays. McQueen was simply out of touch with the ways of the world.

"McQueen," the governor said. "It was turkey roll."

"What, sur?"

"What you ate. It was turkey roll."

McQueen considered the possibility.

"It's a process, McQueen. A modern process. You take a lot of turkeys and make them into a turkey roll. With machinery. You *refine* the turkeys."

"How do ye do that, sur?"

The governor looked away.

"You. Pass them through machinery."

"What? Everything, sur?"

"How would I know, McQueen? I suppose you take the feathers off.

Just accept the fact, man. Everybody else does. It was turkey roll."

"It wasn't turkey, sur."

"McQueen. Turkey roll *is* turkey. Everybody accepts that. It's what a lot of people eat."

"Then they're not eatin' turkey, sur. Turkey roll, as ye call it, isn't turkey. It may be *like* turkey. But it's not turkey."

"It is turkey! What else would it be?"

McQueen was taking the question seriously.

"See when they refine it, sur? What is the exact process?"

The governor was watching McQueen, realising something. But McQueen was too caught up in pursuit of his own ideas to notice. The governor observed him from a distance, like a business-manager full of grave responsibilities looking out of his office window to see a grown-up layabout, who should know better, chasing after butterflies in the park.

"See what I mean, sur? What happens when they turn a turkey into turkey roll? What is it they do, sur? Do you know? Do I know? Do any of the ordinary people know? They take out the bones. Right? They must take out the bones, sur. But nowadays, who knows? Maybe they powder them, sur. And mix it in with the whole mish-mash. But what *exactly* do they do? What is the machinery *like*, sur? And." McQueen paused with the look of a man who has found the incontrovertible point, the argument with which you must agree. "What else do they *put in*? It's guaranteed they put in something, sur. If turkey roll's not a substitute for turkey, why not just have the turkey? Eh?" McQueen was smiling in triumph. "It's cheaper. And what are they doing to make it cheaper? They could put any kind of crap in there, sur, and we wouldn't know. Preservatives. Bits of dead dogs for all we know. We're being had, sur. Everybody's being had. Turkey roll isn't turkey. Sur."

The governor was looking at McQueen. What he had realised was that McQueen was enjoying this. All the men did that. Let out of their routine for any purpose, they contrived to make an event of it. It was part of the emotional economy of prison, like a man going to be hanged who decides he'll try to enjoy the walk to the gallows. The governor understood that.

But McQueen's was an extreme case. He had just been brought up from solitary on a very grave breach of discipline. It could be incitement to riot. And he had contrived to turn his appearance before the governor into a metaphysical discussion on what constitutes a turkey. Was he serious?

The governor studied McQueen, who let himself be studied without apparent discomfort. The intensity of McQueen's commitment to the great turkey question seemed unreal but his reaction to the Christmas dinner had been real enough. You had to wonder if round turkeys were just an excuse but when you looked at McQueen they sure enough felt like a reason.

Prison magnified trivia. Everything came at you as if it was under a microscope. If a man you didn't like raised his forefinger, it looked like an obelisk. The governor had known a man who was killed for not paying the tobacco he owed. The tobacco, carefully used, would have made five cigarettes. The governor had a blessedly brief vision of the terrible complexities with which he was dealing. Habit came to his rescue.

"McQueen," the governor said. "That's it? Because the turkey was round?"

"It wasn't turkey, sur."

"It was turkey roll."

"We were promised turkey."

"Everybody else seemed satisfied."

"That's up to them."

The governor contemplated the strange wildness of McQueen's behaviour and gave it up.

"You're back to solitary, McQueen," he said. "Till I decide. I see no justification for your behaviour. I don't even see that you're sorry for it. Are you? I mean, was that the only way you could express yourself?"

McQueen shrugged.

"You said it yerself, sur. Ye can't complain to the waiter, can ye?"

The governor wondered how he was supposed to have said it himself. Then he remembered having mentioned the idea of a waiter serving from the wrong side. There it was again, tangential attempts to meet. One of us, the governor thought, is wrong. Or perhaps we both are. He hadn't time to pursue the thought.

"McQueen. I'm disappointed in you. You know the score here. Every man in here is a long-termer from another place. This is where you get a chance to prepare for outside. You know this is an easy ticket. We're trying to make a transition here. From hard jails to the real world."

"That's the real world, sur? Broken promises? Synthetic turkey?"

"The interview's over, McQueen. Don't you understand that? And you didn't get the job. I've tried to give you a chance. We'll do it my way now. And you'll just listen. In the meantime you're back yourself. I don't want any rotten apples in my barrel. You're a mug. You've maybe just worked your ticket to a real jail. I'll let you know. In the meantime, stew in your juice. I hope you enjoy it. Thing is, you're not even a violent man. Then you do this. Hoof it."

As McQueen turned, one thing was still niggling at the governor's mind.

"McQueen!"

McQueen stopped, turned round.

"You ate the turkey."

"Sorry, sur?"

"You ate the turkey. And then you ate the pudding. Was the pudding all right, by the way? Was that to your taste?"

"It wasn't really, sur."

"Oh. What was wrong with that?"

"Ah don't like a cold thing and a warm thing put together."

"You mean the ice-cream and the hot apple tart?"

"That's right, sur."

"I hope you like the menu better where you're going."

McQueen was turning away again.

"But you miss the point," the governor said.

McQueen turned back, practised in patience.

"You *ate* the turkey," the governor said. "You *ate* the pudding. You ate everything. And then you made your protest. Why?"

McQueen gave him that habitual look that suggested the world was out to con him.

"Ah was hungry, sur," he said.

The governor was left staring into the remark. It opened like a window on to a place he had never been. He saw McQueen sitting eating his meal in the big hall. Around him were faces that wouldn't have been out of place on Notre Dame Cathedral. McQueen was grumbling but nobody else was giving him any support. McQueen was hungry, so he ate everything and then exploded. The precision was where the governor had never been, the precision of passion, the risk of choosing the moment when you try to express utterly what you feel. McQueen, the governor understood with a dismay that would quickly bury the understanding in disbelief like dead leaves, was capable of something of which the governor was not. McQueen was capable of freedom.

The assistant governor opened the door and looked in.

"Well?" he said.

"We'll see. He goes back down today. Then I'll decide."

"It's a bad one. We don't need that stuff here."

"I know that. We'll see."

The assistant governor contrived to make a nod look negative and went out.

The governor started to sign his mail. When he was finished, he would inspect the kitchens. Then he would have lunch with the assistant governor and Mrs. Caldwell, the teacher. They would discuss which inmates might be capable of sitting an external examination, the advisability of an evening creative writing class under a visiting teacher and the case of Branson, who believed he was a genius not being published simply because he was in prison. The afternoon was exactly scheduled. He would leave a little early this evening because he was speaking to the Rotary Club in the nearest town, where he lived. Catriona and the children would be asleep by the time he got back. It was an early rise tomorrow. It was his day off and it was their day for visiting his parents. The drive was long and boring and it only gave them three hours at his parents' house. But maybe that was just as well. His mother was a woman who had turned into a compendium of elusive ailments which she recited as if they were conversation. His father would sit apparently stunned into silent awe at the agonies she went through. They would all get back just in time for bed. As he worked, the governor was vaguely aware of an image prowling the perimeter of his interlocking thoughts. The image was the rumpled figure of McQueen.

McQueen sat very still in his cell. With an almost mystical intensity, he was thinking himself beyond the enmeshing smell of urine mixed with disinfectant that had always for him meant prison. He had a method for doing this. He recreated in his mind big houses he had seen. This one was a big detached white house with a semi-circular balcony on the first floor. It faced the sea-front of an Ayrshire coastal town. Sometimes in McQueen's head they were hard to get into. This one had been easy. He put shaving foam on the burglar alarm and forced the kitchen window.

McQueen landed on his stockinged feet on the kitchen floor. His shoes were on the draining board. He tied their specially long laces together and hung them round his neck. He listened. His eyes became accustomed to the darkness. Something brushed against his leg and he almost called out. It was a cat. McQueen bent down and stroked it gently. He straightened and looked slowly round the kitchen. The kitchen was well appointed, rich in the shining surfaces of affluence. It glowed dimly like the entrance to Ali Baba's cave.

McQueen moved without sound towards the hall. He was wondering what he would find.

The Meeting

JORGE LUIS BORGES

What are the possible consequences of a duel fought between reluctant combatants? This story provides one answer.

Anyone leafing his way through the morning paper does so either to escape his surroundings or to provide himself with small talk for later in the day, so it is not to be wondered at that no one any longer remembers—or else remembers as in a dream—the famous and once widely discussed case of Maneco Uriarte and of Duncan. The event took place, furthermore, back around 1910, the year of the comet and the Centennial, and since then we have had and have lost so many things. Both protagonists are now dead; those who witnessed the episode solemnly swore silence. I, too, raised my hand for the oath, feeling the importance of the ritual with all the romantic seriousness of my nine or ten years. I do not know whether the others noticed that I had given my word; I do not know whether they kept theirs. Anyway, here is the story, with all the inevitable variations brought about by time and by good or bad writing.

My cousin Lafinur took me to a barbecue that evening at a country house called The Laurels, which belonged to some friends of his. I cannot fix its exact location; let us take any of those suburban towns lying just to the north, shaded and quiet, that slope down to the river and that have nothing in common with sprawling Buenos Aires and its surrounding prairie. The journey by train lasted long enough to seem endless to me, but time for children—as is well known—flows slowly. It was already dark when we passed through the villa's main gate. Here, I felt, were all the ancient, elemental things: the smell of meat cooking golden brown, the trees, the dogs, the kindling wood, and the fire that brings men together.

The guests numbered about a dozen; all were grown-ups. The eldest, I learned later, was not yet thirty. They were also—this I was soon to find out—well versed in matters about which I am still somewhat backward: race horses, the right tailors, motorcars, and notoriously expensive women. No one ruffled my shyness, no one paid any attention to me. The lamb, slowly and skillfully prepared by one of the hired men, kept us a long time in the big dining room. The dates of vintages were argued back and forth. There was a guitar; my cousin, if I remember correctly, sang a couple of Elías Regules' ballads about gauchos in the back country of Uruguay and some verses in dialect, in the incipient *lunfardo* of those days, about a knife fight in a brothel on Junín Street. Coffee and Havana cigars were brought in. Not a word about getting back. I felt (in the words of the poet Lugones) the fear of what is suddenly too late. I dared not look at the clock. In order to disguise my boyish loneliness among grown-ups, I put away—not really liking it—a glass or two of wine. Uriarte, in a loud voice, proposed to Duncan a two-handed game of poker. Someone objected that that kind of play made for a poor game and suggested a hand of four. Duncan agreed, but Uriarte, with a stubbornness that I did not understand and that I did not try to understand, insisted on the first scheme. Outside of *truco*—a game whose real aim is to pass time with mischief and verses—and of the modest mazes of solitaire, I never enjoyed cards. I slipped away without anyone's noticing. A rambling old house, unfamiliar and dark (only in the dining room was there light), means more to a boy than a new country means to a traveler. Step by step, I explored the rooms; I recall a billiard room, a long gallery with rectangular and diamond-shaped panes, a couple of rocking chairs, and a window from which you could just make out a summer-house. In the darkness I lost my way; the owner of the house, whose name, as I recall after all these years, may have been Acevedo or Acebal, finally came across me somehow. Out of kindness or perhaps out of a collector's vanity, he led me to a display cabinet. On lighting a lamp, I saw the glint of steel. It was a collection of knives that had once been in the hands of famous fighters. He told me that he had a bit of land somewhere to the north around Pergamino, and that he had been picking up these things on his travels back and forth across the province. He opened the cabinet and, without looking at what was written on the tags, he began giving me accounts of each item; they were more or less the same except for dates and place names. I asked him whether among the weapons he might have the dagger of Juan Moreira, who was in that day the archetype of the gaucho, as later Martín Fierro and Don Segundo Sombra would be. He had to confess that he hadn't but that he could show me one like it, with a U-shaped crosspiece in the hilt. He was interrupted by the sound of angry voices. At once he shut the cabinet and turned to leave; I followed him.

Uriarte was shouting that his opponent had tried to cheat him. All the others stood around the two players. Duncan, I remember, was a taller man than the rest of the company, and was well built, though somewhat round-shouldered; his face was expressionless, and his hair was so light it was almost white. Maneco Uriarte was nervous, dark, with perhaps a touch of Indian blood, and wore a skimpy, petulant moustache. It was obvious that everybody was drunk; I do not know whether there were two or three emptied bottles on the floor or whether an excess of movies suggests this false memory to me. Uriarte's insults did not let up; at first sharp, they now grew obscene. Duncan appeared not to hear, but finally, as though weary, he got up and threw a punch. From the floor, Uriarte snarled that he was not going to take this outrage, and he challenged Duncan to fight.

Duncan said no, and added, as though to explain, "The trouble is I'm afraid of you."

Everybody howled with laughter.

Uriarte, picking himself up, answered, "I'm going to have it out with you, and right now."

Someone—may he be forgiven for it—remarked that weapons were not lacking.

I do not know who went and opened the glass cabinet. Maneco Uriarte picked out the showiest and longest dagger, the one with the U-shaped crosspiece; Duncan, almost absentmindedly, picked a wooden-handled knife with the stamp of a tiny tree on the blade. Someone said it was just like Maneco to play it safe, to choose a sword. It astonished no one that his hand began shaking; what was astonishing is that the same thing happened with Duncan.

Tradition demands that men about to fight should respect the house in which they are guests, and step outside. Half on a spree, half seriously, we all went out into the damp night. I was not drunk—at least, not on wine—but I was reeling with adventure; I wished very hard that someone would be killed, so that later I could tell about it and always remember it. Maybe at that moment the others were no more adult than I was. I also had the feeling that an overpowering current was dragging us on and would drown us. Nobody believed the least bit in Maneco's accusation; everyone saw it as the fruit of an old rivalry, exacerbated by the wine.

We pushed our way through a clump of trees, leaving behind the summerhouse. Uriarte and Duncan led the way, wary of each other. The rest of us strung ourselves out around the edge of an opening of lawn. Duncan had stopped there in the moonlight and said, with mild authority, "This looks like the right place."

The two men stood in the center, not quite knowing what to do. A voice rang out: "Let go of all that hardware and use your hands!"

But the men were already fighting. They began clumsily, almost as if they were afraid of hurting each other; they began by watching the blades, but later their eyes were on one another. Uriarte had laid aside his anger, Duncan his contempt or aloofness. Danger, in some way, had transfigured them; these were now two men fighting, not boys. I had imagined the fight as a chaos of steel; instead, I was able to follow it, or almost follow it, as though it were a game of chess. The intervening years may, of course, have exaggerated or blurred what I saw. I do not know how long it lasted; there are events that fall outside the common measure of time.

Without ponchos to act as shields, they used their forearms to block each lunge of the knife. Their sleeves, soon hanging in shreds, grew black with blood. I thought that we had gone wrong in supposing that they knew nothing about this kind of fencing. I noticed right off that they handled themselves in different ways. Their weapons were unequal. Duncan, in order to make up for his disadvantage, tried to stay in close to the other man; Uriarte kept stepping back to be able to lunge out with long, low thrusts. The same voice that had called attention to the display cabinet shouted out now: "They're killing each other! Stop them!"

But no one dared break it up. Uriarte had lost ground; Duncan charged him. They were almost body to body now. Uriarte's weapon sought Duncan's face. Suddenly the blade seemed shorter, for it was piercing the taller man's chest. Duncan lay stretched out on the grass. It was at this point that he said, his voice very low. "How strange. All this is like a dream."

He did not shut his eyes, he did not move, and I had seen a man kill another man.

Maneco Uriarte bent over the body, sobbing openly, and begged to be forgiven. The thing he had just done was beyond him. I know now that he regretted less having committed a crime than having carried out a senseless act.

I did not want to look anymore. What I had wished for so much had happened, and it left me shaken. Lafinur told me later that they had had to struggle hard to pull out the weapon. A makeshift council was formed. They decided to lie as little as possible and to elevate this

duel with knives to a duel with swords. Four of them volunteered as seconds, among them Acebal. In Buenos Aires anything can be fixed; someone always has a friend.

On top of the mahogany table where the men had been playing, a pack of English cards and a pile of bills lay in a jumble that nobody wanted to look at or to touch.

In the years that followed, I often considered revealing the story to some friend, but always I felt that there was a greater pleasure in being the keeper of a secret than in telling it. However, around 1929, a chance conversation suddenly moved me one day to break my long silence. The retired police captain, Don José Olave, was recalling stories about men from the tough riverside neighborhood of the Retiro who had been handy with their knives; he remarked that when they were out to kill their man, scum of this kind had no use for the rules of the game, and that before all the fancy playing with daggers that you saw now on the stage, knife fights were few and far between. I said I had witnessed one, and gave him an account of what had happened nearly twenty years earlier.

He listened to me with professional attention, then said, "Are you sure Uriarte and What's-His-Name never handled a knife before? Maybe they had picked up a thing or two around their fathers' ranches."

"I don't think so," I said. "Everybody there that night knew one another pretty well, and I can tell you they were all amazed at the way the two men fought."

Olave went on in his quiet manner, as if thinking aloud. "One of the weapons had a U-shaped crosspiece in the handle. There were two daggers of that kind which became quite famous—Moreira's and Juan Almada's. Almada was from down south, in Tapalquén."

Something seemed to come awake in my memory. Olave continued. "You also mentioned a knife with a wooden handle, one with the Little Tree brand. There are thousands of them, but there was one—"

He broke off for a moment, then said, "Señor Acevedo had a big property up around Pergamino. There was another of these famous toughs from up that way—Juan Almanza was his name. This was along about the turn of the century. When he was fourteen, he killed his first man with one of these knives. From then on, for luck, he stuck to the same one. Juan Almanza and Juan Almada had it in for each other, jealous of the fact that many people confused the two. For a long time they searched high and low for one another, but they never met. Juan Almanza was killed by a stray bullet during some election brawl or other. The other man, I think, died a natural death in a hospital bed in Las Flores."

Nothing more was said. Each of us was left with his own conclusions.

Nine or ten men, none of whom is any longer living, saw what my eyes saw—that sudden stab and the body under the night sky— but perhaps what we were really seeing was the end of another story, an older story. I began to wonder whether it was Maneco Uriarte who killed Duncan or whether in some uncanny way it could have been the weapons, not the men, which fought. I still remember how Uriarte's hand shook when he first gripped his knife, and the same with Duncan, as though the knives were coming awake after a long sleep side by side in the cabinet. Even after their gauchos were dust, the knives—the knives, not their tools, the men—knew how to fight. And that night they fought well.

Things last longer than people; who knows whether these knives will meet again, who knows whether the story ends here.

Translated by Norman Thomas di Giovanni

---

lunfardo: thieves' slang; language of the underworld

The Poor

ROBERTO SOSA

The poor are many.
That's why
we cannot forget them.

Surely
they see
in the morning light
many buildings
they would like
to live in with their children.

They can
shoulder
the coffin of a star.
They can
rip up the air like furious birds,
blot out the sun.

But not knowing their treasures
they enter and leave by mirrors of blood;
they walk, and die, slowly.

That's why
we cannot forget them.

Translated by Jim Lindsey

Decomposition

ZULFIKAR GHOSE

I have a picture I took in Bombay
of a beggar asleep on the pavement:
grey-haired, wearing shorts and a dirty shirt,
his shadow thrown aside like a blanket.

His arms and legs could be cracks in the stone,
routes for the ants' journeys, the flies' descents.
Brain-washed by the sun into exhaustion,
he lies veined into stone, a fossil man.

Behind him, there is a crowd passingly
bemused by a pavement trickster and quite
indifferent to this very common sight
of an old man asleep on the pavement.

I thought it then a good composition
and glibly called it *The Man in the Street*,
remarking how typical it was of
India that the man in the street lived there.

His head in the posture of one weeping
into a pillow chides me now for my
presumption at attempting to compose
art out of his hunger and solitude.

What's a Bum, Mom?

KATHLEEN ROCKWELL LAWRENCE

How does a mother feel when she can't answer her daughter's questions?

That one is a bum. That one is a drug addict." Isabelle, at five, has a firm grip on verities that have eluded me these last few years. I am walking her and my daughter through the five blocks of sidewalk from kindergarten to ballet class. Isabelle is our guide. We've walked around three men lying asleep on the sidewalk, stepping over a streak of urine that has made its way from one man to the curb. ("Are they asleep? Are they sick? Are they dead? What's the matter with them?" my daughter asks. "They're bums," Isabelle explains.) We've declined to give money to a woman who has asked us for 25 cents. I excuse myself to myself by saying that my hands are full with the children's hands.

"Why does she want 25 cents, Mom? Can't she get 25 cents herself? Why didn't you give her 25 cents if she needs money?"

"We're late for ballet," I say. How can I stop now to rummage in my pockets for quarters? And what if I don't have a quarter? I'm getting real good at excuses.

"Thank you," says the woman. "God bless you."

We wait for the light at 14th. Opposite us, a man wearing ripped high tops and a sheer slip is also waiting. His beard is matted filth and his head is bandaged. He is shouting and gesticulating. I feel baby hands tighten on mine. Their bodies lean against my legs. As he passes us in the crosswalk he lurches toward us. The girls grab my arms and scream. "Yuk," says Isabelle, when we are safely past. "That one stinks!" He does, and the stench of him fouls even the air he has gone from.

"What is a bum, Mom? I mean, how do you know?" my daughter asks that night. She needs an explanation for the people that she sees on the streets. She has to know why. She has to find out about human misery. It is all around her.

"I'm taking you to the Precinct," a man tells me the next afternoon as I'm walking my daughter home. "You ragged five dollars off me."

"Walk fast," I tell my daughter, but I didn't have to. I figure once we're past, he'll go to the next passer-by. But he doesn't. His deranged mind has singled me out. He grabs my arm as I turn to go into my building. My terrified daughter is hanging onto my other arm. Just then my neighbour Shelley comes out of our building with her three-year-old daughter. I want her to go back in, but she is too good a friend, and too brave.

"Sir, you leave her alone! I'm going to call the police."

"I'm taking her to the Precinct. She ragged five dollars off me."

"She didn't rag five dollars off anyone, sir!"

I should scream, but I cannot. Though my reflexes have worked in other emergencies, having my daughter as a hostage in this one has rendered me immobile. I am mute, thinking dumbly, as if at the distance I wish I were:

Shelley is my good, good friend.

I should have gone to the Precinct.

Shelley is calling him "sir."

Shelley knew right away what "ragged" meant.

Does he have a knife?

His face is menacing, filled with hatred. I know he is going to hurt me, but I am frozen, listening to my daughter, who is screaming, crying.

A large man in a sweatshirt comes from somewhere and pulls him from me, but he grabs me again. The large man has to hit him, actually deck him in front of our little daughters, before we can escape.

"He thought you took his five dollars, Mom? Did somebody really take his five dollars? Why didn't you give him five dollars and he would go away? He's in jail now, right? How long will they keep him in jail? Until he knows not to hurt somebody?"

I have another story, of another mother and her teen-age daughter who live on the ground floor of a lovely old building in the West Village. There is a moatlike depression in the front of the building. A homeless man built a house for himself in the moat, from discarded plywood. The house the man built was right outside the daughter's window. She heard him in the night the way my daughter hears her hamster. In the morning he was gone, and she and her mother dismantled his house.

In the afternoon, when they returned home, they found his house rebuilt. That evening he threw a rock through their front window.

I take after my daughter. I've got a lot of questions. Why were these women forced into this situation? What is it like, taking down a man's house before the winter? They had to do it, anyone would have done it, but did they cry while they were doing it?

Why are thousands of people without homes in this city? Why are deranged people on the streets where they will harm or be harmed? Why have they not been given the dignity of a place?

I've lived too long and seen too much for Isabelle's answers. A woman defecating in the waiting room at Penn Station. A man, clearly sick and in pain, ushered between two security guards from the place in front of their building where he had been lying, to a sidewalk across the street. Bouncers at the doors of our libraries keeping them out. A supermarket manager bodily removing a man who came in to redeem a few scavenged deposit bottles.

From a bus window I saw a woman with oozing ankles shuffle in pain and pieces of shoes as she carried her bags. She stopped at a wastebasket and retrieved a large discarded sketch book. She flipped through it until she found a blank page. Standing on the corner of Sixth and 14th, she reached into one of her bags and found a marker. She made one deft stroke, then another, on the page another artist left her. My bus moved on.

I can no longer say *bum* or *bag lady*. And, that most invidious term *street people*, with its implication that the street is where they are happiest, doing their thing, merrily rifling for rotted food in the supermarket garbage bins, gladly searching out a place to wash their bodies. So I tell my daughter that they are homeless and try to explain what that means. I try to explain why. Some of them can't think right. Some of them can hurt people. All of them are hungry. I do not tell her that there are children among them. I do not tell her that many of these people are sick and some are dying from hunger and exposure and neglect.

I have plenty more questions than I have answers. I've always been good at putting questions to others. It's right: there's need here, there's agony, there's blame. But now I have a daughter who demands answers from me and *will* get them. She observes her mother far too closely. The only true response for her is the one she sees me make to those whose anguished lives are being lived so close to hers.

Dives

EDWARD KAMAU BRATHWAITE

Before they built the deep water harbour
sinking an island to do it
we used to row out in our boats

to the white liners, great ocean-going floats,
to dive for coins. women with bracelets,
men with expensive tickers on their wrists,

watched us through bland sun glasses
so that their blue stares never blinked.
they tossed us pennies. the spinning flat
metallic bird would hit the water with a little

flap and wing zig-zagging down the water's track.
our underwater eyes would watch it like a cat
as it dark bottomed soundwards like a pendulum
winging from side to side, now black

now bright, now black, now bright,
catching the dying daylight down
the coal dark tides of the ship.
every shadow we saw was a possible shark

but we followed that flat dark light
even if the propellers would suddenly turn
burning the water to murderous cold
we would never come nearer to gold.

No Witchcraft for Sale

DORIS LESSING

Powerful ties of loyalty and gratitude bind Gideon and his masters. But there are secrets the faithful servant cannot reveal, even to the missus or the baas.

The Farquars had been childless for years when little Teddy was born; and they were touched by the pleasure of their servants, who brought presents of fowls and eggs and flowers to the homestead when they came to rejoice over the baby, exclaiming with delight over his downy golden head and his blue eyes. They congratulated Mrs Farquar as if she had achieved a very great thing, and she felt that she had—her smile for the lingering, admiring natives was warm and grateful.

Later, when Teddy had his first haircut, Gideon the cook picked up the soft gold tufts from the ground, and held them reverently in his hand. Then he smiled at the little boy and said: "Little Yellow Head." That became the native name for the child. Gideon and Teddy were great friends from the first. When Gideon had finished his work, he would lift Teddy on his shoulders to the shade of a big tree, and play with him there, forming curious little toys from twigs and leaves and grass, or shaping animals from wetted soil. When Teddy learned to walk it was often Gideon who crouched before him, clucking encouragement, finally catching him when he fell, tossing him up in the air till they both became breathless with laughter. Mrs Farquar was fond of the old cook because of his love for her child.

There was no second baby; and one day Gideon said: "Ah missus, missus, the Lord above sent this one; Little Yellow Head is the most good thing we have in our house." Because of that "we" Mrs Farquar felt a warm impulse towards her cook; and at the end of the month she raised his wages. He had been with her now for several years; he was one of the few natives who had his wife and children in the compound and never wanted to go home to his kraal, which was some hundreds of miles away. Sometimes a small piccanin who had been born the same time as Teddy could be seen peering from the edge of the bush, staring in awe at the little white boy with his miraculous fair hair and northern blue eyes. The two little children would gaze at each other with a wide, interested gaze, and once Teddy put out his hand curiously to touch the black child's cheeks and hair.

Gideon, who was watching, shook his head wonderingly, and said: "Ah, missus, these are both children, and one will grow up to be a baas, and one will be a servant;" and Mrs Farquar smiled and said sadly, "Yes, Gideon, I was thinking the same." She sighed. "It is God's will," said Gideon, who was a mission boy. The Farquars were very religious people; and this shared feeling about God bound servant and masters even closer together.

Teddy was about six years old when he was given a scooter, and discovered the intoxications of speed. All day he would fly around the homestead, in and out of flowerbeds, scattering squawking chickens and irritated dogs, finishing with a wide dizzying arc into the kitchen door. Then he would cry: "Gideon, look at me!" And Gideon would laugh and say: "Very clever, Little Yellow Head." Gideon's youngest son, who was now a herdsboy, came especially up from the compound to see the scooter. He was afraid to come near it, but Teddy showed off in front of him.

"Piccanin," shouted Teddy, "get out of my way!" And he raced in circles around the black child until he was frightened, and fled back to the bush.

"Why did you frighten him?" asked Gideon, gravely reproachful.

Teddy said defiantly: "He's only a black boy," and laughed. Then, when Gideon turned away from him without speaking, his face fell. Very soon he slipped into the house and found an orange and brought it to Gideon, saying: "This is for you." He could not bring himself to say he was sorry; but he could not bear to lose Gideon's affection either. Gideon took the orange unwillingly and sighed. "Soon you will be going away to school, Little Yellow Head," he said wonderingly, "and then you will be grown up." He shook his head gently and said, "And that is how our lives go." He seemed to be putting a distance between himself and Teddy, not because of resentment, but in the way a person accepts something inevitable. The baby had lain in his arms and smiled up into his face: the tiny boy had swung from his shoulders, had played with him by the hour. Now Gideon would not let his flesh touch the flesh of the white child. He was kind, but there was a grave formality in his voice that made Teddy pout and sulk away. Also it made him into a man: with Gideon he was polite, and carried himself formally, and if he came into the kitchen to ask for something, it was in the way a white man uses towards a servant, expecting to be obeyed.

But on the day Teddy came staggering into the kitchen with his fists to his eyes, shrieking with pain, Gideon dropped the pot full of hot soup that he was holding, rushed to the child, and forced aside his fingers. "A snake!" he exclaimed. Teddy had been on his scooter, and had come to a rest with his foot on the side of a big tub of plants. A tree snake, hanging by its tail from the roof, had spat full into his eyes. Mrs Farquar came running when she heard the commotion. "He'll go blind," she sobbed, holding Teddy close against her. "Gideon, he'll go blind!" Already the eyes, with perhaps half an hour's sight left in them, were swollen to the size of fists: Teddy's small white face was distorted by great purple oozing protuberances. Gideon said: "Wait a minute, missus, I'll get some medicine." He ran off into the bush.

Mrs Farquar lifted the child into the house and bathed his eyes with permanganate. She had scarcely heard Gideon's words; but when she saw that her remedies had no effect at all, and remembered how she had seen natives with no sight in their eyes, because of the spitting of a snake, she began to look for the return of the cook, remembering what she had heard of the efficacy of native herbs. She stood by the window, holding the terrified, sobbing little boy in her arms, and peered helplessly into the bush. It was not more than a few minutes before she saw Gideon come bounding back, and in his hand he held a plant.

"Do not be afraid, missus," said Gideon, "this will cure Little Yellow Head's eyes." He stripped the leaves from the plant, leaving a small white fleshy root. Without even washing it he put the root in his mouth, chewed it vigorously, and then held the spittle there while he took the child forcibly from Mrs Farquar. He gripped Teddy down between his knees, and pressed the balls of his thumbs into the swollen eyes, so that the child screamed and Mrs Farquar cried out in protest: "Gideon, Gideon!" But Gideon took no notice. He knelt over the writhing child, pushing back the puffy lids till chinks of eyeball showed, and then he spat hard, again and again, into first one eye, and then the other. He finally lifted Teddy gently into his mother's arms, and said: "His eyes will get better." But Mrs Farquar was weeping with terror, and she could hardly thank him: it was impossible to believe that Teddy could keep his sight. In a couple of hours the swellings were gone; the eyes were inflamed and tender but Teddy could see. Mr and Mrs Farquar went to Gideon in the kitchen and thanked him over and over again. They felt helpless because of

their gratitude: it seemed they could do nothing to express it. They gave Gideon presents for his wife and children, and a big increase in wages, but these things could not pay for Teddy's now completely cured eyes. Mrs Farquar said: "Gideon, God chose you as an instrument for His goodness," and Gideon said: "Yes, missus, God is very good."

Now, when such a thing happens on a farm, it cannot be long before everyone hears of it. Mr and Mrs Farquar told their neighbours and the story was discussed from one end of the district to the other. The bush is full of secrets. No one can live in Africa, or at least on the veld, without learning very soon that there is an ancient wisdom of leaf and soil and season—and, too, perhaps most important of all, of the darker tracts of the human mind—which is the black man's heritage. Up and down the district people were telling anecdotes, reminding each other of things that had happened to them.

"But I saw it myself, I tell you. It was a puff adder bite. The kaffir's arm was swollen to the elbow, like a great shiny black bladder. He was groggy after half a minute. He was dying. Then suddenly a kaffir walked out of the bush with his hands full of green stuff. He smeared something on the place, and next day my boy was back at work, and all you could see was two small punctures in the skin."

This was the kind of tale they told. And, as always, with a certain amount of exasperation, because while all of them knew that in the bush of Africa are waiting valuable drugs locked in bark, in simple-looking leaves, in roots, it was impossible to ever get the truth about them from the natives themselves.

The story eventually reached town; and perhaps it was at a sundowner party, or some such function, that a doctor who happened to be there, challenged it. "Nonsense," he said. "These things get exaggerated in the telling. We are always checking up on this kind of story, and we draw a blank every time."

Anyway, one morning there arrived a strange car at the homestead, and out stepped one of the workers from the laboratory in town, with cases full of test-tubes and chemicals.

Mr and Mrs Farquar were flustered and pleased and flattered. They asked the scientist to lunch, and they told the story all over again, for the hundredth time. Little Teddy was there too, his blue eyes sparkling with health, to prove the truth of it. The scientist explained how humanity might benefit if this new drug could be offered for sale; and the Farquars were even more pleased; they were kind, simple people, who liked to think of something good coming about because of them. But when the scientist began talking of the money that might result, their manner showed discomfort. Their feelings over the miracle (that was how they thought of it) were so strong and deep and religious, that it was distasteful to them to think of money. The scientist, seeing their faces, went back to his first point, which was the advancement of humanity. He was perhaps a trifle perfunctory: it was not the first time he had come salting the tail of a fabulous bush-secret.

Eventually, when the meal was over, the Farquars called Gideon into their living-room and explained to him that this baas, here, was a Big Doctor from the Big City, and he had come all that way to see Gideon. At this Gideon seemed afraid; he did not understand; and Mrs Farquar explained quickly that it was because of the wonderful thing he had done with Teddy's eyes that the Big Baas had come.

Gideon looked from Mrs Farquar to Mr Farquar, and then at the little boy, who was showing great importance because of the occasion. At last he said grudgingly: "The Big Baas wants to know what medicine I used?" He spoke incredulously, as if he could not believe his old friends could so betray him. Mr Farquar began explaining how a useful medicine could be made out of the root, and how it could be put on sale, and how thousands of people, black and white, up and down the continent of Africa, could be saved by the medicine when that spitting snake filled their eyes with poison. Gideon listened, his eyes bent on the ground, the skin of his forehead puckering in discomfort. When Mr Farquar had finished he did not reply. The scientist, who all this time had been leaning back in a big chair, sipping his coffee and smiling with sceptical good-humour, chipped in and explained all over again, in different words, about the making of drugs and the progress of science. Also, he offered Gideon a present.

There was silence after this further explanation, and then Gideon remarked indifferently that he could not remember the root. His face was sullen and hostile, even when he looked at the Farquars, whom he usually treated like old friends. They were beginning to feel annoyed; and this feeling annulled the gilt that had been sprung into life by Gideon's accusing manner. They were beginning to feel that he was unreasonable. But it was at that moment that they all realized he would never give in. The magical drug would remain where it was, unknown and useless except for the tiny scattering of Africans who had the knowledge, natives who might be digging a ditch for the municipality in a ragged shirt and a pair of patched shorts, but who were still born to healing, hereditary healers, being the nephews or sons of the old witch doctors whose ugly masks and bits of bone and all the uncouth properties of magic were the outward signs of real power and wisdom.

The Farquars might tread on that plant fifty times a day as they passed from house to garden, from cow kraal to mealie field, but they would never know it.

But they went on persuading and arguing, with all the force of their exasperation; and Gideon continued to say that he could not remember, or that there was no such root, or that it was the wrong season of the year, or that it wasn't the root itself, but the spittle from his mouth that had cured Teddy's eyes. He said all these things one after another, and seemed not to care they were contradictory. He was rude and stubborn. The Farquars could hardly recognize their gentle, lovable old servant in this ignorant, perversely obstinate native, standing there in front of them with lowered eyes, his hands twitching his cook's apron, repeating over and over whichever one of the stupid refusals that first entered his head.

And suddenly he appeared to give in. He lifted his head, gave a long, blank angry look at the circle of whites, who seemed to him like a circle of yelping dogs pressing around him, and said: "I will show you the root."

They walked single file away from the homestead down a kaffir path. It was a blazing December afternoon, with the sky full of hot rain-clouds. Everything was hot: the sun was like a bronze tray whirling overhead, there was a heat shimmer over the fields, the soil was scorching underfoot, the dusty wind blew gritty and thick and warm in their faces. It was a terrible day, fit only for reclining on a verandah with iced drinks, which is where they would normally have been at that hour.

From time to time, remembering that on the day of the snake it had taken ten minutes to find the root, someone asked: "Is it much further, Gideon?" And Gideon would answer over his shoulder, with angry politeness: "I'm looking for the root, baas." And indeed, he would frequently bend sideways and trail his hand among the grasses with a gesture that was insulting in its perfunctoriness. He walked them through the bush along unknown paths for two hours, in the melting destroying heat, so that the sweat trickled coldly down them and their heads ached. They were all quite silent: the Farquars because they were angry, the scientist because he was being proved right again; there was not such plant. His was a tactful silence.

At last, six miles from the house, Gideon suddenly decided they had had enough; or perhaps his anger evaporated at that moment. He picked up, without an attempt at looking anything but casual, a handful of blue flowers from the grass, flowers that had been growing plentifully all down the paths they had come.

He handed them to the scientist without looking at him, and marched off by himself on the way home, leaving them to follow him if they chose.

When they got back to the house, the scientist went to the kitchen to thank Gideon: he was being very polite, even though there was an amused look in his eyes. Gideon was not there. Throwing the flowers casually into the back of his car, the eminent visitor departed on his way back to his laboratory.

Gideon was back in his kitchen in time to prepare dinner, but he was sulking. He spoke to Mrs Farquar like an unwilling servant. It was days before they liked each other again.

The Farquars made enquiries about the root from their labourers. Sometimes they were answered with distrustful stares. Sometimes the natives said: "We do not know. We have never heard of the root." One, the cattle boy, who had been with them a long time, and had grown to trust them a little, said: "Ask your boy in the kitchen. Now, there's a doctor for you. He's the son of a famous medicine man who used to be in these parts, and there's nothing he cannot cure." Then he added politely: "Of course, he's not as good as the white man's doctor, we know that, but he's good for us."

After some time, when the soreness had gone from between the Farquars and Gideon, they began to joke: "When are you going to show us the snake-root, Gideon?" and he would laugh and shake his head, saying, a little uncomfortably: "But I did show you, missus, have you forgotten?"

Much later, Teddy, as a schoolboy, would come into the kitchen and say: "You old rascal, Gideon! Do you remember that time you tricked us all by making us walk miles all over the veld for nothing? It was so far my father had to carry me!"

And Gideon would double up with polite laughter. After much laughing, he would suddenly straighten himself up, wipe his old eyes, and look sadly at Teddy, who was grinning mischievously at him across the kitchen: "Ah, Little Yellow Head, how you have grown! Soon you will be grown up with a farm of your own . . . "

---

baas, missus: master and mistress

kraal: separate village for blacks

mealie: corn

piccanin: a small black child (now considered an insulting term)

veld: open grassland

R · O · O · T · S

eyes washed by a new rain

Roots

RIENZI CRUSZ

for Cleta Marcellina Nora Serpanchy

What the end usually demands
is something of the beginning,
and so
I conjure history from a cup
of warm Portuguese blood
from my forefathers,
black diamond eyes, charcoal hair
from my Sinhalese mothers;
the beached catamaran,
gravel voices of the fishermen,
the catch still beating like a heart
under the pelting sun;
how the pariah-dogs looked urgent
with fish-meal in their brains,
the children romped, sagged,
then melted into the sand.

A Portuguese captain holds
the soft brown hand of my Sinhala mother.
It's the year 1515 A.D.,
when two civilizations kissed and merged,
and I, burgher of that hot embrace,
write a poem of history
as if it were only the romance
of a lonely soldier on a crowded beach
in Southern Ceylon.

The **Sinhalese** form the majority of the population of Sri Lanka (formerly Ceylon).

A Horse and Two Goats

R.K. NARAYAN

Speaking only English, an American tourist attempts to buy a statue from an old goatherd who speaks only Tamil. Ludicrous? Absolutely!

The village was so small that it found no mention in any atlas. On the local survey map it was indicated by a tiny dot. It was called Kiritam, which in the Tamil language means "crown" (preferably diamond-studded)—a rather gorgeous conception, readily explained by any local enthusiast convinced beyond doubt that this part of India is the apex of the world. In proof thereof, he could, until quite recently, point in the direction of a massive guardian at the portals of the village, in the shape of a horse moulded out of clay, baked, burnt, and brightly coloured. The horse reared his head proudly, prancing, with his forelegs in the air and his tail looped up with a flourish. Beside the horse stood a warrior with scythe-like moustaches, bulging eyes, and an aquiline nose. The image-makers of old had made the eyes bulge out when they wished to indicate a man of strength, just as the beads around the warrior's neck were meant to show his wealth. Blobs of mud now, before the ravages of sun and rain they had had the sparkle of emerald, ruby and diamond. The big horse looked mottled, but at one time it was white as a dhobi-washed sheet, its back enveloped in a checkered brocade of pure red and black. The lance in the grip of the warrior had been covered with bands of gay colour, and the multicoloured sash around his waist contrasted with every other colour in these surroundings. This statue, like scores of similar ones scattered along the countryside, was forgotten and unnoticed, with lantana and cactus growing around it. Even the youthful vandals of the village left the statue alone, hardly aware of its existence. On this particular day, an old man was drowsing in the shade of a nearby cactus and watching a pair of goats graze in this arid soil; he was waiting for the sight of a green

bus lumbering down the hill road in the evening, which would be the signal for him to start back home, and he was disturbed by a motorist, who jammed on his brakes at the sight of the statue, and got out of his car, and went up to the mud horse.

"Marvellous!" he cried, pacing slowly around the statue. His face was sunburned and red. He wore a khaki-coloured shirt and shorts. Noticing the old man's presence, he said politely in English, "How do you do?"

The old man replied in pure Tamil, his only means of communication, "My name is Muni, and the two goats are mine and mine only; no one can gainsay it, although the village is full of people ready to slander a man."

The red-faced man rested his eyes for a moment in the direction of the goats and the rocks, took out a cigarette, and asked, "Do you smoke?"

"I never even heard of it until yesterday," the old man replied nervously, guessing that he was being questioned about a murder in the neighbourhood by this police officer from the government, as his khaki dress indicated.

The red-faced man said, "I come from New York. Have you heard of it? Have you heard of America?"

The old man would have understood the word "America" (though not "New York") if the name had been pronounced as he knew it—"Ah Meh Rikya"—but the red-faced man pronounced it very differently, and the old man did not know what it meant. He said respectfully, "Bad characters everywhere these days. The cinema has spoiled the people

166

and taught them how to do evil things. In these days anything may happen."

"I am sure you must know when this horse was made," said the red-faced man, and smiled ingratiatingly.

The old man reacted to the relaxed atmosphere by smiling himself, and pleaded, "Please go away, sir. I know nothing. I promise I will hold him for you if I see any bad character around, but our village has always had a clean record. Must be the other village."

"Please, please, I will speak slowly. Please try to understand me," the red-faced man said. "I arrived three weeks ago and have travelled five thousand miles since, seeing your wonderful country."

The old man made indistinct sounds in his throat and shook his head. Encouraged by this, the other went on to explain at length, uttering each syllable with care and deliberation, what brought him to this country, how much he liked it, what he did at home, how he had planned for years to visit India, the dream of his life and so forth—every now and then pausing to smile affably. The old man smiled back and said nothing, whereupon the red-faced man finally said, "How old are you? You have such wonderful teeth. Are they real? What's your secret?"

The old man knitted his brow and said mournfully, "Sometimes our cattle, too, are lost; but then we go and consult our astrologer. He will look at a camphor flame and tell us in which direction to search for the lost animals . . . I must go home now." And he turned to go.

The other seized his shoulder and said earnestly, "Is there no one—absolutely no one—here to translate for me?" He looked up and down the road, which was deserted on this hot afternoon. A sudden gust of wind churned up the dust and the dead leaves on the roadside into a ghostly column and propelled it toward the mountain road. "Is this statue yours? Will you sell it to me?"

The old man understood that the other was referring to the horse. He thought for a second and said, "I was an urchin of this height when I heard my grandfather explain this horse and warrior, and my grandfather himself was of this height when he heard his grandfather, whose grandfather . . . " Trying to indicate the antiquity of the statue, he got deeper and deeper into the bog of reminiscence, and then pulled himself out by saying, "But my grandfather's grandfather's uncle had first-hand knowledge, although I don't remember him."

"Because I really do want this statue," the red-faced man said, "I hope you won't drive a hard bargain."

"This horse," the old man continued, "will appear as the tenth avatar at the end of the Yuga."

The red-faced man nodded. He was familiar with the word "avatar."

"At the end of this Kali Yuga, this world will be destroyed, and all the worlds will be destroyed, and it is then that the Redeemer will come, in the form of a horse called Kalki, and help the good people, leaving the evil ones to perish in the great deluge. And this horse will come to life then, and that is why this is the most sacred village in the whole world."

"I am willing to pay any price that is reasonable . . ."

This statement was cut short by the old man, who was now lost in the visions of various avatars. "God Vishnu is the highest god, so our pandit at the temple has always told us, and He has come nine times before, whenever evil-minded men troubled this world."

"But please bear in mind that I am not a millionaire."

"The first avatar was in the shape of a fish," the old man said, and explained the story of how Vishnu at first took the form of a little fish, which grew bigger each hour and became gigantic, and supported on its back the holy scriptures, which were about to be lost in the ocean. Having launched on the first avatar, it was inevitable that he should go on with the second one, a tortoise, and the third, a boar on whose tusk the world was lifted up when it had been carried off and hidden at the bottom of the ocean by an extraordinary vicious conqueror of the earth.

"Transportation will be my problem, but I will worry about that later. Tell me, will you accept a hundred rupees for the horse only? Although I am charmed by the moustached soldier, I will have to come next year for him. No space for him now."

"It is God Vishnu alone who saves mankind each time such a thing has happened. He incarnated himself as Rama, and He alone could destroy Ravana, the demon with ten heads who shook all the worlds. Do you know the story of Ramayana?"

"I have my station wagon, as you see. I can push the seat back and take the horse in. If you'll just lend me a hand with it."

"Do you know Mahabharata? Krishna was the eighth avatar of Vishnu, incarnated to help the Five Brothers regain their kingdom. When Krishna was a baby, he danced on the thousand-hooded, the giant serpent, and trampled it to death . . ."

At this stage the mutual mystification was complete. The old man chattered away in a spirit of balancing off the credits and debits of conversational exchanges, and said, in order to be on the credit side, "Oh, honourable one, I hope God has blessed you with numerous progeny.

168

I say this because you seem to be a good man, willing to stay beside an old man and talk to him, while all day I have none to talk to except when somebody stops to ask for a piece of tobacco . . . How many children have you?"

"Nothing ventured, nothing gained," the red-faced man said to himself. And then, "Will you take a hundred rupees for it?" Which encouraged the other to go into details.

"How many of your children are boys and how many girls? Where are they? Is your daughter married? Is it difficult to find a son-in-law in your country also?"

The red-faced man thrust his hand into his pocket and brought forth his wallet, from which he took a hundred rupee currency note.

The old man now realized that some financial element was entering their talk. He peered closely at the currency note, the like of which he had never seen in his life; he knew the five and ten by their colours, although always in other people's hands. His own earning at any time was in coppers and nickels. What was this man flourishing the note for? Perhaps for change. He laughed to himself at the notion of anyone's coming to him to change a thousand- or ten-thousand-rupee note. He said with a grin, "Ask our village headman, who is also a money-lender; he can change even a lakh of rupees in gold sovereigns if you prefer it that way. He thinks nobody knows, but dig the floor of his *puja* room and your head will reel at the sight of the hoard. The man disguises himself in rags just to mislead the public."

"If that's not enough, I guess I could go a little higher," the red-faced man said.

"You'd better talk to him yourself, because he goes mad at the sight of me. Someone took away his pumpkins with the creeper and he thinks it was me and my goats. That's why I never let my goats be seen anywhere near the farms," the old man said, with his eyes travelling to his goats as they were nosing about, attempting to wrest nutrition out of minute greenery peeping out of rock and dry earth.

The red-faced man followed his look and decided it would be a sound policy to show an interest in the old man's pets. He went up to them casually and stroked their backs.

Now the truth dawned on the old man. His dream of a lifetime was about to be realized: the red-faced man was making him an offer for the goats. He had reared them up in the hope of selling them some day and with the capital opening a small shop on this very spot; under a thatched roof he would spread out a gunny sack and display on it fried nuts, coloured sweets, and green coconut for thirsty and hungry

169

wayfarers on the highway. He needed for this project a capital of twenty rupees, and he felt that with some bargaining he could get it now; they were not prize animals worthy of a cattle show, but he had spent his occasional savings to provide them some fancy diet now and then, and they did not look too bad.

Saying, "It is all for you, or you may share it if you have a partner," the red-faced man placed on the old man's palm one hundred and twenty rupees in notes.

The old man pointed at the station wagon.

"Yes, of course," said the other.

The old man said, "This will be their first ride in a motor car. Carry them off after I get out of sight; otherwise they will never follow you but only me, even if I am travelling on the path to the Underworld." He laughed at his own joke, brought his palms together in a salute, turned round, and was off and out of sight beyond a clump of bushes.

The red-faced man looked at the goats grazing peacefully and then perched himself on the pedestal of the horse, as the westerly sun touched off the ancient faded colours of the statue with a fresh splendour. "He must be gone to fetch some help," he remarked, and settled down to wait.

---

avatar: In Hindu mythology, the descent of a god or released soul to earth in bodily form

dhobi: a washerman or washerwoman

Kali: the most terrifying of Hindu goddesses, wife of Siva

lakh: a hundred thousand rupees

pandit (pundit): a Hindu term for a learned expert or teacher

puja: a Hindu rite of worship; a prayer

Yuga: (Hindu) one of the four ages that make up the cycle of history

American Dreams

PETER CAREY

The strange story of how one small meek man took his revenge on a whole town, and taught the people to regret their "American dreams."

N
o-one can, to this day, remember what it was we did to offend him. Dyer the butcher remembers a day when he gave him the wrong meat and another day when he served someone else first by mistake. Often when Dyer gets drunk he recalls this day and curses himself for his foolishness. But no-one seriously believes that it was Dyer who offended him.

But one of us did something. We slighted him terribly in some way, this small meek man with the rimless glasses and neat suit who used to smile so nicely at us all. We thought, I suppose, he was a bit of a fool and sometimes he was so quiet and grey that we ignored him, forgetting he was there at all.

When I was a boy I often stole apples from the trees at his house up in Mason's Lane. He often saw me. No, that's not correct. Let me say I often sensed that he saw me. I sensed him peering out from behind the lace curtains of his house. And I was not the only one. Many of us came to take his apples, alone and in groups, and it is possible that he chose to exact payment for all these apples in his own peculiar way.

Yet I am sure it wasn't the apples.

What has happened is that we all, all eight hundred of us, have come to remember small transgressions against Mr. Gleason who once lived amongst us.

My father, who has never borne malice against a single living creature, still believes that Gleason meant to do us well, that he loved the town more than any of us. My father says we have treated the town badly in our minds. We have used it, this little valley, as nothing more than a stopping place. Somewhere on the way to somewhere else. Even those of us who have been here many years have never taken the town seriously. Oh yes, the place is pretty. The hills are green and the woods thick. The stream is full of fish. But it is not where we would rather be.

For years we have watched the films at the Roxy and dreamed, if not of America, then at least of our capital city. For our own town, my father says, we have nothing but contempt. We have treated it badly, like a whore. We have cut down the giant shady trees in the main street to make doors for the school house and seats for the football pavilion. We have left big holes all over the countryside from which we have taken brown coal and given back nothing.

The commercial travellers who buy fish and chips at George the Greek's care for us more than we do, because we all have dreams of the big city, of wealth, of modern houses, of big motor cars: American dreams, my father has called them.

Although my father ran a petrol station he was also an inventor. He sat in his office all day drawing strange pieces of equipment on the back of delivery dockets. Every spare piece of paper in the house was covered with these little drawings and my mother would always be very careful about throwing away any piece of paper no matter how small. She would look on both sides of any piece of paper very carefully and always preserved any that had so much as a pencil mark.

I think it was because of this that my father felt that he understood Gleason. He never said as much, but he implied that he understood Gleason because he, too, was concerned with similar problems. My father was working on plans for a giant gravel crusher, but occasionally he would become distracted and become interested in something else.

There was, for instance, the time when Dyer the butcher bought a new bicycle with gears, and for a while my father talked of nothing else but the gears. Often I would see him across the road squatting down beside Dyer's bicycle as if he were talking to it.

We all rode bicycles because we didn't have the money for anything better. My father did have an old Chev truck, but he rarely used it and it occurs to me now that it might have had some mechanical problem that was impossible to solve, or perhaps it was just that he was saving it, not wishing to wear it out all at once. Normally, he went everywhere on his bicycle and, when I was younger, he carried me on the cross bar, both of us dismounting to trudge up the hills that led into and out of the main street. It was a common sight in our town to see people pushing bicycles. They were as much a burden as a means of transport.

Gleason also had his bicycle and every lunchtime he pushed and pedalled it home from the shire offices to his little weatherboard house out at Mason's Lane. It was a three-mile ride and people said that he went home for lunch because he was fussy and wouldn't eat either his wife's sandwiches or the hot meal available at Mrs. Lessing's café.

But while Gleason pedalled and pushed his bicycle to and from the shire offices everything in our town proceeded as normal. It was only when he retired that things began to go wrong.

Because it was then that Mr. Gleason started supervising the building of the wall around the two-acre plot up on Bald Hill. He paid too much for this land. He bought it from Johnny Weeks, who now, I am sure, believes the whole episode was his fault, firstly for cheating Gleason, secondly for selling him the land at all. But Gleason hired some Chinese and set to work to build his wall. It was then that we knew that we'd offended him. My father rode all the way out to Bald Hill and tried to talk Mr. Gleason out of his wall. He said there was no need for us to build walls. That no one wished to spy on Mr. Gleason or whatever he wished to do on Bald Hill. He said no-one was the least bit interested in Mr. Gleason. Mr. Gleason, neat in a new sportscoat, polished his glasses and smiled vaguely at his feet. Bicycling back, my father thought that he had gone too far. Of course we had an interest in Mr. Gleason. He pedalled back and asked him to attend a dance that was to be held on the next Friday, but Mr. Gleason said he didn't dance.

"Oh well," my father said, "any time, just drop over."

Mr. Gleason went back to supervising his family of Chinese labourers on his wall.

Bald Hill towered high above the town and from my father's small filling station you could sit and watch the wall going up. It was an interesting sight. I watched it for two years, while I waited for customers who rarely came. After school and on Saturdays I had all the time in the world to watch the agonizing progress of Mr. Gleason's wall. It was as painful as a clock. Sometimes I could see the Chinese labourers running at a jog-trot carrying bricks on long wooden planks. The hill was bare, and on this bareness Mr. Gleason was, for some reason, building a wall.

In the beginning people thought it peculiar that someone would build such a big wall on Bald Hill. The only thing to recommend Bald Hill was the view of the town, and Mr. Gleason was building a wall that denied that view. The top soil was thin and bare clay showed through in places. Nothing would ever grow there. Everyone assumed that Gleason had simply gone mad and after the initial interest they accepted his madness as they accepted his wall and as they accepted Bald Hill itself.

Occasionally someone would pull in for petrol at my father's filling station and ask about the wall and my father would shrug and I would see, once more, the strangeness of it.

"A house?" the stranger would ask. "Up on that hill?"

"No," my father would say, "chap named Gleason is building a wall."

And the strangers would want to know why, and my father would shrug and look up at Bald Hill once more. "Damned if I know," he'd say.

Gleason still lived in his old house at Mason's Lane. It was a plain weatherboard house with a rose garden at the front, a vegetable garden down the side, and an orchard at the back.

At night we kids would sometimes ride out to Bald Hill on bicycles. It was an agonizing, muscle-twitching ride, the worst part of which was a steep, unmade road up which we finally pushed our bikes, our lungs rasping in the night air. When we arrived we found nothing but walls. Once we broke down some of the brickwork and another time we threw stones at the tents where the Chinese labourers slept. Thus we expressed our frustration at this inexplicable thing.

The wall must have been finished on the day before my twelfth birthday. I remember going on a picnic birthday party up to Eleven Mile Creek and we lit a fire and cooked chops at a bend in the river from where it was possible to see the walls on Bald Hill. I remember standing with a hot chop in my hand and someone saying, "Look, they're leaving!"

We stood on the creek bed and watched the Chinese labourers walking their bicycles slowly down the hill. Someone said they were going to build a chimney up at the mine at A.1 and certainly there is a large brick chimney there now, so I suppose they built it.

When the word spread that the walls were finished most of the town went up to look. They walked around the four walls which were as interesting as any other brick walls. They stood in front of the big wooden gates and tried to peer through, but all they could see was a small blind wall that had obviously been constructed for this special purpose. The walls themselves were ten feet high and topped with broken glass and barbed wire. When it became obvious that we were not going to discover the contents of the enclosure, we all gave up and went home.

Mr. Gleason had long since stopped coming into town. His wife came instead wheeling a pram down from Mason's Lane to Main Street and filling it with groceries and meat (they never bought vegetables, they grew their own) and wheeling it back to Mason's Lane. Sometimes you would see her standing with the pram halfway up the Gell Street hill.

Just standing there, catching her breath. No-one asked her about the wall. They knew she wasn't responsible for the wall and they felt sorry for her, having to bear the burden of the pram and her husband's madness. Even when she began to visit Dixon's hardware and buy plaster of paris and tins of paint and waterproofing compound, no-one asked her what these things were for. She had a way of averting her eyes that indicated her terror of questions. Old Dixon carried the plaster of paris and the tins of paint out to her pram for her and watched her push them away. "Poor woman," he said, "poor bloody woman."

From the filling station where I sat dreaming in the sun, or from the enclosed office where I gazed mournfully at the rain, I would see, occasionally, Gleason entering or leaving his walled compound, a tiny figure way up on Bald Hill. And I'd think "Gleason," but not much more.

Occasionally strangers drove up there to see what was going on, often egged on by locals who told them it was a Chinese temple or some other silly thing. Once a group of Italians had a picnic outside the walls and took some photographs of each other standing in front of the closed door. God knows what they thought it was.

But for five years between my twelfth and seventeenth birthdays there was nothing to interest me in Gleason's walls. Those years seem lost to me now and I can remember very little of them. I developed a crush on Susy Markin and followed her back from the swimming pool on my bicycle. I sat behind her in the pictures and wandered past her house. Then her parents moved to another town and I sat in the sun and waited for them to come back.

We became very keen on modernization. When coloured paints became available the whole town went berserk and brightly coloured houses blossomed overnight. But the paints were not of good quality and quickly faded and peeled, so that the town looked like a garden of dead flowers. Thinking of those years, the only real thing I recall is the soft hiss of bicycle tyres on the main street. When I think of it now it seems very peaceful, but I remember then that the sound induced in me a feeling of melancholy, a feeling somehow mixed with the early afternoons when the sun went down behind Bald Hill and the town felt as sad as an empty dance hall on a Sunday afternoon.

And then, during my seventeenth year, Mr. Gleason died. We found out when we saw Mrs. Gleason's pram parked out in front of Phonsey Joy's Funeral Parlour. It looked very sad, that pram, standing by itself in the windswept street. We came and looked at the pram and felt sad for Mrs. Gleason. She hadn't had much of a life.

Phonsey Joy carried old Mr. Gleason out to the cemetery by the

Parwan Railway Station and Mrs. Gleason rode behind in a taxi. People watched the old hearse go by and thought, "Gleason," but not much else.

And then, less than a month after Gleason had been buried out at the lonely cemetery by the Parwan Railway Station, the Chinese labourers came back. We saw them push their bicycles up the hill. I stood with my father and Phonsey Joy and wondered what was going on.

And then, I saw Mrs. Gleason trudging up the hill. I nearly didn't recognize her, because she didn't have her pram. She carried a black umbrella and walked slowly up Bald Hill and it wasn't until she stopped for breath and leant forward that I recognized her.

"It's Mrs. Gleason," I said, "with the Chinese."

But it wasn't until the next morning that it became obvious what was happening. People lined the main street in the way they do for a big funeral but, instead of gazing towards the Grant Street corner, they all looked up at Bald Hill.

All that day and all the next people gathered to watch the destruction of the walls. They saw the Chinese labourers darting to and fro, but it wasn't until they knocked down a large section of the wall facing the town that we realized there really was something inside. It was impossible to see what it was, but there was something there. People stood and wondered and pointed out Mrs. Gleason to each other as she went to and fro supervising the work.

And finally, in ones and twos, on bicycles and on foot, the whole town moved up to Bald Hill. Mr. Dyer closed up his butcher shop and my father got out the old Chev truck and we finally arrived up at Bald Hill with twenty people on board. They crowded into the back tray and hung onto the running boards and my father grimly steered his way through the crowds of bicycles and parked just where the dirt track gets really steep. We trudged up this last steep track, never for a moment suspecting what we would find at the top.

It was very quiet up there. The Chinese labourers worked diligently, removing the third and fourth walls and cleaning the bricks which they stacked neatly in big piles. Mrs. Gleason said nothing either. She stood in the only remaining corner of the walls and looked defiantly at the townspeople who stood open-mouthed where another corner had been.

And between us and Mrs. Gleason was the most incredibly beautiful thing I had ever seen in my life. For one moment I didn't recognize it. I stood open-mouthed and breathed the surprising beauty of it. And then I realized it was our town. The buildings were two feet high and they were a little rough but very correct. I saw Mr. Dyer nudge my father and whisper that Gleason had got the faded "U" in the BUTCHER sign of his shop.

I think at that moment everyone was overcome with a feeling of simple joy. I can't remember ever having felt so uplifted and happy. It was perhaps a childish emotion but I looked up at my father and saw a smile of such warmth spread across his face that I knew he felt just as I did. Later he told me that he thought Gleason had built the model of our town just for this moment, to let us see the beauty of our own town, to make us proud of ourselves and to stop the American Dreams we were so prone to. For the rest, my father said, was not Gleason's plan and he could not have foreseen the things that happened afterwards.

I have come to think that this view of my father's is a little sentimental and also, perhaps, insulting to Gleason. I personally believe that he knew everything that would happen. One day the proof of my theory may be discovered. Certainly there are in existence some personal papers, and I firmly believe that these papers will show that Gleason knew exactly what would happen.

We had been so overcome by the model of the town that we hadn't noticed what was the most remarkable thing of all. Not only had Gleason built the houses and the shops of our town, he had also peopled it. As we tip-toed into the town we suddenly found ourselves. "Look," I said to Mr. Dyer, "there you are."

And there he was, standing in front of his shop in his apron. As I bent down to examine the tiny figure I was staggered by the look on its face. The modelling was crude, the paint work was sloppy, and the face a little too white, but the expression was absolutely perfect: those pursed, quizzical lips and the eyebrows lifted high. It was Mr. Dyer and no-one else on earth.

And there beside Mr. Dyer was my father, squatting on the footpath and gazing lovingly at Mr. Dyer's bicycle's gears, his face marked with grease and hope.

And there was I, back at the filling station, leaning against a petrol pump in an American pose and talking to Brian Sparrow who was amusing me with his clownish antics.

Phonsey Joy standing beside his hearse. Mr. Dixon sitting inside his hardware store. Everyone I knew was there in that tiny town. If they were not in the streets or in their backyards they were inside their houses, and it didn't take very long to discover that you could lift off the roofs and peer inside.

We tip-toed around the streets peeping into each other's windows, lifting off each other's roofs, admiring each other's gardens, and, while we did it, Mrs. Gleason slipped silently away down the hill towards Mason's Lane. She spoke to nobody and nobody spoke to her.

I confess that I was the one who took the roof from Cavanagh's house. So I was the one who found Mrs. Cavanagh in bed with young Craigie Evans.

I stood there for a long time, hardly knowing what I was seeing. I stared at the pair of them for a long, long time. And when I finally knew what I was seeing I felt such an incredible mixture of jealousy and guilt and wonder that I didn't know what to do with the roof.

Eventually it was Phonsey Joy who took the roof from my hands and placed it carefully back on the house, much, I imagine, as he would have placed the lid on a coffin. By then other people had seen what I had seen and the word passed around very quickly.

And then we all stood around in little groups and regarded the model town with what could only have been fear. If Gleason knew about Mrs. Cavanagh and Craigie Evans (and no-one else had), what other things might he know? Those who hadn't seen themselves in the town began to look a little nervous and were unsure of whether to look for themselves or not. We gazed silently at the roofs and felt mistrustful and guilty.

We all walked down the hill then, very quietly, the way people walk away from a funeral, listening only to the crunch of the gravel under our feet while the women had trouble with their high-heeled shoes.

The next day a special meeting of the shire council passed a motion calling on Mrs. Gleason to destroy the model town on the grounds that it contravened building regulations.

It is unfortunate that this order wasn't carried out before the city newspapers found out. Before another day had gone by the government had stepped in.

The model town and its model occupants were to be preserved. The minister for tourism came in a large black car and made a speech to us in the football pavilion. We sat on the high, tiered seats eating potato chips while he stood against the fence and talked to us. We couldn't hear him very well, but we heard enough. He called the model town a work of art and we stared at him grimly. He said it would be an invaluable tourist attraction. He said tourists would come from everywhere to see the model town. We would be famous. Our businesses would flourish. There would be work for guides and interpreters and caretakers and taxi drivers and people selling soft drinks and ice creams.

The Americans would come, he said. They would visit our town in buses and in cars and on the train. They would take photographs and bring wallets bulging with dollars. American dollars.

We looked at the minister mistrustfully, wondering if he knew about Mrs. Cavanagh, and he must have seen the look because he said that certain controversial items would be removed, had already been removed. We shifted in our seats, like you do when a particularly tense part of a film has come to its climax, and then we relaxed and listened to what the minister had to say. And we all began, once more, to dream our American dreams.

We saw our big smooth cars cruising through cities with bright lights. We entered expensive night clubs and danced till dawn. We made love to women like Kim Novak and men like Rock Hudson. We drank cocktails. We gazed lazily into refrigerators filled with food and prepared ourselves lavish midnight snacks which we ate while we watched huge television sets on which we would be able to see American movies free of charge and forever.

The minister, like someone from our American dreams, re-entered his large black car and cruised slowly from our humble sportsground, and the newspaper men arrived and swarmed over the pavilion with their cameras and note books. They took photographs of us and photographs of the models up on Bald Hill. And the next day we were all over the newspapers. The photographs of the model people side by side with photographs of the real people. And our names and ages and what we did were all printed there in black and white.

They interviewed Mrs. Gleason but she said nothing of interest. She said the model town had been her husband's hobby.

We all felt good now. It was very pleasant to have your photograph in the paper. And, once more, we changed our opinion of Gleason. The shire council held another meeting and named the dirt track up Bald

Hill, "Gleason Avenue". Then we all went home and waited for the Americans we had been promised.

It didn't take long for them to come, although at the time it seemed an eternity, and we spent six long months doing nothing more with our lives than waiting for the Americans.

Well, they did come. And let me tell you how it has all worked out for us.

The Americans arrive every day in buses and cars and sometimes the younger ones come on the train. There is now a small airstrip out near the Parwan cemetery and they also arrive there, in small aeroplanes. Phonsey Joy drives them to the cemetery where they look at Gleason's grave and then up to Bald Hill and then down to the town. He is doing very well from it all. It is good to see someone doing well from it. Phonsey is becoming a big man in town and is on the shire council.

On Bald Hill there are half a dozen telescopes through which the Americans can spy on the town and reassure themselves that it is the same down there as it is on Bald Hill. Herb Gravney sells them ice creams and soft drinks and extra film for their cameras. He is another one who is doing well. He bought the whole model from Mrs. Gleason and charges five American dollars admission. Herb is on the council now too. He's doing very well for himself. He sells them the film so they can take photographs of the houses and the model people and so they can come down to the town with their special maps and hunt out the real people.

To tell the truth most of us are pretty sick of the game. They come looking for my father and ask him to stare at the gears of Dyer's bicycle. I watch my father cross the street slowly, his head hung low. He doesn't greet the Americans anymore. He doesn't ask them questions about colour television or Washington D.C. He kneels on the footpath in front of Dyer's bike. They stand around him. Often they remember the model incorrectly and try to get my father to pose in the wrong way. Originally he argued with them, but now he argues no more. He does what they ask. They push him this way and that and worry about the expression on his face which is no longer what it was.

Then I know they will come to find me. I am next on the map. I am very popular for some reason. They come in search of me and my petrol pump as they have done for four years now. I do not await them eagerly because I know, before they reach me, they will be disappointed.

"But this is not the boy."

"Yes," says Phonsey, "this is him all right." And he gets me to show them my certificate.

They examine the certificate suspiciously, feeling the paper as if it might be a clever forgery. "No," they declare. (Americans are so confident.) "No," they shake their heads, "this is not the real boy. The real boy is younger."

"He's older now. He used to be younger." Phonsey looks weary when he tells them. He can afford to look weary.

The Americans peer at my face closely. "It's a different boy."

But finally they get their cameras out. I stand sullenly and try to look amused as I did once. Gleason saw me looking amused but I can no longer remember how it felt. I was looking at Brian Sparrow. But Brian is also tired. He finds it difficult to do his clownish antics and to the Americans his little act isn't funny. They prefer the model. I watch him sadly, sorry that he must perform for such an unsympathetic audience.

The Americans pay one dollar for the right to take our photographs. Having paid the money they are worried about being cheated. They spend their time being disappointed and I spend my time feeling guilty, that I have somehow let them down by growing older and sadder.

The Chosen One

CATHERINE LIM

With modern shops and changing ways threatening to put her out of business, Chow Ah Sum prays to the goddess of mercy for deliverance. The results? Miraculous!

I used to see many of them—now there do not appear to be many anymore—old women in their faded black long-sleeved cotton blouses and loose pants, sitting patiently behind little wooden trestles on which they had set up their wares—small bottles of sweets, packets of dried ginger and plums, cigarettes in loose sticks of five or six stuck in a little tin. And there was the inevitable lit joss-stick standing in a tin in front of the meagre wares, a reminder to the gods that they were to be kind to these old women and give them good business. Sitting behind their trestles by the side of the passageways in front of shops and houses, and largely ignored by the flow of people shopping and going about their business in the city, they became a separate, pathetic little world unto themselves. Only occasionally was their existence acknowledged—by a hurrying pedestrian in need of a quick smoke, by a child who wanted a sweet or some dried plums. But by and large, they were forgotten in the pitiless hustle of city life, for with the modern shops which sold everything, who would want to buy the pitiably inadequate wares of an old woman?

And so she sat, tired and forlorn, waiting all day, and the large pocket inside her blouse was without the little coins she had dreamed would fill it. In her old age she wept easily, and so she shed tears over the sweets and small biscuits going soft and sticky for want of anybody to buy them. She put a larger joss-stick in the tin, her lips moving desolately in prayer, imploring the great goddess Kuan Yin to have mercy on her, an old woman of sixty, alone in the world. She had never married and therefore had no children to take care of her in her old age. There would be no one to offer prayers for her after her death.

And now death appeared as a desirable way out of her misery and bitterness. "Kuan Yin, Most Merciful Goddess, come and take me away to Heaven to live with you forever."

Her prayer was answered. That night she had a dream in which she saw the goddess Kuan Yin—how beautiful she was—slowly come down from heaven to her. And Kuan Yin told her, "My daughter, your prayer is heard. You are a pure soul. Get ready to come with me on the seventh day. I shall make you one of my fourteen handmaidens in heaven."

When she awoke, the tears of joy were still in her eyes, and re-collecting the dream in all its vividness of detail, she wept afresh. She began to prepare for Kuan Yin's coming for her in seven days as the goddess had promised. First she went to the temple to cleanse herself and offer fruits and scented flowers. Then she went to the rusty biscuit tin that she kept by her side all day, counted the notes and coins inside and found she had enough for a coffin. She had the coffin placed upwards, leaning against the wall of the unused space of the tenement house in which she shared a room with many other old people, so that when placed in the coffin in death her body would point heavenwards.

The word spread rapidly—first through the tenement house, then the neighbourhood, then even through the country by way of newspapers eager for news—of an old woman named Chow Ah Sum, aged sixty, who had had a vision of the Goddess of Mercy, Kuan Yin, and had been promised that she would die on a specified day, at a specified time, and thence be taken to heaven. A coffin was ready; the old woman sat near it day and night, ready for her appointment with death.

The crowds came, the young out of curiosity and cynicism, the old out of a touching reconciliation with the notion of death. But the old woman's unshakeable faith in the truth of her dream had the effect of reducing the large crowds to a state of awed silence; even the young hoodlums, with their fancy clothes and tattooed arms, merely gaped. There were two reporters there, rather pleased with the unusual nature of the event, taking quick notes and photographs, but the old woman sat still and impassive through it all, as if there were nobody around, for she was waiting, waiting for the first signs of the coming of the goddess Kuan Yin for her.

Only one more day and she would be free and happy at last! The suspense was great—the more imaginative asked among themselves whether Chow Ah Sum would be lifted bodily to heaven by the goddess. On that much-awaited day, the telephone board in the national newspaper office was actually jammed with calls from the public, anxiously asking whether the old woman was dead.

She wasn't; the evening of the same day, she wept in disappointment and bitterly complained that the goddess Kuan Yin could not keep her promise because the atmosphere was not pure—how many impure, unchaste people were there, surrounding her and her coffin! Chow Ah Sum pleaded with them to leave her alone, to let her die in peace.

Then the news spread again. On the day that the goddess Kuan Yin was to appear, something miraculous had happened. A strange, wonderful plant had suddenly burst into bloom on a small piece of waste land behind the house. Some said the flower was as big as a man's head, others that it gave a lovely scent. Nobody of course was interested in the botanical name that was used for it in the papers (a young, enthusiastic reporter had done some quick research), or in the information that it was a rare tropical variety, probably first brought over from South America, that it seldom flowered and when it did, its petals were light purple, bulbous, and so on. What was infinitely more interesting was that the old woman claimed that the flower was a sign from heaven for her—a sign that the goddess Kuan Yin had decreed that she remain on earth longer, to do good deeds among the people. The good deeds were quickly attested to and described, and the news spread in a fever of excitement and wonder. Chow Ah Sum was working miracles, by the power of the goddess Kuan Yin! She could cure the sick—a woman claimed that she felt much better after drinking the water into which Chow Ah Sum had dropped the ashes from a piece of prayer-writing. Another woman whom she muttered prayers over exclaimed that she was cured of her disease!

    And so the crowds came. Chow Ah Sum sat cross-legged on a mat with the altar of the goddess Kuan Yin beside her, surrounded by joss-sticks. In front of her was the rusty biscuit tin into which grateful devotees could drop their tokens of appreciation. And the biscuit tin was filling up nicely. Chow Ah Sum, her eyes closed and her lips moving in trance-like prayer, was happy at last.

---

joss-stick: fragrant tinder burnt as incense

Kuan Yin: goddess of mercy

The Sacrificial Egg

CHINUA ACHEBE

Julius Obi believed he was above all that "superstitious stuff"—until he stepped on a sacrificial egg and broke it.

Julius Obi sat gazing at his typewriter. The fat chief clerk, his boss, was snoring at his table. Outside, the gatekeeper in his green uniform was sleeping at his post. No customer had passed through the gate for nearly a week. There was an empty basket on the giant weighing machine. A few palm kernels lay in the dust around the machine.

Julius went to the window that overlooked the great market on the banks of the Niger. This market, like all Ibo markets, had been held on one of the four days of the week. But with the coming of the white man and the growth of Umuru into a big palm-oil port, it had become a daily market. In spite of that, however, it was still busiest on its original Nkwo day, because the deity that presided over it cast her spell only on that day. It was said that she appeared in the form of an old woman in the centre of the market just before cockcrow and waved her magic fan in the four directions of the earth—in front of her, behind her, to the right, and to the left—to draw to the market men and women from distant clans. And they came, these men and women, bringing the produce of their lands: palm-oil and kernels, kola nuts, cassava, mats, baskets, and earthenware pots. And they took home many-coloured cloths, smoked fish, iron pots and plates.

Others came by the great river bringing yams and fish in their canoes. Sometimes it was a big canoe with a dozen or more people in it; sometimes it was just a fisherman and his wife in a small vessel from the swift-flowing Anambara. They moored their canoe on the bank and sold their fish, after much haggling. The woman then walked up the steep banks of the river to the heart of the market to buy salt and oil and, if the sales had been good, a length of cloth. And for her children at home she bought bean cakes or *akara* and *mai-mai*, which the Igara women cooked. As evening approached, they took up their paddles and paddled away, the water shimmering in the sunset and their canoe becoming smaller and smaller in the distance until it was just a dark crescent on the water's face and two dark bodies swaying forwards and backwards in it.

Julius Obi was not a native of Umuru. He came from a bush village twenty or so miles away. But having passed his Standard Six in a mission school in 1920 he came to Umuru to work as a clerk in the offices of the Niger Company, which dealt in palm-oil and kernels. The offices were situated beside the famous Umuru market, so that in his first two or three weeks Julius had to learn to work against the background of its noise. Sometimes when the chief clerk was away or asleep he walked to the window and looked down on the vast anthill activity. Most of these people were not there yesterday, he thought, and yet the market was as full. There must be many, many people in the world. Of course they say that not everyone who came to the great market was a real person. Janet's mother had said so.

"Some of the beautiful young women you see squeezing through the crowds are not real people but *mammy-wota* from the river," she said.

"How does one know them?" asked Julius, whose education placed him above such superstitious stuff. But he took care not to sound unbelieving. He had long learned that it was bad policy to argue with Ma on such points.

"You can always tell," she explained, "because they are beautiful with a beauty that is not of this world. You catch a glimpse of them with the tail of your eye, then they disappear in the crowd."

Julius thought about these things as he now stood at the window looking down at the empty market. Who would have believed that the great market could ever be so empty? But such was the power of *Kitikpa*, or smallpox.

When Umuru had been a little village, it had been swept and kept clean by its handful of inhabitants. But now it had grown into a busy, sprawling, crowded, and dirty river port. And *Kitikpa* came. No other disease is feared by the Ibo people as much as they fear *Kitikpa*. It is personified as an evil deity. Its victims are not mourned lest it be offended. It put an end to the coming and going between neighbours and between villages. They said, "*Kitikpa* is in that village," and immediately it was cut off by its neighbours.

Julius was worried because it was almost a week since he had seen Janet, the girl he was going to marry. Ma had explained to him very gently that he should no longer come to see them "until this thing is over by the power of Jehovah." Ma was a very devout Christian, and one reason why she approved of Julius for her only daughter was that he sang in the church choir.

"You must keep to your rooms," she had said. "You never know whom you might meet on the streets. That family has got it." She pointed at the house across the road. "That is what the yellow palm frond at the doorway means. The family were all moved away today in the big government lorry."

Janet walked a short way with him, and they said good night. And they shook hands, which was very odd.

Julius did not go straight home. He went to the bank of the river and just walked up and down it. He must have been there a long time, because he was still there when the *ekwe*, or wooden gong, of the night spirit sounded. He immediately set out for home, half walking and half running. He had about half an hour to get home before the spirit ran its race through the town.

As Julius hurried home he stepped on something that broke with a slight liquid explosion. He stopped and peeped down at the footpath. The moon was not yet up, but there was some faint light which showed that it would not be long delayed. In this light Julius saw that he had stepped on a sacrificial egg. There were young palm fronds around it. Someone oppressed by misfortune had brought the offering to the cross-roads in the dusk. And he had stepped on it, and taken the sufferer's ill luck to himself. "Nonsense," he said and hurried away. But it was too late; the night spirit was already abroad. Its voice rose high and clear in the still, black air. It was a long way away, but Julius knew that distance did not apply to these beings. So he made straight for the cocoyam farm beside the road and threw himself on his belly. He had hardly done this when he heard the rattling staff of the spirit and a thundering stream of esoteric speech. He shook all over. The sounds came bearing down on him. And then he could hear the footsteps. It was as if twenty men were running together. In no time at all the sounds had passed and disappeared in the distance on the other side of the road.

As Julius stood at the window looking out on the empty market he lived through that night again. It was only a week ago, but already it seemed to be separated from the present by a vast emptiness. This emptiness deepened with the passage of time. On this side stood Julius, and on the other Ma and Janet, who were carried away by the smallpox.

---

akara: fried bean cake

cocoyam: small white yam with a dark jacket (similar to a potato)

Ibo: largest group of Nigerian people

mai-mai: steamed bean cake

mammy-wota: river goddesses

Niger: the main river of Nigeria

Standard Six: an exam taken at the end of elementary school

The Novelist as Teacher

CHINUA ACHEBE

African writers, says Achebe, need to reach out to their readers—to help African people regain pride in themselves, their past, and their future.

Writing of the kind I do is relatively new in my part of the world and it is too soon to try and describe in detail the complex of relationships between us and our readers. However, I think I can safely deal with one aspect of these relationships which is rarely mentioned. Because of our largely European education our writers may be pardoned if they begin by thinking that the relationship between European writers and their audience will automatically reproduce itself in Africa. We have learnt from Europe that a writer or an artist lives on the fringe of society—wearing a beard and a peculiar dress and generally behaving in a strange, unpredictable way. He is in revolt against society, which in turn looks on him with suspicion if not hostility. The last thing society would dream of doing is to put him in charge of anything.

All that is well known, which is why some of us seem too eager for our society to treat us with the same hostility or even behave as though it already does. But I am not interested now in what writers expect of society; that is generally contained in their books, or should be. What is not so well documented is what society expects of its writers.

I am assuming, of course, that our writer and his society live in the same place. I realize that a lot has been made of the allegation that African writers have to write for European and American readers because African readers where they exist at all are only interested in reading textbooks. I don't know if African writers always have a foreign audience in mind. What I do know is that they don't have to. At least I know that I don't have to. Last year the pattern of sales in *Things Fall Apart* in the cheap paperback edition was as follows: about 800 copies in Britain; 20,000 in Nigeria; and about 2,500 in all other places. The same pattern was true also of *No Longer at Ease*.

Most of my readers are young. They are either in school or college or have only recently left. And many of them look to me as a kind of teacher. Only the other day I received this letter from Northern Nigeria:

> Dear C. Achebe,
> I do not usually write to authors, no matter how interesting their work is, but I feel I must tell you how much I enjoyed your editions of *Things Fall Apart* and *No Longer at Ease*. I look forward to reading your new edition *Arrow of God*. Your novels serve as advice to us young. I trust that you will continue to produce as many of this type of books. With friendly greetings and best wishes.
>
> Yours sincerely,
I. Buba Yero Mafindi

It is quite clear what this particular reader expects of me. Nor is there much doubt about another reader in Ghana who wrote me a rather pathetic letter to say that I had neglected to include questions and answers at the end of *Things Fall Apart* and could I make these available to him to ensure his success at next year's school certificate examination. This is what I would call in Nigerian pidgin "a how-for-do" reader and I hope there are not very many like him. But also in Ghana I met a young woman teacher who immediately took me to task for not making the hero of my *No Longer at Ease* marry the girl he is in love with. I made the kind of vague noises I usually make whenever a wise critic comes along to tell me I should have written a different book to the one I wrote. But my woman teacher was not going to be shaken off so easily. She was in deadly earnest. Did I know, she said, that there were many women in the kind of situation I had described and that I could have served them well if I had shown that it was possible to find one man with enough guts to go against custom?

I don't agree, of course. But this young woman spoke with so much feeling that I couldn't help being a little uneasy at the accusation (for it was indeed a serious accusation) that I had squandered a rare opportunity for education on a whimsical and frivolous exercise. It is important to say at this point that no self-respecting writer will take dictation from his audience. He must remain free to disagree with his society and go into rebellion against it if need be. But I am for choosing my cause very carefully. Why should I start waging war as a Nigerian newspaper editor was doing the other day on the "soulless efficiency" of Europe's industrial and technological civilization when the very thing my society needs may well be a little technical efficiency?

My thinking on the peculiar needs of different societies was sharpened when not long ago I heard an English pop song which I think was entitled "*I Ain't Gonna Wash for a Week*." At first I wondered why it should occur to anyone to take such a vow when there were so many much more worthwhile resolutions to make. But later it dawned on me that this singer belonged to the same culture which in an earlier age of self-satisfaction had blasphemed and said that cleanliness was next to godliness. So I saw him in a new light—as a kind of divine administrator of vengeance. I make bold to say, however, that his particular offices would not be required in my society because we did not commit the sin of turning hygiene into a god.

Needless to say, we do have our own sins and blasphemies recorded against our name. If I were God I would regard as the very worst our acceptance—for whatever reason—of racial inferiority. It is too late in the day to get worked up about it or to blame others, much as they may deserve such blame and condemnation. What we need to do is to look back and try and find out where we went wrong, where the rain began to beat us.

Let me give one or two examples of the result of the disaster brought upon the African psyche in the period of subjection to alien races. I remember the shock felt by Christians of my father's generation in my village in the early 1940s when for the first time the local girls' school performed Nigerian dances at the anniversary of the coming of the gospel. Hitherto they had always put on something Christian and civilized which I believe was called the Maypole dance. In those days—when I was growing up—I also remember that it was only the poor benighted heathen who had any use for our local handicraft, e.g., our pottery. Christians and the well-to-do (and they were usually the same people) displayed their tins and other metalware. We never carried water pots to the stream. I had a small cylindrical biscuit-tin suitable to my years while the older members of our household carried four-gallon kerosene tins.

Today, things have changed a lot, but it would be foolish to pretend that we have fully recovered from the traumatic effects of our first confrontation with Europe. Three or four weeks ago my wife, who teaches English in a boys' school, asked a pupil why he wrote about winter when he meant the harmattan. He said the other boys would call him a bushman if he did such a thing! Now, you wouldn't have thought, would you, that there was something shameful in your weather? But apparently we do. How can this great blasphemy be purged? I think it is part of my business as a writer to teach that boy that there is nothing disgraceful about the African weather, that the palm tree is a fit subject for poetry.

Here then is an adequate revolution for me to espouse—to help my society regain belief in itself and put away the complexes of the years of denigration and self-abasement. And it is essentially a question of education, in the best sense of that word. Here, I think, my aims and the deepest aspirations of my society meet. For no thinking African can escape the pain of the wound in our soul. You have all heard of the "African personality"; of African democracy, of the African way to socialism, of negritude, and so on. They are all props we have fashioned at different times to help us get on our feet again. Once we are up we shan't need any of them anymore. But for the moment it is in the nature of things that we may need to counter racism with what Jean-Paul Sartre has called an anti-racist racism, to announce not just that we are as good as the next man but that we are much better.

The writer cannot expect to be excused from the task of re-education and regeneration that must be done. In fact, he should march right in front. For he is, after all—as Ezekiel Mphahlele says in his African Image—the sensitive point of his community. The Ghanaian professor of philosophy, William Abraham, puts it this way:

> Just as African scientists undertake to solve some of the scientific problems of Africa, African historians go into the history of Africa, African political scientists concern themselves with the politics of Africa; why should African literary creators be exempted from the services that they themselves recognize as genuine?

I for one would not wish to be excused. I would be quite satisfied if my novels (especially the ones I set in the past) did no more than teach my readers that their past—with all its imperfections—was not one long night of savagery from which the first Europeans acting on God's behalf delivered them. Perhaps what I write is applied art as distinct from pure. But who cares? Art is important, but so is education of the kind I have in mind. And I don't see that the two need be mutually exclusive. In a recent anthology a Hausa folk tale, having recounted the usual fabulous incidents, ends with these words:

> They all came and they lived happily together. He had several sons and daughters who grew up and helped in raising the standard of education of the country.

As I said elsewhere, if you consider this ending a naïve anticlimax then you cannot know very much about Africa.

---

harmattan: a dusty wind that blows on the coast of West Africa from December to February

Hausa: people of the Sudan and northern Nigeria

The Women's Swimming Pool

HANAN AL SHAYKH

Working in the tobacco fields, the girl dreams constantly of the sea. Now at last she has a chance to see it, and to swim in the women-only pool in faraway Beirut.

I am in the tent for threading the tobacco amidst the mounds of tobacco plants and the skewers. Cross-legged, I breathe in the green odor, threading one leaf after another. I find myself dreaming and growing thirsty and dreaming. I open the magazine: I devour the words and surreptitiously gaze at the pictures. Exasperated at being in the tent, my exasperation then turns to sadness.

Thirsty, I rise to my feet. I hear Abu Ghalib say, "Where are you off to, little lady?" I make my way to the cistern, stumbling in the sandy ground. I see the greenish blue waters. I stretch out my hand and wipe it across my brow and face and neck, across my chest. Before being able to savor its relative coldness, I hear my name and see my grandmother standing in her black dress at the doorway of the tent. Aloud I express the wish that someone else had called to me. We have become like an orange and its navel: my grandmother has welded me so close to her that the village girls no longer dare to make friends with me, perhaps for fear of rupturing this close union.

I return to the tent, growing thirsty and dreaming, with the sea ever in my mind. What were its waters like? What color would they be now? If only this week would pass in a flash for I had at last persuaded my grandmother to go down to Beirut and the sea, after my friend Sumayya had sworn that the swimming pool she'd been to had been for women only.

My grandmother sat on the edge of a jagged slab of stone, leaning on my arm. Her hand was hot and rough. She sighed as she chased away a fly.

What is my grandmother gazing at? There was nothing in front of us but the asphalt road, which, despite the sun's rays, gave off no light, and the white marble tombs that stretched along the high mountainside, while the houses of Upper Nabatieh looked like deserted Crusader castles, their alleyways empty, their windows of iron. Our house likewise seemed to be groaning in its solitude, shaded by the fig tree. The washing line stirs with the wind above the tomb of my grandfather, the celebrated religious scholar, in the courtyard of the house. What is my grandmother staring at? Or does someone who is waiting not stare?

Turning her face toward me, she said, "Child, what will we do if the bus doesn't come?" Her face, engraved in my mind, seemed overcast, also her half-crossed eyes and the blue tattoo mark on her chin. I didn't answer her for fear I'd cry if I talked. This time I averted my gaze from the white tombs; moving my foot away from my grandmother's leg clothed in thick black stockings, I began to walk about, my gaze directed to the other side where lay the extensive fields of green tobacco, their leaves glinting under the sun, leaves that were imprinted on my brain, and with the marks of them still showing on my hands, towering and gently swaying.

My gaze reached out behind the thousands of plants, then beyond them, moving away till it arrived at the tent where the tobacco was threaded. I came up close to my grandmother, who was still sitting in her place, still gazing in front of her. As I drew close to her, I heard her give a sigh. A sprinkling of sweat lay on the pouches under her eyes. "Child, what do you want with the sea? Don't you know that the sea puts a spell on people?" I didn't answer her: I was so worried that the morning would pass, that noonday would pass and that I wouldn't see the green bus come to a stop by the stone my grandmother sat on and take us with it to the sea, to Beirut. Again I heard my grandmother mumbling, "That devil Sumayya . . . " I pleaded with her to stop, and my thoughts rose up and left the stone upon which my grandmother sat, the rough road, left everything. I went back to my dreams, to the sea.

The sea had remained my preoccupation ever since I had seen it for the first time inside a colored ball; with its blue color it was like a magic lantern, wide open, the surface of its water unrippled unless you tilted the piece of glass, with its small shells and white specks like snow. When I first became aware of things, it was this ball, which I had found in the parlor, that was the sole thing that animated and amused me. The more I gazed at it the more cold I could feel its waters, the more they invited me to bathe myself in them; they knew that I had been born amidst dust and mud and the stench of tobacco.

If only the green bus would come along—and I shifted my bag from one hand to the other. I heard my grandmother wail, "Child, bring up a stone and sit down. Put down the bag and don't worry." My distress increased and I was no longer able to stop it turning into tears that flowed freely down my face, veiling it from the road. I stretched up to wipe them with my sleeve: in this heat I still had to wear that dress with long sleeves, that head-covering over my plaits, despite the hot wind that set the tobacco plants and the sparse poplars swaying. Thank God I had resisted her and refused to wear my stockings. I gave a deep sigh as I heard the bus's horn from afar. Fearful and anxious, I shouted at my grandmother as I helped her to her feet, turning round to make sure that my bag was still in my hand and my grandmother's hand in the other. The bus came to a stop and the conductor helped my grandmother on. When I saw myself alongside her and the stone on its own, I tightened my grip on my bag, in which lay Sumayya's bathing costume, a sleeveless dress, and my money.

I noticed as the bus slowly made its way along the road that my anxiety was still there, that it was in fact increasing. Why didn't the bus pass by all these trees and fallow land like lightning? Why was it crawling along? My anxiety was still there and increased till it predominated over my other sensations, such as nausea and curiosity.

How would we find our way to the sea? Would we see it as soon as we arrived in Beirut? Was it at the other end of it? Would the bus stop in the district of Zeytouna, at the door of the women's swimming pool? Why, I wondered, was it called Zeytouna? Were there olive trees there? I leaned toward my grandmother with her silent face and long nose, which almost met up with her mouth. Thinking that I wanted a piece of cane sugar, she put her hand to her bosom to take out a small twist of cloth. Impatiently I asked her if she was sure that Maryam al-Taweela knew Zeytouna, to which she answered, her mouth sucking at the cane sugar and making a noise with her tongue, "God will look after everything." Then she broke the silence by saying, "All this trouble is that devil Sumayya's fault—it was she who told you she'd seen with her own eyes the swimming pool just for women and not for men."

"Yes, Grandma," I answered her.

She said, "Swear by your mother's grave."

I thought to myself absentmindedly, Why only my mother's grave?

What about my father's? Or did she acknowledge only her daughter's death? "By my mother's grave, it's for women."

She inclined her head and still munching the cane sugar and making a noise with her tongue, she said, "If any man were to see you, you'd be done for, and so would your mother and father and your grandfather, the religious scholar—and I'd be done for more than anyone because it's I who agreed to you and helped you."

I would have liked to say to her, They've all gone, they've all died, so what do we have to be afraid of? But I knew what she meant: that she was frightened they wouldn't go to heaven.

I began to sweat and my heart again contracted as Beirut came into view with its lofty buildings, car horns, the bared arms of the women, the girls' hair, the tight trousers they were wearing. People were sitting on chairs in the middle of the pavement eating and drinking; the trams; the roasting chickens revolving on spits. Ah, these dresses for sale in the windows, would anyone be found actually to wear them? I see a Japanese man, the first ever member of the yellow races outside of books; the Martyrs' monument, Riad Solh Square. I was wringing wet with sweat and my heart pounded—it was as though I regretted having come to Beirut, perhaps because I was accompanied by my grandmother. It was soon all too evident that we were outsiders to the capital. We began walking after my grandmother had asked the bus driver the whereabouts of the district of Khandak al-Ghamik where Maryam al-Taweela lived. Once again my body absorbed all the sweat and allowed my heart to flee its cage. I find myself treading on a pavement on which for long years I have dreamed of walking; I hear sounds that have been engraved on my imagination, and everything I see I have seen in daydreams at school or in the tobacco-threading tent. Perhaps I shouldn't say that I was regretting it, for after this I would never forget Beirut. We begin walking and losing our way in a Beirut that never ends, leads nowhere. We begin asking and walking and losing our way, and my going to the sea seems an impossibility; the sea is fleeing from me. My grandmother comes to a stop and leans against a lamppost, or against the litter bin attached to it, and against my shoulders, and puffs and blows. I have the feeling that we shall never find Maryam al-Taweela's house. A man we had stopped to ask the way walks with us. When we knock at the door and no one opens to us, I become convinced that my bathing in the sea is no longer possible. The sweat again pours off me, my throat contracts. A woman's voice brings me back to my senses as I drown in a lake of anxiety, sadness, and fear; then it drowns me once again. It was not Maryam al-Taweela but her neighbour who is asking us to wait at her place. We go down the steps to the neighbour's outdoor stone bench, and my grandmother sits down by the door but gets to her feet again when the woman entreats her to sit in the cane chair. Then she asks to be excused while she finishes washing down the steps. While she is cursing the heat of Beirut in the summer, I notice the tin containers lined up side by side containing red and green peppers. We have a long wait, and I begin to weep inwardly as I stare at the containers.

I wouldn't be seeing the sea today, perhaps not for years, but the thought of its waters would not leave me, would not be erased from my dreams. I must persuade my grandmother to come to Beirut with Sumayya. Perhaps I should not have mentioned the swimming pool in front of her. I wouldn't be seeing the sea today—and once again I sank back into a lake of doubt and fear and sadness. A woman's voice again brought me back to my senses: it was Maryam al-Taweela, who had stretched out her long neck and had kissed me, while she asked my grandmother, "She's the child of your late daughter, isn't she?"—and she swore by the Imam that we must have lunch with her, doing so before we had protested, feeling perhaps that I would do so. When she stood up and took the Primus stove from under her bed and brought out potatoes and tomatoes and bits of meat, I had a feeling of nausea, then of frustration. I nudged my grandmother, who leaned over and whispered, "What is it, dear?" at which Maryam al-Taweela turned and asked, "What's your granddaughter want—to go to the bathroom?" My mouth went quite dry and my tears were all stored up waiting for a signal from my heartbeats to descend. My grandmother said with embarrassment, "She wants to go to the sea, to the women's swimming pool—that devil Sumayya put it into her head." To my amazement Maryam al-Taweela said loudly, "And why not? Right now Ali Mousa, our neighbour, will be coming and he'll take you, he's got a car"—and Maryam al-Taweela began peeling the potatoes at a low table in the middle of the room and my grandmother asked, "Where's Ali Mousa from? Where does he live?"

I can't wait, I shan't eat, I shan't drink. I want to go now, now. I remained seated, crying inwardly because I was born in the South, because there's no escape for me from the South, and I go on rubbing my fingers and gnawing at my nails. Again I begin to sweat: I shan't eat, I shan't drink, I shan't reply to Maryam al-Taweela. It was as though I were taking vengeance on my grandmother for some wrong she did not know about. My patience vanished. I stood up and said to my grandmother before I should burst out sobbing, "Come along, Grandma, get up and let's go." I helped her to her feet and Maryam al-Taweela asked

in bewilderment what had suddenly come over me. I went on dragging my grandmother out to the street so that I might stop the first taxi.

Only moments passed before the driver shut off his engine and said, "Zeytouna." I looked about me but saw no sea. As I gave him a lira I asked him, "Where's the women's swimming pool?" He shrugged his shoulders. We got out of the car with difficulty, as was always the case with my grandmother. To my astonishment the driver returned, stretching out his head in concern at us. "Jump in," he said, and we got in. He took us round and round, stopping once at a petrol station and then by a newspaper seller, asking about the women's swimming pool and nobody knowing where it was. Once again he dropped us in the middle of Zeytouna Street.

Then, behind the hotels and the beautiful buildings and the date palms, I saw the sea. It was like a blue line of quicksilver: it was as though pieces of silver paper were resting on it. The sea that was in front of me was more beautiful than it had been in the glass ball. I didn't know how to get close to it, how to touch it. Cement lay between us. We began enquiring about the whereabouts of the swimming pool, but no one knew. The sea remains without waves, a blue line. I feel frustrated. Perhaps this swimming pool is some secret known only to the girls of the South. I began asking every person I saw. I tried to choke back my tears; I let go of my grandmother's hand as though wishing to reproach her, to punish her for having insisted on accompanying me instead of Sumayya. Poor me. Poor Grandma. Poor Beirut. Had my dreams come to an end in the middle of the street? I clasp my bag and my grandmother's hand, with the sea in front of me, separating her from me. My stubbornness and vexation impel me to ask and go on asking. I approached a man leaning against a bus and to my surprise he pointed to an opening between two shops. I hurried back to my grandmother, who was supporting herself against a lamppost, to tell her I'd found it. When I saw with what difficulty she attempted to walk, I asked her to wait for me while I made sure. I went through the opening but didn't see the sea. All I saw was a fat woman with bare shoulders sitting behind a table. Hesitating, I stood and looked at her, not daring to step forward. My enthusiasm had vanished, taking with it my courage.

"Yes," said the woman.

I came forward and asked her, "Is the women's swimming pool here?" She nodded her head and said, "The entrance fee is a lira."

I asked her if it was possible for my grandmother to wait for me here and she stared at me and said, "Of course." There was contempt in the way she looked at me—was it my southern accent or my long-sleeved dress? I had disregarded my grandmother and had taken off my headshawl and hidden it in my bag. I handed her a lira and could hear the sounds of women and children—and still I did not see the sea. At the end of the portico were steps that I was certain led to the roofed-in sea. The important thing was that I'd arrived, that I would be tasting the salty spray of its waters. I wouldn't be seeing the waves; never mind, I'd be bathing in its waters.

I found myself saying to the woman, or rather to myself because no sound issued from my throat, "I'll bring my grandmother." Going out through the opening and still clasping my bag to my chest, I saw my grandmother standing and looking up at the sky. I called to her but she was reciting to herself under her breath as she continued to look upwards: she was praying, right there in the street, praying on the pavement at the door of the swimming pool. She had spread out a paper bag and had stretched out her hands to the sky. I walked off in another direction and stopped looking at her. I would have liked to persuade myself that she had nothing to do with me, that I didn't know her. How, though? She's my grandmother, whom I've dragged with my entreaties from the tobacco-threading tent, from the jagged slab of stone, from the winds of the South; I have crammed her into the bus and been lost with her in the streets as we searched for Maryam al-Taweela's house. And now here were the two of us standing at the door of the swimming pool and she, having heard the call to prayers, had prostrated herself in prayer. She was destroying what lay in my bag, blocking the road between me and the sea. I felt sorry for her, for her knees that knelt on the cruelly hard pavement, for her tattooed hands that lay on the dirt. I looked at her again and saw the passersby staring at her. For the first time her black dress looked shabby to me. I felt how far removed we were from these passersby, from this street, this city, this sea. I approached her and she again put her weight on my hand.

Translated by Denys Johnson-Davies

Imam: cousin and son-in-law of the prophet Mohammed; indicates that the characters in the story are Shi'ite Muslims

Zeytouna: an olive tree in Arabic

Flowers

DENNIS CRAIG

I have never learnt the names of flowers.
From beginning, my world has been a place
Of pot-holed streets where thick, sluggish gutters race
In slow time, away from garbage heaps and sewers
Past blanched old houses around which cowers
Stagnant earth. There, scarce green thing grew to chase
The dull-grey squalor of sick dust; no trace
Of plant save few sparse weeds; just these, no flowers.

One day they cleared a space and made a park
There in the city's slums; and suddenly
Came stark glory like lightning in the dark,
While perfume and bright petals thundered slowly.
I learnt no names, but hue, shape and scent mark
My mind, even now, with symbols holy.

Where The World Began

MARGARET LAURENCE

For every human being, the world begins at home.

A strange place it was, that place where the world began. A place of incredible happenings, splendours and revelations, despairs like multitudinous pits of isolated hells. A place of shadow-spookiness, inhabited by the unknowable dead. A place of jubilation and of mourning, horrible and beautiful.

It was, in fact, a small prairie town.

Because that settlement and that land were my first and for many years my only real knowledge of this planet, in some profound way they remain my world, my way of viewing. My eyes were formed there. Towns like ours, set in a sea of land, have been described thousands of times as dull, bleak, flat, uninteresting. I have had it said to me that the railway trip across Canada is spectacular, except for the prairies, when it would be desirable to go to sleep for several days, until the ordeal is over. I am always unable to argue this point effectively. All I can say is—well, you really have to live there to know that country. The town of my childhood could be called bizarre, agonizingly repressive or cruel at times, and the land in which it grew could be called harsh in the violence of its seasonal changes. But never merely flat or uninteresting. Never dull.

In winter, we used to hitch rides on the back of the milk sleigh, our moccasins squeaking and slithering on the hard rutted snow of the roads, our hands in ice-bubbled mitts hanging onto the box edge of the sleigh for dear life, while Bert grinned at us through his great frosted moustache and shouted the horse into speed, daring us to stay put. Those mornings, rising, there would be the perpetual fascination of the frost feathers on windows, the ferns and flowers and eerie faces traced there during the night by unseen artists of the wind. Evenings, coming back from skating, the sky would be black but not dark, for you could see a cold glitter of stars from one side of the earth's rim to the other. And then the sometime astonishment when you saw the Northern lights flaring across the sky, like the scrawled signature of God. After a blizzard, when the snowploughs hadn't yet got through, school would be closed for the day, the assumption being that the town's young could not possibly flounder through five feet of snow in the pursuit of education. We would then gaily don snowshoes and flounder for miles out into the white dazzling deserts, in pursuit of a different kind of knowing. If you came back too close to night, through the woods at the foot of the town hill, the thin black branches of poplar and chokecherry now meringued with frost, sometimes you heard coyotes. Or maybe the banshee wolf-voices were really only inside your head.

Summers were scorching, and when no rain came and the wheat became bleached and dried before it headed, the faces of farmers and townsfolk would not smile much, and you took for granted, because it never seemed to have been any different, the frequent knocking at the back door and the young men standing there, mumbling or thrusting defiantly their requests for a drink of water and a sandwich if you could spare it. They were riding the freights, and you never knew where they had come from, or where they might end up, if anywhere. The Drought and Depression were like evil deities which had been there always. You understood and did not understand.

Yet the outside world had its continuing marvels. The poplar bluffs and the small river were filled and surrounded with a zillion different grasses, stones, and weed flowers. The meadowlarks sang undaunted from the twanging telephone wires along the gravel highway. Once we found an old flat-bottomed scow, and launched her, poling along the shallow brown waters, mending her with wodges of hastily chewed Spearmint, grounding her among the tangles of yellow marsh marigolds that grew succulently along the banks of the shrunken river, while the sun made our skins smell dusty-warm.

My best friend lived in an apartment above some stores on Main Street (its real name was Mountain Avenue, goodness knows why), an elegant apartment with royal-blue velvet curtains. The back roof, scarcely sloping at all, was corrugated tin, of a furnace-like warmth on a July afternoon, and we would sit there drinking lemonade and looking across the back lane at the Fire Hall. Sometimes our vigil would be rewarded. Oh joy! Somebody's house burning down! We had an almost-perfect callousness in some ways. Then the wooden tower's bronze bell would clonk and toll like a thousand speeded funerals in a time of plague, and in a few minutes the team of giant black horses would cannon forth, pulling the fire wagon like some scarlet chariot of the Goths, while the firemen clung with one hand, adjusting their helmets as they went.

The oddities of the place were endless. An elderly lady used to serve, as her afternoon tea offering to other ladies, soda biscuits spread with peanut butter and topped with a whole marshmallow. Some considered this slightly eccentric, when compared with chopped egg sandwiches, and admittedly talked about her behind her back, but no one ever refused these delicacies or indicated to her that they thought she had slipped a cog. Another lady dyed her hair a bright and cheery orange, by strangers often mistaken at twenty paces for a feather hat. My own beloved step-mother wore a silver fox neckpiece, a whole pelt, *with the embalmed (?) head still on.* My Ontario Irish grandfather said, "sparrow grass," a more interesting term than asparagus. The town dump was known as "the nuisance grounds," a phrase fraught with weird connotations, as though the effluvia of our lives was beneath contempt but at the same time was subtly threatening to the determined and sometimes hysterical pro-priety of our ways.

Some oddities were, as idiom had it, "funny ha ha"; others were "funny peculiar." Some were not so very funny at all. An old man lived, deranged, in a shack in the valley. Perhaps he wasn't even all that old, but to us he seemed a wild Methuselah figure, shambling among the underbrush and the tall couch grass, muttering indecipherable curses or blessings, a prophet who had forgotten his prophesies. Everyone in town knew him, but no one knew him. He lived among us as though only occasionally and momentarily visible. The kids called him Andy Gump, and feared him. Some sought to prove their bravery by tormenting him. They were the mediaeval bear baiters, and he the lumbering be-wildered bear, half blind, only rarely turning to snarl. Everything is to be found in a town like mine. Belsen, writ small but with the same ink.

All of us cast stones in one shape or another. In grade school, among the vulnerable and violet girls we were, the feared and despised were those few older girls from what was charmingly termed "the wrong side of the tracks." Tough in talk and tougher in muscle, they were said to be whores already. And may have been, that being about the only pro-fession readily available to them.

The dead lived in that place, too. Not only the grandparents who had, in local parlance, "passed on" and who gloomed, bearded or bonneted, from the sepia photographs in old albums, but also the uncles, forever eighteen or nineteen, whose names were carved on granite family stones in the cemetery, but whose bones lay in France. My own young mother lay in the graveyard, beside other dead of our kind, and when I was ten, my father, too, only forty, left the living town for the dead dwelling on the hill.

When I was eighteen, I couldn't wait to get out of that town, away from the prairies. I did not know then that I would carry the land and town all my life within my skull, that they would form the mainspring and source of the writing I was to do, wherever and however far away I might live.

This was my territory in the time of my youth, and in a sense my life since then has been an attempt to look at it, to come to terms with it. Stultifying to the mind it certainly could be, and sometimes was, but not to the imagination. It was many things, but it was never dull.

The same, I now see, could be said for Canada in general. Why on earth did generations of Canadians pretend to believe this country dull? We knew perfectly well it wasn't. Yet for so long we did not proclaim what we knew. If our upsurge of so-called nationalism seems odd or irrelevant to outsiders, and even to some of our own people *(what's all the fuss about?)*, they might try to understand that for many years we valued ourselves insufficiently, living as we did under the huge shadows of those two dominating figures, Uncle Sam and Britannia. We have only just begun to value ourselves, our land, our abilities. We have only just begun to recognize our legends and to give shape to our myths.

There are, God knows, enough aspects to deplore about this country. When I see the killing of our lakes and rivers with industrial wastes, I feel rage and despair. When I see our industries and natural resources increasingly taken over by America, I feel an overwhelming discouragement, especially as I cannot simply say "damn Yankees." It should never be forgotten that it is we ourselves who have sold such a large amount of our birthright for a mess of plastic Progress. When I saw the War Measures Act being invoked in 1970, I lost forever the vestigial remains of the naive wish-belief that repression could not happen here, or would not. And yet, of course, I had known all along in the deepest and often hidden caves of the heart that anything can happen anywhere, for the seeds of both man's freedom and his captivity are found everywhere, even in the microcosm of a prairie town. But in raging against our injustices, our stupidities, I do so as *family*, as I did, and still do in writing about those aspects of my town which I hated and which are always in some ways aspects of myself.

The land still draws me more than other lands. I have lived in Africa and in England, but splendid as both can be, they do not have the power to move me in the same way as, for example, that part of southern Ontario where I spent four months last summer in a cedar cabin beside a river. "Scratch a Canadian, and you find a phony pioneer," I used to say to myself in warning. But all the same it is true, I think, that we are not yet totally alienated from physical earth, and let us only pray we do not become so. I once thought that my lifelong fear and mistrust of cities made me a kind of old-fashioned freak; now I see it differently.

The cabin has a long window across its front western wall, and sitting at the oak table there in the morning, I used to look out at the river and at the tall trees beyond, green-gold in the early light. The river was bronze; the sun caught it strangely, reflecting upon its surface the near-shore sand ripples underneath. Suddenly, the crescenting of a fish, gone before the eye could clearly give image to it. The old man next door said these leaping fish were carp. Himself, he preferred muskie, for he was a real fisherman and the muskie gave him a fight. The wind most often blew from the south, and the river flowed toward the south, so when the water was wind-ruffled, and the current was strong, the river seemed to be flowing both ways. I liked this, and interpreted it as an omen, a natural symbol.

A few years ago, when I was back in Winnipeg, I gave a talk at my old college. It was open to the public, and afterward a very old man came up to me and asked me if my maiden name had been Wemyss. I said yes, thinking he might have known my father or my grandfather. But no. "When I was a young lad," he said, "I once worked for your great-grandfather, Robert Wemyss, when he had the sheep ranch at Rae-burn." I think that was a moment when I realized all over again something of great importance to me. My long-ago families came from Scotland and Ireland, but in a sense that no longer mattered so much. My true roots were here.

I am not very patriotic, in the usual meaning of that word. I cannot say "My country right or wrong" in any political, social or literary context. But one thing is inalterable, for better or worse, for life.

This is where my world began. A world which includes the ancestors—both my own and other people's ancestors who become mine. A world which formed me, and continues to do so, even while I fought it in some of its aspects, and continue to do so. A world which gave me my own lifework to do, because it was here that I learned the sight of my own particular eyes.

Belsen: a German village which became a Nazi concentration camp during the Second World War

War Measures Act, 1970: invoked by Prime Minister Pierre Trudeau during separatist activity in Québec

The Natural World

RIGOBERTA MENCHÚ

Rigoberta Menchú, a Guatemalan Indian, explains her people's spiritual attachment to nature and to the earth, their mother.

"We must respect the one God at the heart of the sky, which is the Sun"
—Rigoberta Menchú

"Tojil, in his own natural darkness, struck the leather of his sandal with a stone, and from it, at that very moment, came a spark, then a flash, followed by a flame, and the new fire burned in all its splendour"
—Popul Vuh

From very small children we receive an education which is very different from white children, *ladinos*. We Indians have more contact with nature. That's why they call us polytheistic. But we're not polytheistic . . . or if we are, it's good, because it's our culture, our customs. We worship—or rather not worship but respect—a lot of things to do with the natural world, the most important things for us. For instance, to us, water is sacred. Our parents tell us when we're very small not to waste water, even when we have it. Water is pure, clean, and gives life to man. Without water we cannot survive, nor could our ancestors have survived. The idea that water is sacred is in us children, and we never stop thinking of it as something pure. The same goes for the earth. Our parents tell us: "Children, the earth is the mother of man, because she gives him food." This is especially true for us whose life is based on the crops we grow. Our people eat maize, beans and plants. We can't eat ham, or cheese, or things made with equipment, with machines. So we think of the earth as the mother of man, and our parents teach us to respect the earth. We must only harm the earth when we are in need. This is why, before we sow our maize, we have to ask the earth's permission.

Pom, copal, is a sacred ingredient for our people. We use it to express our feelings for the earth, so that she will allow us to cultivate her. *Copal* is the resin of a tree. It has a smell like incense. We burn it and it gives off a very strong smell: a smoke with a very rich, delicious, aroma. We use the candle, water and lime a great deal in our ceremonies. We use candles to represent the earth, water and maize, which is the food of man. We believe (and this has been passed down to us by our ancestors) that our people are made of maize. We're made of white maize and yellow maize. We must remember this. We put a candle out for man, as the son of the natural world, the universe, and the members of the family join together in prayer. The prayers usually ask the earth for permission to plant our crops at sowing time, to give us a good harvest, and then to give thanks with all our might, with all our being, for a good harvest.

The prayers and ceremonies are for the whole community. We pray to our ancestors, reciting their prayers which have been known to us for a long time—a very, very long time. We evoke the representatives of the animal world; we say the names of dogs. We say the names of the earth, the God of the earth, and the God of water. Then we say the name of the heart of the sky—the Sun. Our grandfathers say we must ask the sun to shine on all its children: the trees, animals, water, man. We ask it to shine on our enemies. To us an enemy is someone who steals or goes into prostitution. So, you see, it's a different world. This is how we make our pleas and our promises. It doesn't refer so much to the real world, but it includes part of our reality. A prayer is made up of all this. We make a definite plea to the earth. We say: "Mother Earth, you who gives us food, whose children we are and on whom we depend, please make this produce you give us flourish and make our children and our animals grow . . .", and other things as well.

Or we say: "We make our vows for ten days so that you concede us permission, your permission, Mother Earth, who are sacred, to feed us and give our children what they need. We do not abuse you, we only beg your permission, you who are part of the natural world and part of the family of our parents and our grandparents." This means we believe, for instance, that the sun is our grandfather, that he is a member of our family. "We respect you and love you and ask that you love us as we love you"—those prayers are specially for the earth. For the sun, we say: "Heart of the sky, you are our father, we ask you to give your warmth and light to our animals, our maize, our beans, our plants, so that they may grow and our children may eat." We evoke the colour of the sun, and this has a special importance for us because this is how we want our children to live—like a light which shines, which shines with generosity. It means a warm heart and it means strength, life-giving strength. It's something you never lose and you find it everywhere. So when we evoke the colour of the sun, it's like evoking all the elements which go to make up our life. The sun, as the channel to the one God, receives the plea from his children that they should never violate the rights of all the other beings which surround them. This is how we renew our prayer which says that men, the children of the one God, must respect the life of the trees, the birds, the animals around us. We say the names of birds and animals—cows, horses, dogs, cats. All these. We mention them all. We must respect the life of every single one of them. We must respect the life, the purity, the sacredness, which is water. We must respect the one God, the heart of the sky, which is the sun. We must not do evil while the sun shines upon his children. This is a promise. Then we promise to respect the life of the one creature, which is man. This is very important. We say: "We cannot harm the life of one of your children, we are your children. We cannot kill any of your creatures, neither trees nor animals." Then we offer up a sheep or chickens, because we believe sheep to be sacred animals, quiet animals, saintly animals, animals which don't harm other animals. They are the most tranquil animals that exist, like birds. So the community chooses certain small animals for the feast after the ceremonies.

Translated by Ann Wright

---

ladinos: today, any Guatemalan who supports the system that suppresses the Indians; person of mixed race

Popul Vuh: author of ancient legends of the Quiché Indians

Our Earth Will Not Die

NIYI OSUNDARE

(To a solemn, almost elegiac tune)

> Lynched
>> the lakes
> Slaughtered
>> the seas
> Mauled
>> the mountains

But our earth will not die

> Here
>> there
>>> everywhere
> a lake is killed by the arsenic urine
> from the bladder of profit factories
> a poisoned stream staggers down the hills
> coughing chaos in the sickly sea
> the wailing whale, belly up like a frying fish,
> crests the chilling swansong of parting waters.

But our earth will not die.

> Who lynched the lakes. Who?
> Who slaughtered the seas. Who?
> Whoever mauled the mountains. Whoever?

Our earth will not die

> And the rain
> the rain falls, acid, on balding forests
> their branches amputated by the septic daggers
> of tainted clouds

> Weeping willows drip mercury tears
> in the eye of sobbing terrains
> a nuclear sun rises like a funeral ball
> reducing man and meadow to dust and dirt.

But our earth will not die.

    Fishes have died in the waters.   Fishes.
    Birds have died in the trees.   Birds.
    Rabbits have died in their burrows.   Rabbits.

But our earth will not die

(Music turns festive, louder)

    Our earth will see again
    eyes washed by a new rain
    the westering sun will rise again
    resplendent like a new coin.
    The wind, unwound, will play its tune
    trees twittering, grasses dancing;
    hillsides will rock with blooming harvests
    the plains batting their eyes of grass and grace.
    The sea will drink its heart's content
    when a jubilant thunder flings open the skygate
    and a new rain tumbles down
    in drums of joy.
    Our earth will see again

    this earth, OUR EARTH.

C·L·A·S·H·E·S

such a bitter taste

The Long March

MAO TSE-TUNG

For our Red Army there was no fear in
meeting hardships of the Long March;
those myriad streams to be crossed,
that maze of mountains to be climbed,
simply a part of the work to be done;
crests of the five ranges rising in front
of us as waves over a stormy sea,
yet taken in our passage
as though they were tiny ripples;
the crossing of the rugged Wumeng range
as if it was a lump of clay;
and there was that river of Golden Sands
running by precipices,
lying warm against the sun;
and the long chains of iron
stretching over the gorge of the Tatu River
cold, so cold in our grasp;
then marching through those miles of snow
on Minshan;
and on the faces of all our fighters
was joy.

Translated by Rewi Alley

The "**Long March**" refers to the Communists' famous twelve-month, 10 000 km
retreat (1934-35) to new headquarters in north-central China.

Lilies

RU ZHIJUAN

After the surrender of the Japanese in 1945, the Chinese Communist Party held talks with the Nationalist Party in an effort to bring peace to the nation. But the agreement failed, and civil war broke out again. That's when this story begins.

Mid-autumn 1946.

The decision was made that day that the troops fighting in the coastal region would launch a general offensive that evening. The other comrades from the production office of our arts ensemble were all assigned work in various combat companies by the commander of the main offensive regiment, but, probably because I was a woman, the commander scratched his head in perplexity for a long time before finally calling a courier to lead me to a first-aid post near the front lines.

I didn't mind being assigned to a first-aid post. Just as long as I wasn't being ushered into a strongbox, I was willing to do anything. I shouldered my pack and set off after the courier.

That morning there had been a shower of rain, and although the sky was now clear, the road was still extremely slippery. But the crops on either side of the track had been washed a brilliant emerald-green and sparkled like jewels in the sunlight. The air carried a fresh, moist fragrance. If it hadn't been for the intermittent explosions of the enemy's blind cannon-fire, I might have imagined myself on the way to market.

The courier walked ahead of me with rapid strides, and right from the start I lagged behind him some fifty or sixty metres. My feet were festering and the road so slippery that no matter how hard I tried, I couldn't catch up with him. I thought of calling to him to wait for me, but I was afraid he would laugh at me for being a frightened coward, and didn't dare. I really was afraid that I wouldn't be able to find the first-aid post on my own. I began to feel angry with him.

But strange to say, he seemed to have eyes in the back of his head, and stopped at the roadside of his own accord, though he kept his face to the front and didn't even glance at me. When I had almost struggled up to where he stood, he set off again by himself, and in a short time had once more left me far behind. I genuinely didn't have the strength to keep up, so simply staggered on slowly behind him. However, it was not so bad this time; he didn't let me lag too far back but he never let me get close to him either, always maintaining the distance between us. If I walked quickly, he would stride ahead, and if I walked slowly, he would vacillate to the right and left before me. What was strange was that I never saw him look back once. I couldn't help feeling rather intrigued by this courier.

I hadn't paid him any attention at the regiment headquarters just now, but by the look of his tall, slender figure and broad shoulders he was a strong young fellow. He wore a faded yellow uniform and puttees that reached to his knees. Several leafy twigs stuck into the barrel of the rifle on his shoulder seemed more a decoration than a means of camouflage.

I hadn't caught up with him, but my swollen feet were burning like twin fires. I suggested to him that we rest for a while, and sat down on a stone at the edge of a field. He sat down with his back to me on another stone a good distance away, acting as if I simply didn't exist. From experience I knew that this was because I was a woman. Women comrades who worked at company level always had these problems. Slightly irritated, I displayed my spirit of resistance by walking over and sitting down directly opposite him. Now I could see his round, childish face. He must have been eighteen at the most. Seeing me sit down near him, he immediately became as alarmed as if a time bomb had been planted nearby. He was clearly ill at ease, knowing that to turn his head away would be impolite, but too embarrassed to face in my direction. He thought of standing up, but then felt that that would make things even more awkward. Fighting hard not to laugh, I casually asked him where he was from. He didn't answer immediately. He blushed a deep crimson like the painted face of the god of war, and only after stuttering incoherently for a while did he manage to make it clear that he was from the Tianmu Mountains. So we were from the same area!

"What do you do at home?"

"I haul bamboo."

Looking at his broad shoulders, a vision of a green, misty sea of bamboo floated before my eyes. Through the trees a narrow, stone-stepped mountain path wound upwards out of sight. A broad-shouldered young man with an old piece of blue cloth cushioning his shoulder was hauling several thick bamboos down the mountain. The tips of the bamboos trailed on the ground far behind him, issuing a rhythmic thud as they fell from step to step. This was the hometown life with which I was so familiar! My heart immediately warmed towards him. I questioned him further.

"How old are you?"

"Nineteen."

"When did you join the revolution?"

"A year ago."

"How did you come to join the revolution?" At this point I suddenly felt that this was more like an interrogation than a conversation, but I still couldn't resist questioning him.

"When the Communist troops pulled out of Jiangnan, I followed them."

"How many in your family?"

"Mum, Dad, younger brothers and sisters, and another girl who lives with us."

"You're not married yet?"

He blushed scarlet and became even more disconcerted, his fingers endlessly counting the eyelets on his belt. After a long pause, he lowered his head with a bashful grin, and shook his head. I was going to ask him if he had a finacée, but seeing the flustered state he was in, swallowed my words.

We sat in silence for a while, then he raised his head and looked at the sky, glancing at me to indicate that we should be on our way.

When I stood up to go, I saw him take off his cap and covertly mop the sweat with a towel. This was all my fault—he hadn't shed a drop of perspiration marching along the road, but his conversation with me brought the sweat pouring off him.

When we arrived at the first-aid station, it was already past two in the afternoon. The first-aid post had been set up in a primary school about a kilometre from the battle front. Six buildings of various sizes were arranged in a rough triangle with a yard in the centre overgrown with weeds. Obviously the school had been closed for some time. When we arrived, several health workers were preparing gauze bandages and cotton wool. The rooms were filled with doors propped up on piles of bricks that were to serve as hospital beds.

We hadn't been there long when a county cadre arrived. His eyes were heavily bloodshot from lack of sleep, and he had stuck a piece of card under the front of his tattered felt cap to shade them from the sunlight. He came in puffing and panting, with a rifle on one shoulder and a steelyard on the other, a basket of eggs in his left hand and a large cooking pot in his right. Putting down the things he had brought, he apologized to us and at the same time poured out his troubles. Gulping breathlessly from drinking down a cup of water, he pulled a lump of cooked rice from inside his jacket and took a large bite. I was so astonished by the speed with which he did all this that I didn't catch what he was saying. He seemed to be saying that we would have to go and borrow cotton quilts ourselves. One of the health workers told me that the army quilts had still not been issued, but because it was essential that the wounded be kept warm, we would have to borrow quilts from the villagers. Even if we could only get a dozen or so strips of quilt padding, that would be better than nothing. I had been feeling frustrated at not being able to lend a hand, so I volunteered to undertake the task, and, afraid that I wouldn't have time to complete it on my own, randomly asked my townsman to help me mobilize a few households before he went back. After a moment's hesitation, he followed me out of the door.

We went first to a nearby village, he covering the eastern side and I the western. In a short time I had written out three receipts and borrowed two strips of cotton padding and one cotton quilt. My arms were full and I was elated. I was just going to take the bedding back to the first-aid post and come back for more, when the courier, his arms empty, came up from the opposite direction.

"What? You couldn't borrow any?" I was puzzled. I felt that the villagers' political awareness here was very high. They were very open-hearted. How could he possibly have not borrowed any?

"Comrade, you go and borrow them . . . the villagers here are strictly feudal . . . "

"Which house? You take me there." I guessed that he had certainly said something inappropriate and put the people's backs up. Not being able to borrow a cotton quilt was a trifling matter, but to offend the ordinary people was of serious concern. I called him to take me to have a look, but he stubbornly lowered his head and stood as if nailed to the spot, unwilling to move. I went over to him and in a low voice explained to him the importance of making a good impression on the masses. Hearing what I said, without further ado he led me to the house.

When we entered the courtyard, we found the main room of the house empty. The door to the inner room, which was screened by a piece of blue cloth on a red yoke, was framed to the right and left with an antithetical couplet written on bright red paper. We had no choice but to stand outside calling out "Elder Sister," "Sister-in-law." There was no answer, but there was the sound of movement within. After a moment the curtain was flicked aside, and a young woman appeared. She was very attractive: her eyebrows curved gracefully above a high-bridged nose, and a soft fringe covered her forehead. Although her clothes were of coarse cloth, they were all new.

Seeing that her hair was done up in the stiff bun of a married woman, I addressed her as "Elder Sister-in-law," and apologized to her, asking her not to take offence if this comrade had said something out of turn when he was here just now. She stood there listening with her face turned away slightly and a smile on her tightly closed lips. She didn't make a sound, even when I stopped speaking, but kept her head down, biting her lips as if holding back gales of laughter about something incredibly amusing. Now I began to feel awkward. What should I say next? I glanced at the courier at my side, and saw him gazing at me unblinkingly as if watching the company commander giving a demonstration. All I could do was brace myself and somewhat sheepishly ask if we could borrow the quilt, explaining that the troops of the Communist Party were fighting for the ordinary people. As I talked she stopped smiling and listened carefully, glancing towards the house now and then. When I fell silent, she looked first at me and then at the courier as if weighing up my words, then after long consideration, turned and went into the house to fetch the quilt.

The courier seized this opportunity to express his indignation. "That's exactly what I said just now, but she wouldn't lend it to me. Don't you think it's strange?"

I hastily threw him a disdainful glance to stop him talking, but it was already too late. The young woman with the quilt had already reached the doorway. As soon as I saw the quilt I understood why she had been so reluctant to lend it just now: it was completely new. The cover was of wine-coloured synthetic satin, patterned all over with white lilies. As if deliberately wanting to annoy the courier, she held the quilt out to me saying, "Here, take it!"

My arms were already full of quilts, so I motioned to the courier with my lips that he should take it. Quite unexpectedly, he gazed up at the sky, pretending that he hadn't seen, and I was obliged to call to him before he finally took it with eyes cast down and a look of displeasure on his face. Highly flustered, he turned on his heel and shot out the street door. But as he passed the door, we heard a sharp ripping sound as his uniform caught on the door hook, leaving a sizeable piece of torn cloth hanging down from his shoulder. The young woman burst out laughing and hastily searched out a needle and cotton to stitch

it up for him, but he wouldn't allow it on any account, and left with the quilt under his arm.

We hadn't gone far when someone told us that the young woman was a new bride of only three days. This quilt was her entire dowry. I began to feel sorry that we had borrowed it, and the courier knitted his brows too, gazing silently at the quilt in his arms. I guessed he felt the same way as I did. Sure enough, as we walked along he began to mutter, "We didn't understand the situation. It's really not right to borrow someone's bridal quilt!" I couldn't resist playing a joke on him, and deliberately assumed a serious air. "You're right! Who knows how many mornings she got up early and how many evenings she stayed up late doing extra jobs to save up for this quilt? For all we know she might have spent sleepless nights on account of it. But some people still curse her as strictly feudal . . . "

Hearing this, he suddenly halted, and after a moment's silence said, "Then . . . then let's take it back to her!"

"Since we've already borrowed it, to take it back now would only hurt her feelings." His earnest, embarrassed expression was both amusing and endearing. Unaccountably, I had already given my heart to this simple young townsfellow of mine.

Hearing that my explanation seemed reasonable, he thought for a moment, then said resolutely, "OK, then we'll leave it at that, but when we've finished with it we must wash it really clean for her." Having made this decision, he grabbed all the quilts out of my arms and with them hung over his shoulders went striding off at a rapid pace.

Back at the first-aid post, I told him to return to the regimental headquarters. He brightened up immediately, and after giving me a farewell salute, raced off. He had only gone a few paces when he suddenly thought of something, and feeling around in his shoulder bag pulled out two steamed bread rolls which he waved at me, then placed on a boulder at the roadside. "Have something to eat!" he called, then sped off, his feet scarcely touching the ground. I went over to pick up the two hard, dry rolls, and noticed that at some time a wild chrysanthemum had been added to the greenery in his rifle barrel, and was now nodding at his ear.

He was already disappearing into the distance, but I could still see that torn patch of cloth hanging from his shoulder flapping in the breeze. I regretted not stitching it up for him before he had left. Now he would have to spend at least one night with a bared shoulder.

There were very few staff to run the first-aid post, so the county cadre mobilized several of the village women to fetch water, boil the cauldrons and do various other odd jobs. Our young woman came as well, smiling with closed lips as she had before. She occasionally stole a glance at me from the corner of her eye, but she frequently looked around her as if searching for something. Finally she asked me outright, "Where has that little comrade gone?" I told her he wasn't a member of the staff here and had gone to the front lines. She laughed in embarrassment and said, "When he came to borrow the quilt just now, I'm afraid he felt the sharp edge of my tongue!" She closed her eyes in another smile, then set to work to lay the borrowed quilts and cotton padding out neatly on the doors and tables (two tables side by side served as a bed). I saw her put her own new lily-patterned quilt on a door outside under the eaves.

Night fell and a full moon rose above the horizon. Our general offensive had not yet been launched. As usual the enemy, dreading the night, had set great patches of the countryside ablaze and was continuing its barrage of blind shelling. Flare after flare was fired into the sky, nakedly exposing everything on the ground as if countless kerosene lamps had been lit under the moon. To launch an attack on a bright night like this presented enormous difficulties and would have to be paid for at considerable cost. I even began to hate that clear, bright moon.

The county cadre returned, bringing us several home-made dried-vegetable moon-cakes as a reward for our labours. It had slipped my mind that today was Mid-autumn Festival.

Ah—Mid-autumn Festival! At this moment outside every door in my home village would be placed a table on which was arranged incense, candles and several dishes of candied melon moon-cakes. The children would be impatiently longing for the incense to burn out so as to divide the things laid out for the enjoyment of the Moon Girl as soon as possible. They would be hopping and skipping beside the table and singing, "Moon, moon, bright and dandy, beat the gongs and buy some candy" . . . or perhaps, "Moon, moon is our nanny, shines on you and shines on me . . ." Thinking of the children, my thoughts turned to my young fellow townsman; several years ago the young man who hauled bamboos might very well have sung just those songs! . . . I took a bit of the delicious home-made moon-cake and thought that he was probably at this moment lying behind the fortifications or at the regimental command post— or maybe he was running through those winding communication trenches.

A short time later our cannons sounded and several red signal flares streaked through the sky. The attack had begun. Not long afterwards an intermittent stream of wounded men began to arrive at the first-aid post, and the atmosphere immediately became tense.

I took a notebook and began to register their names and units. Those with light wounds I could ask, but for the severely wounded I had to find their identification tags or look for a name on the inside of their jackets. Pulling out the identification tag of one badly wounded soldier, the word "courier" sent a sudden shiver down my spine, and my heart began to pound. Only after I had pulled myself together did I see below it, "X Battalion." Ah! It wasn't him. My townsfellow was the regimental headquarters courier. But I felt an unaccountable desire to ask someone: might there be any wounded on the battlefield who had been missed? Apart from carrying messages, what else did couriers do on the battlefield? I didn't know myself why I should be asking these meaningless questions.

For the first hour or so of battle everything went smoothly. The wounded brought with them news that we had crossed the abatis; we had crossed the wire entanglement; we had occupied the enemy's front line fortifications and driven the assault into the town. But then the news suddenly stopped. The wounded coming in would only answer briefly, "We're still fighting," or, "We're fighting in the streets." But from their mud-covered bodies, their look of utter exhaustion and even from the stretchers that looked as if they had been just dug out of a mud pit, everyone was well aware just what kind of battle was being fought at the front.

The first-aid post ran out of stretchers, and several badly wounded men who should have been sent immediately to the rear area hospital were unavoidably delayed. We could do nothing to relieve their pain; all we could do was wash their hands and faces with the aid of the village women, feed the ones who could eat, and put dry clothes on those who still carried their knapsacks. For some of them we also had to undo their clothing and wipe their bodies clean of mud and clotting blood.

I was accustomed to this kind of work, but the village women were both bashful and frightened. They were unwilling to touch the wounded men, and vied for the task of boiling the cauldrons—particularly that young bride. I talked to her for a long time before she assented with a blush, but she would only agree to be my assistant.

The sound of gunfire from the front had already become sporadic, and it felt as if dawn should soon break, yet it was only midnight. Outside the moon shone brilliantly, and seemed to have risen higher in the sky than usual. Another badly wounded soldier was brought in from the front. The beds inside were all filled, so I directed that he be put on the door outside under the eaves. The stretcher bearers lifted him on to the makeshift bed, but remained at his side, unwilling to leave. An elderly stretcher bearer seized me by the shoulder, thinking I was a doctor. "Doctor! Whatever happens you must find a way to save this comrade. If you can save him, I . . . our whole stretcher bearer corps will publicly commend you . . ." As he spoke, I discovered that all the other stretcher bearers were also gazing at me unblinkingly, as if a nod of my head would bring the wounded man instantaneous recovery. I wanted to explain the situation to them, but the young bride, who had just approached the bed-head with a bowl of water, suddenly gave a short scream. I pushed them aside and found myself looking down at a round, childish face, its once ruddy brown skin now an ashen yellow. His eyes were serenely closed, and at his shoulder, below the gaping hole in his uniform, that piece of torn cloth was still hanging limply.

"He did it all for us," the elderly stretcher bearer spoke with a heavy burden of guilt. "A dozen of us stretcher bearers were crowded into a small alley waiting for the chance to move forward. He was behind us. Then all of a sudden, from God knows which rooftop, one of those bastard reactionaries dropped a hand grenade right on top of us. While it was still smoking and rolling around, this comrade shouted to us to duck down, and leapt on top of it, covering it with his body."

The young woman gave another short scream. I fought back my tears and spoke to the stretcher bearers, sending them on their way. Turning back, I saw that the young bride had already quietly moved an oil lamp to the bedside and had undone his clothing; her recent

223

bashfulness had completely disappeared and she was solemnly and piously washing his body. The tall young courier lay there without uttering a sound.

I suddenly came to my senses and leaping up, stumbled off to fetch the doctor. When the doctor and I hurried up with needle and syringe, the young woman was sitting down facing the bed.

Her head was lowered as stitch by stitch she repaired the hole in the shoulder of his uniform. The doctor listened to the courier's heart, then stood up slowly. "There's no need to give him an injection." I went forward and felt his hand: it was icy cold. But the young woman, as if seeing and hearing nothing, continued with her work, finely and closely stitching up the hole. I really couldn't stand the sight of it, and said in a low voice, "Don't stitch it!" She threw me a peculiar glance, then lowered her head and continued to sew methodically, stitch after stitch. I wanted to pull her away, wanted to break through this cloying atmosphere, wanted to see him sit up, see him bashfully smile. But unwittingly my hand knocked against something next to me. I stretched out my hand to feel it. It was the meal he had left me—two hard, dry, steamed rolls.

A health worker called someone to bring a coffin, and took the quilt from the courier's body ready to place him inside. At this the young woman, her face ashen, seized the quilt from his hands and glaring at him fiercely, laid half of the quilt smoothly over the bottom of the coffin, and folded the remainder to cover the length of the courier's body. The health worker protested awkwardly, "The quilt . . . was borrowed from the people."

"It's mine," she shouted furiously, then wrenched her head away. In the moonlight I saw the tears shining in her eyes. I saw too that wine-coloured quilt with its sprinkling of lilies—the symbols of purity and love—covering the face of that ordinary young man who hauled bamboos.

Translated by R.A. Roberts

---

abatis: a defence barrier made of felled trees with the boughs pointing outwards

"Everything Is Plundered . . ."

ANNA AKHMATOVA

Everything is plundered, betrayed, sold,
Death's great black wing scrapes the air,
Misery gnaws to the bone.
Why then do we not despair?

By day, from the surrounding woods,
cherries blow summer into town;
at night the deep transparent skies
glitter with new galaxies.

And the miraculous comes so close
to the ruined, dirty houses—
something not known to anyone at all,
but wild in our breast for centuries.

Translated by Stanley Kunitz
and Max Hayward

1921 brought great turbulence to the new USSR. In the spring, peasant revolts and workers' strikes had to be put down by Lenin. The summer brought famine, followed by economic collapse.

Last Comes the Raven

ITALO CALVINO

He was just a village boy, the picture of innocence, but he aimed his rifle with the deadly accuracy of a bird of prey.

The stream was a net of limpid, delicate ripples, with the water running through the mesh. From time to time, like a fluttering of silver wings, the back fin of a trout flashed on the surface, the fish at once plunging zigzag down into the water.

"Full of trout," one of the men said.

"If we toss a grenade in, they'll all come floating to the top, bellies up," said the other; he detached a grenade from his belt and started to unscrew the baseplate.

Then the boy, who had stood looking on, walked over, a mountain youth with an apple-look to his face. "Let me have it," he said, taking the rifle from one of the men. "What does he want to do?" the man said, intending to re-claim the rifle. But the boy was leveling it at the water, in search of a target, it seemed. "If you shoot, you'll only scare the fish away," the man started to say, but did not have time. A trout had surfaced, flashing, and the boy had pumped a bullet into it as though having anticipated the fish's exact point of appearance. Now, with its white underside exposed, the trout floated lifeless on the surface. "Cripes," the men said. The boy reloaded the rifle and swung it around. The air was crisp and tensed: one could distinguish the pine needles on the opposite bank and the knitted texture of the stream. A ripple broke the surface: another trout. He fired: now it floated dead. The men glanced briefly at the fish, briefly at the boy. "He shoots well," they said.

The boy swung the barrel again, into the air. It was curious, to think of it, that they were encompassed by air, actually cut off from other things by meters of air. But when the boy aimed the rifle, the air then became an invisible straight line stretching from the muzzle to the thing

. . . to the hawk, for instance, floating above on wings that seemed scarcely to move. As he pressed the trigger, the air continued crystalline and as clear as ever, but at the upper end of the line the kestrel folded its wings, then dropped like a stone. The open breech emitted a fine smell of powder.

He asked for more cartridges. The number of men watching had now swelled behind him on the bank of the stream. The cones at the top of the pine trees on the other bank—why were they visible and withal out of reach? Why that empty span between him and them? Why were the cones, although a part of him, in the chamber of his eye—why were they *there*, so distant? And yet if he aimed the rifle that empty span was clearly a deception: he touched the trigger and at that instant a cone, severed at the stem, fell. The feeling was one of caressive emptiness: the emptiness of the rifle bore which extended off into the air and was occupied by the shot, straight to the pine cone, the squirrel, the white stone, the flowering poppy. "He doesn't miss a one," the men said, and no one had the audacity to laugh.

"Come, come along with us," the leader said. "You give me the rifle then," the boy returned. "All right. Certainly."

So he went.

He left with a haversack filled with apples and two rounds of cheese. His village was a patch of slate, straw, and cattle muck in the valley bottom. And going away was wonderful, for at every turn there was something new to be seen, trees with cones, birds flitting among the branches, lichen-encrusted rocks, everything in the shaft of the false distances, of the distances occupied by gunshot that gulped up the air between. But he wasn't to shoot, they told him: those were places to be passed in silence, and the cartridges were for fighting. But at a certain point a leveret, frightened by the footsteps, scampered across the trail, amid shouts and the bustle of the men. It was just about to vanish into the underbrush when the boy stopped it with a shot. "A good shot," the leader himself conceded, "but this is not a pleasure hunt. You're not to shoot again, even if you see a pheasant."

But scarcely an hour had elapsed before there were more shots from the column.

"It's the boy again!" the leader stormed, going forward to overtake him.

The boy grinned with his rosy and white apple-face.

"Partridges," he said, displaying them. They had flushed up from a hedge.

"Partridges, crickets, or whatever else, I gave you fair warning. Now

227

let me have the rifle. And if you make me lose my temper once more, back to the village you go."

The boy sulked a little; it was no fun to be hiking without a rifle, but so long as he remained with them he might hope to have it again.

In the night they bedded down in a herdsmen's shelter. The boy awakened as soon as the sky grew light, while the others still slept. He took their finest rifle and loaded his knapsack with cartridges and went out. The air was gentle and clear, as one may discover it in the early morning. Not far from the house stood a mulberry tree. It was the hour in which jays were arriving. There, he saw one! He fired, ran to pick it up, and stuffed it into his haversack. Without moving from where the jay had fallen, he looked about for another target. A dormouse! Startled by the first shot, it was scurrying toward safety in the crown of a chestnut tree. Dead, it was simply a large mouse with a gray tail that shed shocks of fur at the touch. From beneath the chestnut tree he sighted, in a field off below him, a mushroom, red with white prickles and poisonous. He crumbled it with a shot, then went to see if he had really got it. What fun it was, going from one target to another like that: one might in time go all the way round the world! He spied a large snail on a rock; he sighted on its shell, and when he went over to it noticed nothing but the shattered rock and a spot of iridescent spittle. Thus did he wander from the shelter down through unfamiliar fields.

From the stone he saw a lizard on a wall, from the wall a puddle and a frog, from the puddle a signboard on the zigzagging road, and beneath it: beneath it men in uniform advancing on him with arms at the ready. When the boy came forth with his rifle, smiling, his face rosy and white like an apple, they shouted, raising their guns. But the boy had already seen and fired at one of the gold buttons on the chest of one of them. He heard the man scream and then bullets, in a hail and in single shots, whistling over his head: he had already flattened to the ground behind a pile of rocks on the hem of the road, in a dead angle. The rock pile was long and he could move about; and he was able to peep out from unexpected points, see the flash of the soldiers' musketry, the gray and gloss of their uniforms, and fire at a chevron, at an insigne, then quickly scramble along the ground to fire from a new position.

Then he heard a burst of fire behind him, raking over his head into the ranks of the soldiers: his comrades had appeared on the rescue with machine guns. "If the boy hadn't awakened us with his firing . . ." they were saying.

228

Covered by his comrades, the boy was better able to see. Suddenly a bullet grazed his cheek. He turned: a soldier had got to the road above him. He threw himself into the drainage ditch, gaining shelter again, at the same time firing; the bullet, though failing to hit the soldier, glanced off his riflestock. Now, from the sounds he heard, he could tell that his adversary's rifle had jammed; the soldier flung it to the ground. Then the boy rose up. The soldier had taken to his heels and the boy fired at him, popping an epaulette into the air.

The boy gave chase. The soldier dashed into the woods, at first vanishing but presently reappearing within range. The boy burned a crease in the dome of the soldier's helmet, next shot off a belt loop. One after the other, they had meanwhile come into a dale, to which they were both of them strangers, and where the din of the battle was no longer heard. In time the soldier found himself without any more trees before him, instead a glade overgrown with knotted thicket clumps. And the boy was himself about to come out of the woods.

In the middle of the clearing stood a large rock. The soldier barely made it, jumping behind and doubling up with his head between his knees. There, for the time being, he felt, he was out of danger: he had some grenades with him, and the boy would have to maintain a respectful distance; he could do no more than keep him pinned down with his rifle, insuring that he did not escape. Certainly, had it been possible for him simply to dive into the thickets, he would be safe, able then to slide down the heavily overgrown slope. But there was that open space to cross. How long would the boy wait? And would he continue to keep his rifle trained on him? The soldier decided to try an experiment: he put his helmet on his bayonet and stuck it out from behind the rock. There was a shot and the helmet, pierced through, bowled along the ground.

The soldier kept his wits about him; doubtless, aiming at the rock and the area around it was quite easy, but the soldier would not get hit if he was nimble enough. Just then a bird raced overhead, a hoopoe perhaps. One shot and it fell. The soldier wiped sweat from around his neck. Another bird, a missel thrush, went over: it fell too. The soldier swallowed. This was very likely a flyway, for other birds continued to go over, all of them different, and as the boy fired, they fell. A thought came to the soldier: "If he's watching birds, then he can't be watching me. Just as he fires I'll jump for the bushes." But it might be well to test his plan first. He picked up his helmet and placed it back on the tip of his bayonet. Two birds flew over this time: snipes. Waiting, the soldier regretted wasting so fine an occasion on the test. The boy fired at one of the snipes; the soldier raised his helmet. A second shot rang out and he saw the helmet leap into the air. The soldier's mouth tasted of lead; he had no sooner noticed this than the second bird fell. He must not lose his head: behind the rock, with his grenades, he was safe. And why then, even though hidden, couldn't he try to get the boy with a grenade? He lay on his back and, taking care not to be seen, stretched back his arm, primed his strength, and pitched the grenade. A good throw; it would go some distance; but describing only half a parabola, still in midair, it was exploded by a rifle blast. The soldier flattened himself against the ground to escape the shrapnel.

When next the soldier raised himself the raven had come.

He saw, circling lazily above him, a bird, a raven perhaps. The boy would certainly shoot it down. But no shot followed. Was the raven perhaps too high? And yet he had brought down higher and swifter birds than that. Finally, he fired: now it would drop. No. Unperturbed, it continued to soar in the sky, slowly, round and round. A pine cone toppled from a near-by tree. Had he taken to shooting at pine cones? One by one, as he hit them, the cones fell, striking with a dry crunch. At each report the soldier glanced up at the raven: was it falling? Not yet. Lower and lower, the black bird continued to circle overhead. Could it be, really, that the boy didn't see it? Or perhaps the raven didn't exist at all, was only a hallucination. But perhaps—perhaps a man near death sees all the birds fly over . . . and when he sees the raven it means that the hour has come. In any case, he must tell the boy, who went on shooting at mere pine cones.

The soldier rose to his feet and pointed up at the black bird: "There's the raven!" he shouted in his own language. The bullet struck him through the heart of the spread eagle embroidered on his jacket.

The raven came down slowly, wheeling.

Translated by Ben Johnson

The Wall-Reader

FIONA BARR

When you live in a country torn by warring factions, any conversation may be seen as sinister—especially if it's between a Catholic woman and a British soldier.

S hall only our rivers run free?" The question jumped out from the cobbled wall in huge white letters, as The People's taxi swung round the corner at Beechmount. "Looks like paint is running freely enough down here," she thought to herself, as other slogans glided past in rapid succession. Reading Belfast's grim graffiti had become an entertaining hobby for her, and she often wondered, was it in the dead of night that groups of boys huddled round a paint tin daubing walls and gables with tired political slogans and clichés? Did anyone ever see them? Was the guilty brush ever found? The brush is mightier than the bomb, she declared inwardly, as she thought of how celebrated among journalists some lines had become. "Is there a life before death?" Well, no one had answered that one yet, at least, not in this city.

The shapes of Belfast crowded in on her as the taxi rattled over the ramps outside the fortressed police barracks. Dilapidated houses, bricked-up terraces. Rosy-cheeked soldiers, barely out of school, and quivering with high-pitched fear. She thought of the thick-lipped youth who came to hijack the car, making his point by showing his revolver under his anorak, and of the others, jigging and taunting every July, almost sexual in their arrogance and hatred. Meanwhile, passengers climbed in and out at various points along the road, manoeuvring between legs, bags of shopping and umbrellas. The taxi swerved blindly into the road. No Highway Code here. As the woman's stop approached, the taxi swung up to the pavement, and she stepped out.

She thought of how she read walls—like tea-cups, she smiled to herself. Pushing her baby in the pram to the supermarket, she had to pass under a motorway bridge that was peppered with lines, some in irregular lettering with the paint dribbling down the concrete, others written with felt-tip pen in minute secretive hand. A whole range of human emotions splayed itself with persistent anarchy on the walls. "One could do worse than be a reader of walls," she thought, twisting Frost's words. Instead, though, the pram was rushed past the intriguing mural with much gusto. Respectable housewives don't read walls!

The "Troubles," as they were euphemistically named, remained for this couple as a remote, vaguely irritating wart on their life. They were simply ordinary (she often groaned at the oppressive banality of the word), middle-class, and hoping the baby would marry a doctor, thereby raising them in their autumn days to the select legions of the upper class. Each day their lives followed the same routine—no harm in that sordid little detail, she thought. It helps structure one's existence. He went to the office, she fed the baby, washed the rapidly growing mound of nappies, prepared the dinner and looked forward to the afternoon walk. She had convinced herself she was happy with her lot, and yet felt disappointed at the pangs of jealousy endured on hearing of a friend's glamorous job or another's academic and erudite husband. If only someone noticed her from time to time, or even wrote her name on a wall declaring her existence worthwhile; "A fine mind" or "I was once her lover." That way, at least, she would have evidence she was having impact on others. As it was, she was perpetually bombarded with it. Marital successes, even marital failures evoked a response from her. All one-way traffic.

That afternoon she dressed the baby and started out for her walk. "Fantasy time" her husband called it. "Wall-reading time" she knew it to be. On this occasion, however, she decided to avoid those concrete temptations and, instead, visit the park. Out along the main road she trundled, pushing the pram, pausing to gaze into the hardware store's window, hearing the whine of the Saracen as it thundered by, waking the baby and making her feel uneasy. A foot patrol of soldiers strolled past, their rifles, lethal even in the brittle sunlight of this March day, lounged lovingly and relaxed in the arms of their men. One soldier stood nonchalantly, almost impertinent, against a corrugated railing and stared at her. She always blushed on passing troops.

The park is ugly, stark and hostile. Even in summer, when courting couples seek out secluded spots like mating cats, they reject Musgrave. There are a few trees, clustered together, standing like skeletons, ashamed of their nakedness. The rest is grass, a green wasteland speckled with puddles of gulls squawking over a worm patch. The park is bordered

by a hospital with a military wing which is guarded by an army billet. The beauty of the place, it has only this, is its silence.

The hill up to the park bench was not the precipice it seemed, but the baby pram was heavy. Ante-natal self-indulgence had taken its toll— her midriff was now most definitely a bulge. With one final push, pram, baby and mother reached the green wooden seat, and came to rest. The baby slept soundly with the soother touching her velvet pink cheeks, hand on pillow, a picture of purity. The woman heard a coughing noise coming from the nearby gun turret, and managed to see the tip of a rifle and a face peering out from the darkness. Smells of cabbage and burnt potatoes wafted over from behind the slanting sheets of protective steel.

"Is that your baby?" an English voice called out. She could barely see the face belonging to the voice. She replied yes, and smiled. The situation reminded her of the confessional. Dark and supposedly anonymous, "Is that you, my child?" She knew the priest personally. Did he identify her sins with his "Good morning, Mary," and think to himself, "and I know what you were up to last night!" She blushed at the secrets given away during the ceremony. Yes, she nervously answered again, it was her baby, a little girl. First-time mothers rarely resist the temptation to talk about their offspring. Forgetting her initial shyness, she told the voice of when the baby was born, the early problems of all-night crying, now teething, how she could crawl backwards and gurgle.

The voice responded. It too had a son, a few months older than her child, away in Germany at the army base at Munster. Factory pipes, chimney tops, church spires, domes all listened impassively to the Englishman's declaration of paternal love. The scene was strange, for although Belfast's sterile geography slipped into classical forms with dusk and heavy rain-clouds, the voice and the woman knew the folly of such innocent communication. They politely finished their conversation, said goodbye, and the woman pushed her pram homewards. The voice remained in the turret, watchful and anxious. Home she went, past vanloads of workers leering out at the pavement, past the uneasy presence of foot patrols, past the church. "Let us give each other the sign of peace," they said at Mass. The only sign Belfast knew was two fingers pointing towards Heaven. Life was self-contained, the couple often declared, just like flats. No need to go outside.

She did go outside, however. Each week the voice and the woman learned more of each other. No physical contact was needed, no face-to-face encounter to judge reaction, no touching to confirm amity, no threat of dangerous intimacy. It was a meeting of minds, as she explained later to her husband, a new opinion, a common bond, an opening of vistas. He disclosed his ambitions to become a pilot, to watch the land, fields and horizons spread out beneath him—a patchwork quilt of dappled colours and textures. She wanted to be remembered by writing on walls, about them that is, a world-shattering thesis on their psychological complexities, their essential truths, their witticisms and intellectual genius. And all the time the city's skyline and distant buildings watched and listened.

It was April now. More slogans had appeared, white and dripping, on the city walls. "Brits out. Peace in." A simple equation for the writer. "Loose talk claims lives," another shouted menacingly. The messages, the woman decided, had acquired a more ominous tone. The baby had grown and could sit up without support. New political solutions had been proposed and rejected, inter-paramilitary feuding had broken out and subsided, four soldiers and two policemen had been blown to smithereens in separate incidents, and a building a day had been bombed by the Provos. It had been a fairly normal month by Belfast's standards. The level of violence was no more or less acceptable than at other times.

One day—it was, perhaps, the last day in April—her husband returned home panting and trembling a little. He asked had she been to the park, and she replied she had. Taking her by the hand, he led her to the wall on the left of their driveway. She felt her heart sink and thud against her. She felt her face redden. Her mouth was suddenly dry. She could not speak. In huge angry letters the message spat itself out,

"TOUT."

The four-letter word covered the whole wall. It clanged in her brain, its venom rushed through her body. Suspicion was enough to condemn. The job itself was not well done, she had seen better. The letters were uneven, paint splattered down from the cross T, the U looked a misshapen O. The workmanship was poor, the impact perfect.

Her husband led her back into the kitchen. The baby was crying loudly in the living-room but the woman did not seem to hear. Like sleepwalkers, they sat down on the settee. The woman began to sob. Her shoulders heaved in bursts as she gasped hysterically. Her husband took her in his arms gently and tried to make her sorrow his. Already he shared her fear.

"What did you talk about? Did you not realise how dangerous it was? We must leave." He spoke quickly, making plans. Selling the house and car, finding a job in London or Dublin, far away from Belfast, mortgages, removals, savings, the tawdry affairs of normal living stunned her, making her more confused. "I told him nothing," she sobbed, "what could I tell? We talked about life, everything, but not about here." She trembled, trying to control herself. "We just chatted about reading walls, families, anything at all. Oh Sean, it was as innocent as that. A meeting of minds we called it, for it was little else."

She looked into her husband's face and saw he did not fully understand. There was a hint of jealousy, of resentment at not being part of their communication. Her hands fell on her lap, resting in resignation. What was the point of explanation? She lifted her baby from the floor. Pressing the tiny face and body to her breast, she felt all her hopes and desires for a better life become one with the child's struggle for freedom. The child's hands wandered over her face, their eyes met. At once that moment of maternal and filial love eclipsed her fear, gave her the impetus to escape.

For nine months she had been unable to accept the reality of her condition. Absurd, for the massive bump daily shifted position and thumped against her. When her daughter was born, she had been overwhelmed by love for her and amazed at her own ability to give life. By nature she was a dreamy person, given to moments of fancy. She wondered at her competence in fulfilling the role of mother. Could it be measured? This time she knew it could. She really did not care if they maimed her or even murdered her. She did care about her daughter. She was her touchstone, her anchor to virtue. Not for her child a legacy of fear, revulsion or hatred. With the few hours' respite the painters had left between judgement and sentence she determined to leave Belfast's walls behind.

The next few nights were spent in troubled, restless sleep. The message remained on the wall outside. The neighbours pretended not to notice and refused to discuss the matter. She and the baby remained indoors despite the refreshing May breezes and blue skies. Her husband had given in his notice at the office, for health reasons, he suggested to his colleagues. An aunt had been contacted in Dublin. The couple did not answer knocks at the door. They carefully examined the shape and size of mail delivered and always paused when they answered the telephone.

The mini-van was to call at eleven on Monday night, when it would be dark enough to park, and pack their belongings and themselves without too much suspicion being aroused. The firm had been very understanding when the nature of their work had been explained. They were Protestant so there was no conflict of loyalties involved in the exercise. They agreed to drive them to Dublin at extra cost, changing drivers at Newry on the way down.

Monday finally arrived. The couple nervously laughed about how smoothly everything had gone. Privately, they each expected something to go wrong. The baby was fed, and played with, the radio listened to and the clock watched. They listened to the news at nine. Huddled together in their anxiety, they kept vigil in the darkening room. Rain had begun to pour from black thunderclouds. Everywhere it was quiet and still. Hushed and cold they waited. Ten o'clock, and it was now dark. A blustery wind had risen, making the lattice separation next door bang and clatter. At ten to eleven, her husband went into the sitting-room to watch for the mini-van. His footsteps clamped noisily on the floorboards as he paced back and forth. The baby slept.

A black shape glided slowly up the street and backed into the driveway. It was eleven. The van had arrived. Her husband asked to see their identification and then they began to load up the couple's belongings. Settee, chairs, television, washing machine—all were dumped hastily, it was no time to worry about breakages. She stood holding the sleeping baby in the living-room as the men worked anxiously between van and house. The scene was so unreal, the circumstances absolutely incredible. She thought, "What have I done?" Recollections of her naivety, her insensibility to historical fact and political climate were stupefying. She had seen women who had been tarred and feathered, heard of people who had been shot in the head, boys who had been knee-capped, all for suspected fraternising with troops. The catalogue of violence spilled out before her and she realised the gravity and possible repercussions of her alleged misdemeanour.

A voice called her, "Mary, come on now. We have to go. Don't worry, we're all together." Her husband led her to the locked and waiting van.

Handing the baby to him, she climbed up beside the driver, took back the baby as her husband sat down beside her and waited for the engine to start. The van slowly manoeuvered out onto the street and down the main road. They felt more cheerful now, a little like refugees seeking safety and freedom not too far away. As they approached the motorway bridge, two figures with something clutched in their hands stood side by side in the darkness. She closed her eyes tightly, expecting bursts of gunfire. The van shot past. Relieved, she asked her husband what they were doing at this time of night. "Writing slogans on the wall," he replied.

The furtiveness of the painters seemed ludicrous and petty as she recalled the heroic and literary characteristics with which she had endowed them. What did they matter? The travellers sat in silence as the van sped past the city suburbs, the glare of police and army barracks, on out and further out into the countryside. Past sleeping villages and silent fields, past whitewashed farmhouses and barking dogs. On to Newry where they said goodbye to their driver as the new one stepped in. Far along the coast with Rostrevor's twinkling lights opposite the bay down to the Border check and a drowsy soldier waving them through. Out of the North, safe, relieved and heading for Dublin.

Some days later in Belfast the neighbours discovered the house vacant, the people next door received a letter and a cheque from Dublin. Remarks about the peculiar couple were made over hedges and cups of coffee. The message on the wall was painted over by the couple who had bought the house when it went up for sale. They too were ordinary people, living a self-contained life, worrying over finance and babies, promotion and local gossip. He too had an office job, but his wife was merely a housekeeper for him. She was sensible, down to earth, and not in the least inclined to wall-reading.

---

the "Provos": the militant wing of the Provisional Irish Republican Army (IRA) who support the Catholic cause

"reader of walls": see Robert Frost's poem, "Mending Wall"

Saracen: an armoured car

TOUT: (rhymes with "out") in this story the word seems to mean "spy" or "traitor"

the "Troubles": since 1968, violent unrest between Catholics and Protestants in Northern Ireland; the British army is stationed there in an attempt to keep peace

War

TIMOTHY FINDLEY

What can a child understand about war? Both too little and too much.

That's my dad in the middle. We were just kids then, Bud on the right and me on the left. That was taken just before my dad went into the army.

Some day that was.

It was a Saturday, two years ago. August, 1940. I can remember I had to blow my nose just before that and I had to use my dad's hankie because mine had a worm in it that I was saving. I can't remember why; I mean, why I was saving that worm, but I can remember why I had to blow my nose, all right. That was because I'd had a long time crying. Not exactly because my dad was going away or anything—it was mostly because I'd done something.

I'll tell you what in a minute, but I just want to say this first. I was ten years old then and it was sort of the end of summer. When we went back to school I was going into the fifth grade and that was pretty important, especially for me because I'd skipped grade four. Right now I can't even remember grade five except that I didn't like it. I should have gone to grade four. In grade five everyone was a genius and there was a boy called Allan McKenzie.

Anyway, now that you know how old I was and what grade I was into, I can tell you the rest.

It was the summer the war broke out and I went to stay with my friend, Arthur Robertson. Looking back on it, Arthur seems a pretty silly name for Arthur Robertson because he was so small. But he was a nice kid and his dad had the most enormous summer cottage you've ever seen. In Muskoka, too.

It was like those houses they have in the movies in Beverly Hills. Windows a mile long—pine trees outside and then a lake and then a red canoe tied up with a yellow rope. There was an Indian, too, who sold little boxes made of birch-bark and porcupine quills. Arthur

Robertson and I used to sit in the red canoe and this Indian would take us for a ride out to the raft and back. Then we'd go and tell Mrs Robertson or the cook or someone how nice he was and he'd stand behind us and smile as though he didn't understand English and then they'd have to buy a box from him. He certainly was smart, that Indian, because it worked about four times. Then one day they caught on and hid the canoe.

Anyway, that's the sort of thing we did. And we swam too, and I remember a book that Arthur Robertson's nurse read to us. It was about dogs.

Then I had to go away because I'd only been invited for two weeks. I went on to this farm where the family took us every summer when we were children. Bud was already there, and his friend, Teddy Hartley.

I didn't like Teddy Hartley. It was because he had a space between his teeth and he used to spit through it. Once I saw him spit two-and-a-half yards. Bud paced it out. And then he used to whistle through it, too, that space, and it was the kind of whistling that nearly made your ears bleed. That was what I didn't like. But it didn't really matter, because he was Bud's friend, not mine.

So I went by train and Mr and Mrs Currie met me in their truck. It was their farm.

Mrs Currie got me into the front with her while Mr Currie put my stuff in the back.

"Your mum and dad aren't here, dear, but they'll be up tomorrow. Buddy is here—and his friend."

Grownups were always calling Bud "Buddy." It was all wrong.

I didn't care too much about my parents not being there, except that I'd brought them each one of those birch-bark boxes. Inside my mother's there was a set of red stones I'd picked out from where we swam. I thought maybe she'd make a necklace out of them. In my dad's there was an old golf ball, because he played golf. I guess you'd have to say I stole it, because I didn't tell anyone I had it—but it was just lying there on a shelf in Mr Robertson's boathouse, and he never played golf. At least I never saw him.

I had these boxes on my lap because I'd thought my mum and dad would be there to meet me, but now that they weren't I put them into the glove compartment of the truck.

We drove to the farm.

Bud and Teddy were riding on the gate, and they waved when we drove past. I couldn't see too well because of the dust but I could hear them shouting. It was something about my dad. I didn't really hear exactly what it was they said, but Mrs Currie went white as a sheet and said: "Be quiet," to Bud.

Then we were there and the truck stopped. We went inside.

And now—this is where it begins.

After supper, the evening I arrived at the Curries' farm, my brother Bud and his friend Teddy Hartley and I all sat on the front porch. In a hammock.

This is the conversation we had.

BUD: (to me) Are you all right? Did you have a good time at Arthur Robertson's place? Did you swim?

ME: (to Bud) Yes.

TEDDY HARTLEY: I've got a feeling I don't like Arthur Robertson. Do I know him?

BUD: Kid at school. Neil's age. (He said that as if it were dirty to be my age.)

TEDDY HARTLEY: Thin kid? Very small?

BUD: Thin and small—brainy type. Hey Neil, have you seen Ted spit?

ME: Yes—I have.

TEDDY HARTLEY: When did you see me spit? (Indignant as hell) I never spat for you.

ME: Yes, you did. About three months ago. We were still in school. Bud—he did too, and you walked it out, too, didn't you?

BUD: I don't know.

TEDDY HARTLEY: I never spat for you yet! Never!

ME: Two yards and a half.

TEDDY HARTLEY: Can't have been me. I spit four.

ME: Four YARDS!!

TEDDY HARTLEY: Certainly.

BUD: Go ahead and show him. Over the rail.

TEDDY HARTLEY: (Standing up) Okay. Look, Neil. Now watch . . . Come on, WATCH!!

ME: All right—I'm watching.

(Teddy Hartley spat. It was three yards-and-a-half by Bud's feet. I saw Bud mark it myself.)

BUD: Three yards and a half a foot.

TEDDY HARTLEY: Four yards. (Maybe his feet were smaller or something.)

BUD: Three-and-foot. Three and *one* foot. No, no. A *half*-a-one. Of a foot.

TEDDY HARTLEY: Four.

BUD: Three!

TEDDY HARTLEY: Four! Four! Four!

BUD: Three! One-two-three-and-a-half-a-foot!!

TEDDY HARTLEY: My dad showed me. It's four! He showed me, and he knows. My dad knows. He's a mathematical teacher—yes, yes, yes, he showed me how to count a yard. I saw him do it. And he knows, my dad!!

BUD: Your dad's a crazy man. It's three yards and a half a foot.

TEDDY HARTLEY: (All red in the face and screaming) You called my dad a nut! You called my dad a crazy-man-nut-meg! Take it back, you. Bud Cable, you take that back.

BUD: Your dad is a matha-nut-ical nutmeg tree.

TEDDY HARTLEY: Then your dad's a . . . your dad's a . . . your dad's an Insane!

BUD: Our dad's joined the army.

That was how I found out.

They went on talking like that for a long time. I got up and left. I started talking to myself, which is a habit I have.

"Joined the army? Joined the army? Joined the ARMY! Our dad?"

Our dad was a salesman. I used to go to his office and watch him selling things over the phone sometimes. I always used to look for what it was, but I guess they didn't keep it around the office. Maybe they hid it somewhere. Maybe it was too expensive to just leave lying around. But whatever it was, I knew it was important, and so that was one thing that bothered me when Bud said about the army—because I knew that in the army they wouldn't let my dad sit and sell things over any old phone—because in the army you always went in a trench and got hurt or killed. I knew that because my dad had told me himself when my uncle died. My uncle was his brother in the first war, who got hit in his stomach and he died from it a long time afterwards. Long enough, anyway, for me to have known him. He was always in a big white bed, and he gave us candies from a glass jar. That was all I knew—except that it was because of being in the army that he died. His name was Uncle Frank.

So those were the first two things I thought of: my dad not being able to sell anything any more—and then Uncle Frank.

But then it really got bad, because I suddenly remembered that my dad had promised to teach me how to skate that year. He was going to make a rink too; in the back yard. But if he had to go off to some old trench in France, then he'd be too far away. Soldiers always went in trenches—and trenches were always in France. I remember that.

Well, I don't know. Maybe I just couldn't forgive him. He hadn't even told me. He didn't even write it in his letter that he'd sent me at Arthur Robertson's. But he'd told Bud—he'd told Bud, but I was the one he'd promised to show how to skate. And I'd had it all planned how I'd really surprise my dad and turn out to be a skating champion and everything, and now he wouldn't even be there to see.

All because he had to go and sit in some trench.

I don't know how I got there, but I ended up in the barn. I was in the hayloft and I didn't even hear them, I guess. They were looking all over the place for me, because it started to get dark.

I don't know whether you're afraid of the dark, but I'll tell you right now, I am. At least, I am if I have to move around in it. If I can just sit still, then I'm all right. At least, if you sit still you know where you are. And that's awful. You never know what you're going to step on next and I always thought it would be a duck. I don't like ducks— especially in the dark or if you stepped on them.

Anyway, I was in the hayloft in the barn and I heard them calling out—"Neil, Neil"—and "Where are you?" But I made up my mind right then I wasn't going to answer. For one thing, if I did, then I'd have to go down to them in the dark—and maybe I'd step on something. And for another, I didn't really want to see anyone anyway.

It was then that I got this idea about my father. I thought that maybe if I stayed hidden for long enough, then he wouldn't join the army. Don't ask me why—right now I couldn't tell you that—but in those days it made sense. If I hid then he wouldn't go away. Maybe it would be because he'd stay looking for me or something.

The trouble was that my dad wasn't even there that night, and that meant that I either had to wait in the hayloft till he came the next day—or else that I had to go down now, and then hide again tomorrow. I decided to stay where I was because there were some ducks at the bottom of the ladder. I couldn't see them but I could tell they were there.

I stayed there all night. I slept most of the time. Every once in a while they'd wake me up by calling out "Neil! Neil!"—but I never answered.

I never knew a night that was so long, except maybe once when I was in the hospital. When I slept I seemed to sleep for a long time, but it never came to morning. They kept waking me up but it was never time.

Then it was.

I saw that morning through a hole in the roof of the hayloft. The sunlight came in through cracks between the boards and it was all dusty; the sunlight, I mean.

They were up pretty early that morning, even for farmers. There seemed to be a lot more people than I remembered—and there were two or three cars and a truck I'd never seen before, too. And I saw Mrs Currie holding onto Bud with one hand and Teddy Hartley with the other. I remember thinking, "If I was down there, how could she hold onto me if she's only got two hands and Bud and Teddy Hartley to look after?" And I thought that right then she must be pretty glad I wasn't around.

I wondered what they were all doing. Mr Currie was standing in the middle of a lot of men and he kept pointing out the scenery around the farm. I imagined what he was saying. There was a big woods behind the house and a cherry and plum-tree orchard that would be good to point out to his friends. I could tell they were his friends from the way they were listening. What I couldn't figure out was why they were all up so early—and why they had Bud and Teddy Hartley up, too.

Then there was a police car. I suppose it came from Orillia or somewhere. That was the biggest town near where the farm was. Orillia.

When the policemen got out of their car, they went up to Mr Currie. There were four of them. They all talked for quite a long time and then everyone started going out in all directions. It looked to me as though Bud and Teddy Hartley wanted to go, too, but Mrs Currie made them go in the house. She practically had to drag Bud. It looked as if he was crying and I wondered why he should do that.

Then one of the policemen came into the barn. He was all alone. I stayed very quiet, because I wasn't going to let anything keep me from going through with my plan about my dad. Not even a policeman.

He urinated against the wall inside the door. It was sort of funny, because he kept turning around to make sure no one saw him, and he didn't know I was there. Then he did up his pants and stood in the middle of the floor under the haylofts.

"Hey! Neil!"

That was the policeman.

He said it so suddenly that it scared me. I nearly fell off from where

I was, it scared me so much. And I guess maybe he saw me, because he started right up the ladder at me.

"How did you know my name?"

I said that in a whisper.

"They told me."

"Oh."

"Have you been here all night?"

"Yes."

"Don't you realize that *everyone* has been looking for you all over the place? Nobody's even been to sleep."

That sort of frightened me—but it was all right, because he smiled when he said it.

Then he stuck his head out of this window that was there to let the air in (so that the barn wouldn't catch on fire)—and he yelled down, "He's all right—I've found him! He's up here."

And I said: "What did you go and do that for? Now you've ruined everything."

He smiled again and said, "I had to stop them all going off to look for you. Now,"—as he sat down beside me—"do you want to tell me what is it you're doing up here?"

"No."

I think that sort of set him back a couple of years, because he didn't say anything for a minute—except "Oh."

Then I thought maybe I had to have something to tell the others anyway, so I might as well make it up for him right now.

"I fell asleep," I said.

"When—last night?"

"Yes."

I looked at him. I wondered if I could trust a guy who did that against walls, when all you had to do was go in the house.

"Why did you come up here in the first place?" he said.

I decided I could trust him because I remembered once when I did the same thing. Against the wall.

So I told him.

"I want to hide on my dad," I said.

"Why do you want to do that? And besides, Mrs Currie said your parents weren't even here."

"Yes, but he's coming today."

"But why hide on him? Don't you like him, or something?"

"Sure I do," I said.

I thought about it.

"But he's . . . he's . . . Do you know if it's true, my dad's joined the army?"

"I dunno. Maybe. There's a war on, you know."

"Well, that's why I hid."

But he laughed.

"Is that why you hid? Because of the war?"

"Because of my dad."

"You don't need to hide because of the war—the Germans aren't coming over here, you know."

"But it's not that. It's my dad." I could have told you he wouldn't understand.

I was trying to think of what to say next when Mrs Currie came into the barn. She stood down below.

"Is he up there, officer? Is he all right?"

"Yes, ma'am, I've got him. He's fine."

"Neil dear, what happened? Why don't you come down and tell us what happened to you?"

Then I decided that I'd really go all out. I had to, because I could tell they weren't going to—it was just *obvious* that these people weren't going to understand me and take my story about my dad and the army and everything.

"Somebody chased me."

The policeman looked sort of shocked and I could hear Mrs Currie take in her breath.

"Somebody chased you, eh?"

"Yes."

"Who?"

I had to think fast.

"Some man. But he's gone now."

I thought I'd better say he was gone, so that they wouldn't start worrying.

"Officer, why don't you bring him down here? Then we can talk."

"All right, ma'am. Come on, Neil, we'll go down and have some breakfast."

They didn't seem to believe me about that man I made up.

We went over to the ladder.

I looked down. A lot of hay stuck out so that I couldn't see the floor.

"Are there any ducks down there?"

"No, dear, you can come down—it's all right."

She was lying, though. There was a great big duck right next to her. I think it's awfully silly to tell a lie like that. I mean, if the duck is standing right there it doesn't even make sense, does it?

But I went down anyway and she made the duck go away.

When we went out, the policeman held my hand. His hand had some sweat on it but it was a nice hand, with hair on the back. I liked that. My dad didn't have that on his hand.

Then we ate breakfast with all those people who'd come to look for me. At least, they ate. I just sat.

After breakfast, Mr and Mrs Currie took me upstairs to the sitting room. It was upstairs because the kitchen was in the cellar.

All I remember about that was a vase that had a potted plant in it. This vase was made of putty and into the putty Mrs Currie had stuck all kinds of stones and pennies and old bits of glass and things. You could look at this for hours and never see the same kind of stone or glass twice. I don't remember the plant.

All I remember about what they said was that they told me I should never do it again. That routine.

Then they told me my mother and my dad would be up that day around lunch time.

What they were really sore about was losing their sleep, and then all those people coming. I was sorry about that—but you can't very well go down and make an announcement about it, so I didn't.

At twelve o'clock I went and sat in Mr Currie's truck. It was in the barn. I took out those two boxes I'd put in the glove compartment and looked at them. I tried to figure out what my dad would do with an old box like that in the army. And he'd probably never play another game of golf as long as he lived. Not in the army, anyway. Maybe he'd use the box for his bullets or something.

Then I counted the red stones I was going to give my mother. I kept seeing them around her neck and how pretty they'd be. She had a dress they'd be just perfect with. Blue. The only thing I was worried about was how to get a hole in them so you could put them on a string. There wasn't much sense in having beads without a string—not if you were going to wear them, anyway—or your mother was.

And it was then that they came.

I heard their car drive up outside and I went and looked from behind the barn door. My father wasn't wearing a uniform yet like I'd thought he would be. I began to think maybe he really didn't want me to know about it. I mean, he hadn't written or anything, and now he was just wearing an old blazer and some gray pants. It made me remember.

I went back and sat down in the truck again. I didn't know what to do. I just sat there with those stones in my hand.

Then I heard someone shout, "Neil!"

I went and looked. Mr and Mrs Currie were standing with my parents by the car—and I saw Bud come running out of the house, and then Teddy Hartley. Teddy Hartley sort of hung back, though. He was the kind of person who's only polite if there are grownups around him. He sure knew how to pull the wool over their eyes, because he'd even combed his hair. Wildroot-cream-oil-Charlie.

Then I noticed that they were talking very seriously and my mother put her hand above her eyes and looked around. I guess she was looking for me. Then my dad started toward the barn.

I went and hid behind the truck. I wasn't quite sure yet what I was going to do, but I certainly wasn't going to go up and throw my arms around his neck or anything.

"Neil. Are you in there, son?"

My dad spoke that very quietly. Then I heard the door being pushed open, and some chicken had to get out of the way, because I heard it making that awful noise chickens make when you surprise them doing something. They sure can get excited over nothing—chickens.

I took a quick look behind me. There was a door there that led into the part of the barn where the haylofts were and where I'd been all night. I decided to make a dash for it. But I had to ward off my father first—and so I threw that stone.

I suppose I'll have to admit that I meant to hit him. It wouldn't be much sense if I tried to fool you about that. I wanted to hit him because when I stood up behind the truck and saw him then I suddenly got mad. I thought about how he hadn't written me, or anything.

It hit him on the hand.

He turned right around because he wasn't sure what it was or where it came from. And before I ran, I just caught a glimpse of his face. He'd seen me and he sure looked peculiar. I guess that now I'll never forget his face and how he looked at me right then. I think it was that he looked as though he might cry or something. But I knew he wouldn't do that, because he never did.

Then I ran.

From the loft I watched them in the yard. My dad was rubbing his hands together and I guess maybe where I'd hit him it was pretty sore. My mother took off her handkerchief that she had round her neck and put it on his hand. Then I guess he'd told them what I'd done, because this time they *all* started toward the barn.

I didn't know what to do then. I counted out the stones I had left and there were about fifteen of them. There was the golf ball, too.

I didn't want to throw stones at all of them. I certainly didn't want to hit my mother—and I hoped that they wouldn't send her in first. I thought then how I'd be all right if they sent in Teddy Hartley first. I didn't mind the thought of throwing at him, I'll tell you that much.

But my dad came first.

I had a good view of where he came from. He came in through the part where the truck was parked, because I guess he thought I was still there. And then he came on into the part where I was now—in the hayloft.

He stood by the door.

"Neil."

I could only just see his head and shoulders—the rest of him was hidden by the edge of the loft.

"Neil, aren't you even going to explain what you're angry about?"

I thought for a minute and then I didn't answer him after all. I looked at him, though. He looked worried.

"What do you want us to do?"

I sat still.

"Neil?"

Since I didn't answer, he started back out the door—I guess to talk to my mother or someone.

I hit his back with another stone. I had to make sure he knew I was there.

He turned around at me.

"Neil, what's the matter? I want to know what's the matter."

He almost fooled me, but not quite. I thought that perhaps he really didn't know for a minute—but after taking a look at him I decided that he did know, all right. I mean, there he was in that blue blazer and everything—just as if he hadn't joined the army at all.

So I threw again and this time it really hit him in the face.

He didn't do anything—he just stood there. It really scared me. Then my mother came in, but he made her go back.

I thought about my rink, and how I wouldn't have it. I thought about being in the fifth grade that year and how I'd skipped from grade three. And I thought about the Indian who'd sold those boxes that I had down in the truck.

"Neil—I'm going to come up."

You could tell he really would, too, from his voice.

I got the golf ball ready.

To get to me he had to disappear for a minute while he crossed under the loft and then when he climbed the ladder. I decided to change my place while he was out of sight. I began to think that was pretty clever and that maybe I'd be pretty good at that war stuff myself. Field Marshal Cable.

I put myself into a little trench of hay and piled some up in front of me. When my dad came up over the top of the ladder, he wouldn't even see me and then I'd have a good chance to aim at him.

The funny thing was that at that moment I'd forgotten why I was against him. I got so mixed up in all that Field Marshal stuff that I really forgot all about my dad and the army and everything. I was just trying to figure out how I could get him before he saw me—and that was all.

I got further down in the hay and then he was there.

He was out of breath and his face was all sweaty, and where I'd hit him there was blood. And then he put his hand with my mother's hankie up to his face to wipe it. And he sort of bit it (the handkerchief). It was as if he was confused or something. I remember thinking he looked then just like I'd felt my face go when Bud had said our dad had joined the army. You know how you look around with your eyes from side to side as though maybe you'll find the answer to it somewhere near you? You never do find it, but you always look anyway, just in case.

Anyway, that's how he was just then, and it sort of threw me. I had that feeling again that maybe he didn't know what this was all about. But then, he had to know, didn't he? Because he'd done it.

I had the golf ball ready in my right hand and one of those stones in the other. He walked toward me.

I missed with the golf ball and got him with the stone.

And he fell down. He really fell down. He didn't say anything—he didn't even say "ouch," like I would have—he just fell down.

In the hay.

I didn't go out just yet. I sat and looked at him. And I listened.

Nothing.

Do you know, there wasn't a sound in that whole place? It was as if everything had stopped because they knew what had happened.

My dad just lay there and we waited for what would happen next.

It was me.

I mean, I made the first noise.

I said: "Dad?"

But nobody answered—not even my mother.

So I said it louder. "*Dad*?"

It was just as if they'd all gone away and left me with him, all alone.

He sure looked strange lying there—so quiet and everything. I didn't know what to do.

"Dad?"

I went over on my hands and knees.

Then suddenly they all came in. I just did what I thought of first. I guess it was because they scared me—coming like that when it was so quiet.

I got all the stones out of my pockets and threw them, one by one, as they came through the door. I stood up to do it. I saw them all running through the door, and I threw every stone, even at my mother.

And then I fell down. I fell down beside my dad and pushed him over on his back because he'd fallen on his stomach. It was like he was asleep.

They came up then and I don't remember much of that. Somebody picked me up, and there was the smell of perfume and my eyes hurt and I got something in my throat and nearly choked to death and I could hear a lot of talking. And somebody was whispering, too. And then I felt myself being carried down and there was the smell of oil and gasoline and some chickens had to be got out of the way again and then there was sunlight.

Then my mother just sat with me, and I guess I cried for a long time. In the cherry and plum-tree orchard—and she seemed to understand because she said that he would tell me all about it and that he hadn't written me because he didn't want to scare me when I was all alone at Arthur Robertson's.

And then Bud came.

My mother said that he should go away for a while. But he said: "I brought something" and she said: "What is it, then?" and now I remember where I got that worm in my handkerchief that I told you about.

It was from Bud.

He said to me that if I wanted to, he'd take me fishing on the lake just before the sun went down. He said that was a good time. And he gave me that worm because he'd found it.

So my mother took it and put it in my hankie and Bud looked at me for a minute and then went away.

The worst part was when I saw my dad again.

My mother took me to the place where he was sitting in the sun and we just watched each other for a long time.

Then he said: "Neil, your mother wants to take our picture because I'm going away tomorrow to Ottawa for a couple of weeks, and she thought I'd like a picture to take with me."

He lit a cigarette and then he said: "I would, too, you know, like that picture."

And I sort of said: "All right."

So they called to Bud, and my mother went to get her camera.

But before Bud came and before my mother got back, we were alone for about ten hours. It was awful.

I couldn't think of anything and I guess he couldn't either. I had a good look at him, though.

He looked just like he does right there in that picture. You can see where the stone hit him on his right cheek—and the one that knocked him out is the one over the eye.

Right then the thing never got settled. Not in words, anyway. I was still thinking about that rink and everything—and my dad hadn't said anything about the army yet.

I wish I hadn't done it. Thrown those stones and everything. It wasn't his fault he had to go.

For another thing, I was sorry about the stones because I knew I wouldn't find any more like them—but I did throw them, and that's that.

They both got those little boxes, though—I made sure of that. And in one there was a string of red beads from Orillia and in the other there was a photograph.

There still is.

Mother, I'm Hungry

YU KWANG-CHUNG

Mother, I'm hungry,
But I cannot swallow.
Such a bitter taste
Chokes my throat all day long:
How can I swallow?

Mother, I'm tired,
But I cannot sleep.
Such a heavy feeling
Weighs on my chest all night long:
How can I sleep?

Mother, I'm dead,
But I'm not resigned.
Such a tortured country
Brands my soul forever;
How can I give up?

Mother, I'm gone.
On Tomb-Sweeping Day
Come back to recall my soul
In democratic years
In Tienanmen Square.

Translated by the poet

Tomb-Sweeping Day is a Chinese festival in spring when family members gather to attend the tomb of the deceased and offer sacrifice.

Tienanmen Square: A Soldier's Story

NIE JIAN-GUO

When soldiers fired on the protesters in Tienanmen Square, the whole world was shocked—the Chinese perhaps most of all. After all, their army was the people's army. An ex-soldier explains why the military acted as they did.

H ow could the People's Liberation Army attack us, the citizens of Beijing?"

"Never in the history of China have the Army's tanks been turned against the Chinese people!"

"Our leaders are like fathers, and the soldiers are like uncles to us—how could they betray us?"

These and many other expressions of shock echoed throughout Beijing the morning after the violent suppression of demonstrations for political freedom in Tienanmen Square on June 4, 1989. After fifty days of jubilant protest by students and workers, many of whom had set up squatters' housing in the square, the demonstration had become the focus of international attention and an embarrassment to the Chinese leaders. Whatever the degree of dissent in the square, however, whatever level of anger the Party leaders might have felt toward the demonstrators, no one believed it possible that the Army would open fire on their own.

Days after that very occurrence, I stood watching the troops marching across the now depopulated square. My mind turned back to the early days of the protest.

Even then I had an uneasy premonition of the violence to come. And when I first spoke with my father about the demonstration, that uneasiness grew. As a retired Army general who had devoted his entire life to the Party and the revolution, Father regarded anyone who questioned the Party as a counter-revolutionary. In his view, the students and workers in the square were intent on dismantling everything he

and his comrades had striven to create for more than fifty years. He listened with tight-lipped disapproval as I described what was happening at Tienanmen.

I knew his attitudes to be in keeping with those of his generation, a reflection of the resentment harbored toward the demonstrators by the gerontocracy in power. My father could not accept the idea that the protesters might be seeking a new vision for China. For him, the issue was black and white: The demonstrators did not respect those who had sacrificed everything for this same China, for the sake of *these very demonstrators* and their happiness. If they respected all that had been done on their behalf, he reasoned, those rebels would not now be embarrassing the Party. I felt my enthusiasm evaporate in the face of his obvious displeasure.

The days wore on and the demonstration flourished. Many became increasingly hopeful that political change and new political freedoms would come peacefully to China. I continued to visit my father, but we found less and less to say to each other.

One night the lights in the square were turned off. No one knew what to make of it. Tanks and armored personnel carriers rolled into the square. Soldiers began firing on the dissenting citizens of Beijing, some of whom were in their makeshift tents. The soldiers, some fresh from the provinces, many with a wild roving fear, fired into the unarmed crowd and people scattered, tripping in the darkness as they tried to escape. People were shaken and stunned. Their assumptions about the Army's role as protector of the people were shattered as surely as the demonstration was brutally overrun. China was a family at war with itself, and Tienanmen was the dragon biting its own tail. But that circular motion of frustration was the outcome of a process that had other beginnings.

Standing now looking at the square, I thought about the soldiers of Tienanmen. I recognized their uniforms, every button and seam; I knew the shape, weight, and capability of their automatic weapons; many times over I had heard the command that caused them to fire. I, too, had once been a soldier in the People's Liberation Army.

I still remember clearly the morning I said good-bye to my father and set off to join the Army. I was all of fourteen. Father had held a high position in the government but had been criticized during the Cultural Revolution and had been sent to the countryside to do manual labor. For a similar reason, Mother had been sent for re-education to a village more than forty miles away. Father and I were living alone in a small hut on a hill overgrown with weeds.

I walked into the hut, pack on my back, to say good-bye. My father was sitting there on the dilapidated bed with a gloomy look on his face. I felt for the first time that I stood before him as a man. I was going to join the Army, his Army, leaving home as he had done more than thirty years earlier.

It was a great day for me. For my generation, which came of age in the 1970s, to become a soldier in the Army and serve the Party was the noblest ideal. Catching a lift on a truck heading toward the train station, I was filled with the passionate certainty that I had taken the first step on the road to my destiny.

Five nights later I was hundreds of miles away, on Shanxi road in Nanjing, in a fashionable neighborhood where high officials lived. I stood on the porch of one of my father's old wartime comrades, a general and a chief of staff to the commander of the Nanjing military district. Fingering the letter of introduction that my father had written for me, I nervously rang the bell. The guard who answered the door told me that the general and his family were at the theatre. I told him the reason for my visit, but he closed the door on me. I sat down beside the door and fell asleep.

I don't know how much time passed before I was jolted awake by a shout. The general and his family had returned home to find someone sitting in the shadows near the door. Thinking I might be an assassin, the general's bodyguard had immediately drawn his gun. Later that night the general apologized and explained that another high official, someone who had been on the wrong side of the political struggle between Chairman Mao and Marshal Lin Biao, had only recently been assassinated in his home.

The general took me with him to military district headquarters a few days later. We walked into the main building, which looked more like a mansion than an office, with its hardwood tables and chairs and comfortable sofas. Another officer arrived with two teenaged boys, also sons of the general's wartime companions. The general had arranged for all three of us to join the Army together.

The general had personally inducted the sons of so many high-level cadres and military officials that they could form an entire company. During the conscription season at the beginning of each year his home was filled with them. The general was a man who valued friendship. In those days there was no better way to prove his friendship than to assist people's children into the Army. Perhaps in the complex web of human relationships it was one of the most important routes of official-dom in China.

The unit I joined was directly attached to the Nanjing military district, and my camp was situated about twenty-five miles southeast of Nanjing. I was introduced to the staff officer, a heavyset man with a kind, avuncular attitude toward his men. He politely asked me what I wanted to do. I said anything at all would be fine: menial duties, cooking, raising pigs. If only I could be a soldier and fight the Russians and Americans, I said, any amount of misery or fatigue wouldn't matter. He looked both surprised and pleased.

He asked me my age. I lied and said that I was sixteen. He thought for a moment and decided to send me to Company X. That was his old outfit, he told me, and I knew from this assignment that he liked me. He summoned a soldier, who escorted me to the company barracks. I was delighted. I was finally a soldier.

In China to say, "I was a soldier" is like saying, "I can take hardship." Not only is military life tense, but the training is primitive and spartan. Chinese soldiers have a saying, "If you sweat a lot in ordinary times, you bleed less in wartime." The principles of training serve to increase the pressure and hardships that the soldier is able to tolerate. This better equips him for war.

Military life was very strictly regulated. Our clothing, the length of our hair, the way we walked, the respect we showed to senior officers—all were specifically regulated. Everyone got up, trained, ate, and went to bed at the same time. If it was not time for lights out, you could not even touch the side of your bed.

Every morning at 5:00 a.m. we would be awakened by a bugle reveille. I would leap out of bed, throw on my shirt, button it up, pull on my trousers and button them up, and then fasten my belt as I rushed out of the room. If I were fast enough there would be time to pee in the big vat around which a line of men had already formed; otherwise I'd have to hold it in while we did our morning run of four to five miles. Needless to say, that was not easy.

Later I became more experienced. When I heard the wake-up signal I pulled on my shirt, trousers, and hat, hung my battle gear around my neck, and raced out of the barracks, buttoning and straightening my uniform as I ran. That way, I wouldn't be late.

Antitank training was an important part of our military training. In those days, when all we had at our disposal were firebombs, hand grenades, and bazookas, we also had a saying: "A squad should swap their equipment and lives to disable an enemy tank." We practised different means of getting close enough to a tank—sometimes even running up to it—to be able to blow it up. Our drills included even more primitive practices such as throwing Molotov cocktails or inserting wooden poles in the tread of a tank to stop it.

It was felt that by using these tactics we could sap the enemy's strength and stop his advance. Like everyone else, I resolved to sacrifice my life for this purpose. Diagrams of the Soviet T62 and the American M1 tanks were posted all over the camp, so all of the soldiers were acquainted with their capabilities and firepower.

In 1970, the year I entered the army, a special effort was made to upgrade the fighting capacity of the troops. The military units set up special training groups called "guidance teams." The members were selected from the technical core of each company, who were given intensive training so that they could return to their units and serve as trainers. I was chosen to be on a regimental guidance team.

Our squad instructor was as strong as an ox and swarthy, brainless but knowledgeable about military technology, an old pro. He had fought in the Civil War. His military record was good, but because he was not educated, he was never promoted. He didn't care a whit about the political discussions bandied about the camp, and it didn't seem to matter to him with whom he was fighting. As long as there was fighting and he had a part in it, he was satisfied.

He was very demanding of the men on his team. He would often point out a high hill and order us to use tactics to secure it within a given number of minutes. When we practised shooting from a prone position, he made us crawl in the hot sun for several hours. If someone got tired and tried to sneak in a little shifting movement, he would give him a swift kick. When he ordered us to charge forward and dive to the ground, he wanted us to dive very fast and continue to slide headlong for a few yards, since that was the only way he could determine our speed. The skin on my knees and elbows would be scraped off, but as he said, the speed with which you can get down is critical on the battlefield, because losing a few seconds could cost your life. He taught us: "To be a good soldier you should stand like a pine tree and sit like a grandfather clock, awe-inspiring and stern." I learned quite a lot about fighting from him.

One of the things I liked least was being taken out of camp to live and train in the open. This type of training began in 1970, when Mao Zedong observed that during the Civil War he himself had never stayed in a military camp. He ordered the Army to train in the wilderness so that we would be tough in time of war.

Thus it happened that every winter all field armies held large-scale maneuvers. Each day we normally marched 20 to 25 miles, sometimes more. Every man had to carry his gun, four hand grenades, more than 100 bullets, a small iron shovel, several pounds of dry rice, and a canteen. In addition we carried a satchel containing a military comforter, a change of uniform, and a pair of rubber-soled shoes. A raincoat that doubled as a tarpaulin was tied to the top of our pack. Taken together, this equipment weighed between 85 and 100 pounds. We also had to take turns carrying the ammunition crates.

These marches involved crossing mountain roads and dirt roads. Sometimes there was no road at all. When crossing mountainous regions we had to use our arms and legs like gorillas, taking a step and then grabbing a tree, or crawling up a cliff.

Hiking at night was particularly dangerous, especially when it was raining in the mountains. All lights were forbidden in order to guard against aerial reconnaissance, so you could only follow the sound of the feet ahead of you and rely on your senses. Slipping and sliding in the mud, I would grit my teeth at every pace, never sure where I might put my foot down.

One night I heard a sloshing sound ahead of me. I reached out and grabbed at what I could, a foot that had slipped, and I slid after it. The file of men ahead of us had made a turn before a precipice, but the soldier in front of me had not seen it and had kept going straight. Three or four of us fell off the cliff with him into a wet rice paddy.

We usually developed bleeding blisters on our feet after a few days of this kind of hiking. Our feet were a mass of soggy peeling flesh and blood, and the pain was almost unbearable. Empty vehicles followed after us, and anyone who wanted to could get a lift, but very few chose to. We considered the physical challenge a means of tempering ourselves for the sake of the Party. That attitude was encouraged by the political cadres, who walked back and forth among the ranks exhorting us: "This is the point at which the Party is testing you." In that kind of situation, no one wanted to look bad.

After walking for ten hours, my pack and the gun on my shoulder seemed to weigh a thousand pounds. My feet felt as if they had been cast in lead. Every step took great effort. My greatest desire was to lie down and rest, even if it was raining or snowing, even if it meant that I would die. Several times I started to doze off; the man behind me would bump into me and wake me up.

Of course, when we had reached our goal we still could not rest. We had to build fortifications, make camouflage, set up a communications system, and in all respects prepare ourselves to fight a battle. It was exhausting.

Once when a platoon commander was trying to make a telephone call the female operator asked why he was so short of breath. He answered grumpily, "We've just marched more than 30 miles; who wouldn't be short of breath?" Later he was reprimanded because of that one sentence: A revolutionary soldier should not care how much he has endured; he must never complain.

We were also required to devote a lot of time to political studies. Our texts were Mao's writings as well as editorials from the official newspapers. Each company had lessons in basic political terms and information, which we were usually required to memorize. When I joined the army the influence of the Cultural Revolution was still strong, and every evening we lined up under Mao's portrait. The squad leader would speak for us, "reporting to Chairman Mao" what we had done for the sake of the revolution that day, what mistakes we had made, and what we resolved to do tommorow.

The Army also had a policy of "recalling the suffering of the old society." The political officers often invited a toothless old woman and other peasants from a neighboring village to tell us about life before the revolution. The old woman would wipe away her tears as she spoke about the cruelty of the past and how the landlord had mistreated the peasants. This kind of indoctrination, repeated day after day, reinforced the belief that life under the Communist Party leadership was the best in the world and that it was our duty as soldiers to preserve the system.

All of these traditions were intended to foster in us a sense of honor at being revolutionary soldiers; to fan our hatred of class enemies; and to teach us restraint, self-sacrifice, and obedience to the Party and the needs of the revolution.

It had a powerful effect. For instance, in the 1970s China and the Soviet Union sent high-range artillery and guided missile units to Vietnam to support the Vietcong. During an American bombing raid it was discovered that the Chinese artillery had too short a range and could not reach the bombers. Destruction over the target area was intense. Despite the ineffectiveness of their weapons, the Chinese soldiers continued to fire upward at the American planes, shouting quotations from Mao: "Be firm in resolve, don't fear sacrifice, push aside all difficulties, fight for victory!" The Soviet guided missile units nearby stared at this with jaws dropping, doubtless thinking that their Chinese colleagues had lost their minds.

And during the days in Tienanmen, once again the soldiers did not complain. They obediently drove forward, aimed, and opened fire on command. In light of their training, how could it be otherwise?

It is interesting, as I sit here in my study in the United States, to think of those soldiers in the square. Many of the protesters that the soldiers faced had themselves been soldiers and received Army training. I believe it was precisely that Army experience that allowed the demonstrators in and around Tienanmen to be so effective in disabling more than 1,000 of the military vehicles that appeared on the streets of Beijing.

When people in the West ask how I feel about the events in Tienanmen Square and the future of China, I am inevitably confronted with the contradiction between repulsion at the political blindness of the troops and the shedding of blood, and the deep affection I have for my time in the military and my life with my comrades. Rage at the soldiers who fought against unarmed protesters is mixed with comprehension of their reflex to obey.

What of my old father, the general? To this day our love is intact even though he still approves of the way the events in the square were handled, making the subject taboo between us. You ask me about China and I will tell you it is as complex as the emotions of a man sent to the fields to do hard labor for crimes he didn't commit, all the while approving of the decision to punish him since it was made by the Party. As complex as a son who wanted nothing more than to serve, but who found that service in challenging the old to bring about the new.

Translated by Jay Sailey

From a Mother

ANTONIO CISNEROS

Some soldiers who were drinking brandy
have told me that now this country
is ours.
They also said
I shouldn't wait for my sons.
So I must
exhange the wooden chairs
for a little oil & some bread.
The land is black as dead ants,
the soldiers said it was ours.
But when the rains begin
I'll have to sell
the shoes & ponchos
of my dead sons.

Some day I'll buy a longhaired mule
& go down to my fields
of black earth
to reap the fruit
of these broad dark lands.

Translated by Maureen Ahern,
William Rowe and David Tipton

Watching Death, Live on Cable

SLAVENKA DRAKULIĆ

The city of Sarajevo, its population mainly Muslim, suffered under constant shelling during the breakup of the former Yugoslavia.

They say a little girl was killed while eating a pie. It seemed that it happened like this: It was morning, bright and chilly. You ask yourself how that woman, her mother, made the pie in Sarajevo? What flour did she use? What oil? In any case, still half-asleep, the 2 1/2-year-old girl had been sitting at the table, eating breakfast. At that moment, she heard the sound of shelling.

Maybe she was frightened by it, so she ran to her mother—but maybe not. The sound of shelling is normal around here. A shell went through the roof of their house and landed in the kitchen. The girl fell to the floor. It all happened with lightning speed and she was dead before her parents or her grandfather had time to understand what was happening. By the time her father took her in his hands and looked for help, it was all over.

Then a television camera arrived on the scene. This happened per-haps only one or two hours after the shelling. We see the small kitchen already without the little girl, the floor is covered with brick and plaster debris, scattered shoes, her little boots. The camera zooms in on the roof, on the hole left by the shell. Sky and cold descend through the gap into the kitchen. The father is sitting with his arms on the table, crying. The camera gets a close-up of his blue eyes and his tears—so that we, the television spectators, can be sure they are real, that he really cried, the little one's father.

He has on a white pullover made of a rough peasant's wool. The camera moves from his eyes to that pullover so that we can see a red stain on it, left where he held his girl when he picked her up from the floor—when it was already too late. The blood is not dry yet, the stain

is bright red, it looks fresh. I know that raw, hand-spun wool that his pullover is made of. I can feel it under my fingers. It takes forever to dry; soaked blood stays wet a long time. Looking at the blood is nauseating. Still, the camera returns to it several times. This is unnecessary. But there is no defence from pictures like this—and no one to tell us how useless they are.

Now we are in the hospital. This is the first time we see the mother, too. She lies on a kind of stretcher, covering her face with her hands. The father comes in, in his white pullover with the red stain, and embraces her. It is clear that this meeting in a hospital room is their first since the little one's death. On camera—for the first time. The mother lets out something. In other circumstances you might call it a cry, a howl. But now it is only a sound of emptiness; with that sound, the woman tells her husband she has just lost everything.

This is the end, this has to be the end. The camera can't go any further into human suffering. Neither we, the spectators, nor the people we can't see behind the camera—a reporter, a cameraman, a soundman—can stand this any longer. This has to stop—I repeat to myself while the camera goes on.

Now we are looking at a white sheet with red spots. Red on white, that's the sign of her death. My God, how very bright her blood is. I don't want the camera to look under that cover hiding her small body. But someone's hand evades my thoughts and lifts the white sheet. Her face, we see her face. Her small deformed face, no longer human, framed by untidy tufts of her black hair, her half-closed eyes. We see a close-up of death.

Then cut, a little coffin in the shallow ground. The report is finished. It has lasted three minutes.

A moment later, we become aware that we have just seen the tragedy of one family, filmed only a couple of hours after they lost their child. The whole tragedy has happened on camera. The only thing we have not witnessed is the moment of death. (A take from outside: The shell hits the roof. Then from inside: The girl falls from her chair, in slow motion, as if she's flying. A piece of pie drops from her hand and rolls on the ground. That's it. The reporter is pleased.) Well, why not? By now we should be able to stand that too. It's all in the name of documenting, which we obviously believe in.

In fact, that's probably the only thing we have not seen so far. We've watched headless corpses being eaten by pigs and dogs; scattered body parts that do not belong to anyone, anything; skeletons and half-rotted skulls. Children without legs, babies killed by sniper fire. A 12-year-old rape victim talking about it on camera. Day after day, death in Bosnia has been well documented. Sarajevo had been shelled by a million shells. In that city 80 000 kids are trapped, which makes it the biggest children's prison in the world. Five thousand of them were killed or simply died.

Fifty years ago this is how the Jews suffered; now it's the Muslims' turn. We remember it all, and because of that memory we have the idea that everything has to be carefully documented. Shameful history must never be repeated. And yet, here they are, generations who have learned at school about concentration camps and factories of death; generations whose parents swear it could never happen again, at least not in Europe, precisely because of the living memory of the recent past. What, then, has all the documentation changed? And what is being changed now by what seems to be the conscious, precise bookkeeping of death?

The biggest change has happened within ourselves: the audience, spectators. We have started to believe this is our role, that it is possible to play the public, as if war is theatre. Slowly, and without noticing it, a hardness has crept over us, an inability to see the truth. These are the signs of our own dying. The close-up of the dead girl's face was one scene too much because it was senseless. To watch war from so near and in its most macabre details makes sense only if we do so to change things for the better.

But today, nothing changes. Documentation has become a perversion, a pornography of dying.

Epaulettes

MARGARET ATWOOD

The author pinpoints some of the reasons why people continue to wage war, and suggests a mock-serious substitute—touché!

When war had finally become too dangerous, and, more to the point, too expensive for everyone, the world leaders met informally to devise a substitute.

"The thing is," said the first speaker, "what purposes did war serve when we had it?"

"It stimulated production in selected areas of the economy," said one.

"It provided clear winners and clear losers," said another, "and it gave men a break from the boring and trivial domestic routine."

"Expansion of territory," said another. "Privileged access to females and other items in demand."

"It was exciting," said a fourth. "Something was at risk."

"Well then," said the first, "these are the benefits our substitute for war must provide."

At first the world leaders focused their attention on sports, and a lively discussion ensued. Baseball, basketball, and cricket were dismissed as too leisurely. Football and hockey were both seriously proposed, until it became evident that no world leader would last two minutes on either Astroturf or ice. One of the world leaders, who was interested in archaeology, suggested an old Mayan game played in sunken ballcourts, in which the loser's head was ceremonially cut off; but the rules of this game were no longer known.

"We are looking in the wrong area," said a world leader from one of the smaller countries. "Forget these rowdy games. We should be thinking birds."

"Birds?" said the others, sneering both politely—in the case of the older and more machiavellian nations—and less politely, in the case of the younger and cruder ones.

"Bird display," said the speaker. "The male birds, in their elaborate and brightly coloured plumage, strut about, sing, ruffle their feathers, and perform dances. The watching female birds choose the winners. This is a simple and I might add a melodious method of competition, and has much to recommend it. Let me just add, gentlemen, that it has worked for the birds."

The great powers were against this proposal, as it would pit their own leaders against those of the smaller nations on a more or less equal footing. But for this same reason the smaller nations were in favour of it, and because there were more of them than there were of the great powers, the resolution was voted in.

Which leads to the happy state of affairs we enjoy today. Once a year, in April, the play-offs begin. Throngs of chattering and expectant women crowd the football, cricket and jai alai stadia of the world. Each is provided with a voting device, with pushbuttons ranging from 0 to 10. The world leaders compete in groups of six, with the winner going on to the next round until, finally, there is only one winner for the entire world.

During the subsequent year the men of the winning country enjoy certain privileges, which include: modified looting (department stores only, and only on Mondays); ordering loudly and banging the tables in restaurants; having the men from all other nations laugh at their witticisms in a grovelling manner; preferential dating; complimentary theatre tickets; and two days of rape and pillage, followed by ritual drunkenness in the streets. (As everyone knows which days are the two chosen ones, people simply board up their windows and go away for the weekend.) Winners also get an improved foreign exchange rate and the best deals on fish processing. Each country enjoys its triumphant status for a year only, and since all know that next year it will be somebody else's turn— the women see to that—the more extreme forms of riotous behaviour are self-policed.

The competition itself is divided into several categories. Each one of these is designed to appeal to the female temperament, though there has been some difficulty in determining exactly what this is. For instance, the 'aroma' category—in which the condensed essences of the competitors' sweat-socks, cigars, used tennis shirts, and so forth, were wafted through the audience—had to be discontinued, as it made too many women sick.

But the name-calling, muscle-flexing and cool-dressing bouts remain. So does joke-telling, since it is well known that women prefer men with a sense of humour, or so they keep telling us. In addition, a song must be sung, a dance must be danced—though a solo on the flute or cello will suffice—a skill-testing question must be answered; and each world leader must describe his favourite hobby, and declare, in a well-modulated exhibition speech, what he intends to do in future for the good of humanity. This is a popular feature, and occasions much giggling and applause.

Best of all is the military uniform category, during which the contestants march along the runway to the sound of recorded brass bands. What colours we see then, what festoons of gold braid, what constellations of metal stars! Gone are the days of muted khaki, even of navy blue: we live in the age of the peacock. Epaulettes have swollen to epic lengths and breadths, headgear is befeathered, beribboned, resplendent! The stimulus to the fashion industry has been prodigious.

From our new system a new type of world leader has emerged. Younger, for one thing. Lighter on the feet. More musical. Funnier.

And history too is being revised. Daring military exploits, mega-deaths, genocides and other such emblems of conquistadorial prowess no longer count for much. The criteria have changed. It is being said, for instance, that Napoleon was practically a catatonic on the dance floor, and that Stalin wore ill-fitting uniforms and could not sing to save his life.

A Man

NINA CASSIAN

While fighting for his country, he lost an arm
and was suddenly afraid:
"From now on, I shall only be able to do things by halves.
I shall reap half a harvest.
I shall be able to play either the tune
or the accompaniment on the piano,
but never both parts together.
I shall be able to bang with only one fist
on doors, and worst of all
I shall only be able to half hold
my love close to me.
There will be things I cannot do at all,
applaud for example,
at shows where everyone applauds."

From that moment on, he set himself to do
       everything with twice as much enthusiasm.
And where the arm had been torn away
a wing grew.

Translated by Roy MacGregor-Hastie

V·I·S·I·O·N·S

The Man Had No Useful Work

RABINDRANATH TAGORE

If you could choose your Paradise, what would it be like? The man in this poem didn't get a chance to choose, and ended up in someone else's idea of heaven.

The man had no useful work, only vagaries of various kinds.

Therefore it surprised him to find himself in Paradise after a life spent perfecting trifles.

Now the guide had taken him by mistake to the wrong Paradise—one meant only for good, busy souls.

In this Paradise, our man saunters along the road only to obstruct the rush of business.

He stands aside from the path and is warned that he tramples on sown seed. Pushed, he starts up: hustled, he moves on.

A very busy girl comes to fetch water from the well. Her feet run on the pavement like rapid fingers over harp-strings. Hastily she ties a negligent knot with her hair, and loose locks on her forehead pry into the dark of her eyes.

The man says to her, "Would you lend me your pitcher?"

"My pitcher?" she asks, "to draw water?"

"No, to paint patterns on."

"I have no time to waste," the girl retorts in contempt.

Now a busy soul has no chance against one who is supremely idle.

Every day she meets him at the well, and every day he repeats the same request, till at last she yields.

Our man paints the pitcher with curious colors in a mysterious maze of lines.

The girl takes it up, turns it round and asks, "What does it mean?"

"It has no meaning," he answers.

The girl carries the pitcher home. She holds it up in different lights and tries to con its mystery.

At night she leaves her bed, lights a lamp, and gazes at it from all points of view.

This is the first time she has met with something without meaning.

On the next day the man is again near the well.

The girl asks, "What do you want?"

"To do more work for you!"

"What work?" she enquires.

"Allow me to weave colored strands into a ribbon to bind your hair."

"Is there any need?" she asks.

"None whatever," he allows.

The ribbon is made, and thenceforward she spends a great deal of time over her hair.

The even stretch of well-employed time in that Paradise begins to show irregular rents.

The elders are troubled; they meet in council.

The guide confesses his blunder, saying that he has brought the wrong man to the wrong place.

The wrong man is called. His turban, flaming with color, shows plainly how great that blunder has been.

The chief of the elders says, "You must go back to the earth."

The man heaves a sigh of relief: "I am ready."

The girl with the ribbon round her hair chimes in: "I also!"

For the first time the chief of the elders is faced with a situation which has no sense in it.

A Very Old Man with Enormous Wings

A Tale for Children

GABRIEL GARCÍA MÁRQUEZ

Here's a question that was hotly debated in medieval times: How many angels can fit on the head of a pin? And now, a story to make you wonder . . . .

On the third day of rain they had killed so many crabs inside the house that Pelayo had to cross his drenched courtyard and throw them into the sea, because the newborn child had a temperature all night and they thought it was due to the stench. The world had been sad since Tuesday. Sea and sky were a single ash-gray thing and the sands of the beach, which on March nights glimmered like powdered light, had become a stew of mud and rotten shellfish. The light was so weak at noon that when Pelayo was coming back to the house after throwing away the crabs, it was hard for him to see what it was that was moving and groaning in the rear of the courtyard. He had to go very close to see that it was an old man, a very old man, lying face down in the mud, who, in spite of his tremendous efforts, couldn't get up, impeded by his enormous wings.

Frightened by that nightmare, Pelayo ran to get Elisenda, his wife, who was putting compresses on the sick child, and he took her to the rear of the courtyard. They both looked at the fallen body with mute stupor. He was dressed like a ragpicker. There were only a few faded hairs left on his bald skull and very few teeth in his mouth, and his pitiful condition of a drenched great-grandfather had taken away any sense of grandeur he might have had. His huge buzzard wings, dirty and half-plucked, were forever entangled in the mud. They looked at him so long and so closely that Pelayo and Elisenda very soon overcame their surprise and in the end found him familiar. Then they dared speak to him, and he answered in an incomprehensible dialect with a strong sailor's voice. That was how they skipped over the inconvenience of the wings and quite intelligently concluded that he was a lonely castaway from some foreign ship wrecked by the storm. And yet, they called in a neighbor woman who knew everything about life and death to see him, and all she needed was one look to show them their mistake.

"He's an angel," she told them. "He must have been coming for the child, but the poor fellow is so old that the rain knocked him down."

On the following day everyone knew that a flesh-and-blood angel was held captive in Pelayo's house. Against the judgment of the wise neighbor woman, for whom angels in those times were the fugitive survivors of a celestial conspiracy, they did not have the heart to club him to death. Pelayo watched over him all afternoon from the kitchen, armed with his bailiff's club, and before going to bed he dragged him out of the mud and locked him up with the hens in the wire chicken coop. In the middle of the night, when the rain stopped, Pelayo and Elisenda were still killing crabs. A short time afterward the child woke up without a fever and with a desire to eat. Then they felt magnanimous and decided to put the angel on a raft with fresh water and provisions for three days and leave him to his fate on the high seas. But when they went out into the courtyard with the first light of dawn, they found the whole neighborhood in front of the chicken coop having fun with the angel, without the slightest reverence, tossing him things to eat through the openings in the wire as if he weren't a supernatural creature but a circus animal.

Father Gonzaga arrived before seven o'clock, alarmed at the strange news. By that time onlookers less frivolous than those at dawn had already arrived and they were making all kinds of conjectures concerning the captive's future. The simplest among them thought that he should be named mayor of the world. Others of sterner mind felt that he should be promoted to the rank of five-star general in order to win all wars. Some visionaries hoped that he could be put to stud in order to implant on earth a race of winged wise men who could take charge of the universe. But Father Gonzaga, before becoming a priest, had been a robust woodcutter. Standing by the wire, he reviewed his catechism in an instant and asked them to open the door so that he could take a close look at that pitiful man who looked more like a huge decrepit hen among the fascinated chickens. He was lying in a corner drying his open wings in the sunlight among the fruit peels and breakfast leftovers that the early risers had thrown him. Alien to the impertinences of the world, he only lifted his antiquarian eyes and murmured something in his dialect when Father Gonzaga went into the chicken coop and said good morning

to him in Latin. The parish priest had his first suspicion of an imposter when he saw that he did not understand the language of God or know how to greet His ministers. Then he noticed that seen close up he was much too human: he had an unbearable smell of the outdoors, the back side of his wings was strewn with parasites and his main feathers had been mistreated by terrestrial winds, and nothing about him measured up to the proud dignity of angels. Then he came out of the chicken coop and in a brief sermon warned the curious against the risk of being ingenuous. He reminded them that the devil had the bad habit of making use of carnival tricks in order to confuse the unwary. He argued that if wings were not the essential element in determining the difference between a hawk and an airplane, they were even less so in the recognition of angels. Nevertheless, he promised to write a letter to his bishop so that the latter would write to his primate so that the latter would write to the Supreme Pontiff in order to get the final verdict from the highest courts.

His prudence fell on sterile hearts. The news of the captive angel spread with such rapidity that after a few hours the courtyard had the bustle of a marketplace and they had to call in troops with fixed bayonets to disperse the mob that was about to knock the house down. Elisenda, her spine all twisted from sweeping up so much marketplace trash, then got the idea of fencing in the yard and charging five cents admission to see the angel.

The curious came from far away. A traveling carnival arrived with a flying acrobat who buzzed over the crowd several times, but no one paid any attention to him because his wings were not those of an angel but, rather, those of a sidereal bat. The most unfortunate invalids on earth came in search of health: a poor woman who since childhood had been counting her heartbeats and had run out of numbers; a Portuguese man who couldn't sleep because the noise of the stars disturbed him; a sleepwalker who got up at night to undo the things he had done while awake; and many others with less serious ailments. In the midst of that shipwreck disorder that made the earth tremble, Pelayo and Elisenda were happy with fatigue, for in less than a week they had crammed their rooms with money and the line of pilgrims waiting their turn to enter still reached beyond the horizon.

The angel was the only one who took no part in his own act. He spent his time trying to get comfortable in his borrowed nest, befuddled by the hellish heat of the oil lamps and sacramental candles that had been placed along the wire. At first they tried to make him eat some mothballs, which, according to the wisdom of the wise neighbor woman, were the food prescribed for angels. But he turned them down, just as he turned down the papal lunches that the penitents brought him, and they never found out whether it was because he was an angel or because he was an old man that in the end he ate nothing but eggplant mush. His only supernatural virtue seemed to be patience. Especially during the first days, when the hens pecked at him, searching for the stellar parasites that proliferated in his wings, and the cripples pulled out feathers to touch their defective parts with, and even the most merciful threw stones at him, trying to get him to rise so they could see him standing. The only time they succeeded in arousing him was when they burned his side with an iron for branding steers, for he had been motionless for so many hours that they thought he was dead. He awoke with a start, ranting in his hermetic language and with tears in his eyes, and he flapped his wings a couple of times, which brought on a whirlwind of chicken dung and lunar dust and a gale of panic that did not seem to be of this world. Although many thought that his reaction had been one not of rage but of pain, from then on they were careful not to annoy him, because the majority understood that his passivity was not that of a hero taking his ease but that of a cataclysm in repose.

Father Gonzaga held back the crowd's frivolity with formulas of maidservant inspiration while awaiting the arrival of a final judgment on the nature of the captive. But the mail from Rome showed no sense of urgency. They spent their time finding out if the prisoner had a navel, if his dialect had any connection with Aramaic, how many times he could fit on the head of a pin, or whether he wasn't just a Norwegian with wings. Those meager letters might have come and gone until the end of time if a providential event had not put an end to the priest's tribulations.

It so happened that during those days, among so many other carnival attractions, there arrived in town the traveling show of the woman who had been changed into a spider for having disobeyed her parents. The admission to see her was not only less than the admission to see the angel, but people were permitted to ask her all manner of questions about her absurd state and to examine her up and down so that no one would ever doubt the truth of her horror. She was a frightful tarantula the size of a ram and with the head of a sad maiden. What was most heartrending, however, was not her outlandish shape but the sincere affliction with which she recounted the details of her misfortune. While still practically a child she had sneaked out of her parents' house to go to a dance, and while she was coming back through the woods after having danced all night without permission, a fearful thunderclap rent the sky in two and through the crack came the lightning bolt of brimstone that changed her into a spider. Her only nourishment came from the meatballs that charitable souls chose to toss into her mouth. A spectacle like that, full of so much human truth and with such a fearful lesson, was bound to defeat without even trying that of a haughty angel who scarcely deigned to look at mortals. Besides, the few miracles attributed to the angel showed a certain mental disorder, like the blind man who didn't recover his sight but grew three new teeth, or the paralytic who didn't get to walk but almost won the lottery, and the leper whose sores sprouted sunflowers. Those consolation miracles, which were more like mocking fun, had already ruined the angel's reputation when the woman who had been changed into a spider finally crushed him completely. That was how Father Gonzaga was cured forever of his insomnia and Pelayo's courtyard went back to being as empty as during the time it had rained for three days and crabs walked through the bedrooms.

The owners of the house had no reason to lament. With the money they saved they built a two-story mansion with balconies and gardens and high netting so that crabs wouldn't get in during the winter, and with iron bars on the windows so that angels wouldn't get in. Pelayo also set up a rabbit warren close to town and give up his job as bailiff for good, and Elisenda bought some satin pumps with high heels and many dresses of iridescent silk, the kind worn on Sunday by the most desirable women in those times. The chicken coop was the only thing that didn't receive any attention. If they washed it down with creolin and burned tears of myrrh inside it every so often, it was not in homage to the angel but to drive away the dungheap stench that still hung everywhere like a ghost and was turning the new house into an old one. At first, when the child learned to walk, they were careful that he not get too close to the chicken coop. But then they began to lose their fears and got used to the smell, and before the child got his second teeth he'd gone inside the chicken coop to play, where the wires were falling apart. The angel was no less standoffish with him than with other mortals, but he tolerated the most ingenious infamies with the patience of a dog who had no illusions. They both came down with the chicken pox at the same time. The doctor who took care of the child couldn't resist the temptation to listen to the angel's heart, and he found so much whistling in the heart and so many sounds in his kidneys that it seemed impossible for him to be alive. What surprised him most, however, was the logic of his wings. They seemed so natural on that completely human organism that he couldn't understand why other men didn't have them too.

When the child began school it had been some time since the sun and rain had caused the collapse of the chicken coop. The angel went dragging himself about here and there like a stray dying man. They would drive him out of the bedroom with a broom and a moment later find him in the kitchen. He seemed to be in so many places at the same time that they grew to think that he'd been duplicated, that he was reproducing himself all through the house, and the exasperated and unhinged Elisenda shouted that it was awful living in that hell full of angels. He could scarcely eat and his antiquarian eyes had also become so foggy that he went about bumping into posts. All he had left were the bare cannulae of his last feathers. Pelayo threw a blanket over him and extended him the charity of letting him sleep in the shed, and only then did they notice that he had a temperature at night, and was delirious with the tongue twisters of an old Norwegian. That was one of the few times they became alarmed, for they thought he was going to die and not even the wise neighbor woman had been able to tell them what to do with dead angels.

And yet he not only survived his worst winter, but seemed improved with the first sunny days. He remained motionless for several days in the farthest corner of the courtyard, where no one would see him, and at the beginning of December some large, stiff feathers began to grow on his wings, the feathers of a scarecrow, which looked more like another misfortune of decrepitude. But he must have known the reason for those changes, for he was quite careful that no one should notice them, that no one should hear the sea chanteys that he sometimes sang under the stars. One morning Elisenda was cutting some bunches of onions for lunch when a wind that seemed to come from the high seas blew into the kitchen. Then she went to the window and caught the angel in his first attempts at flight. They were so clumsy that his fingernails opened a furrow in the vegetable patch and he was on the point of knocking the shed down with the ungainly flapping that slipped on the light and couldn't get a grip on the air. But he did manage to gain altitude. Elisenda let out a sigh of relief, for herself and for him, when she saw him pass over the last houses, holding himself up in some way with the risky flapping of a senile vulture. She kept watching him even when she was through cutting the onions and she kept on watching until it was no longer possible for her to see him, because then he was no longer an annoyance in her life but an imaginary dot on the horizon of the sea.

Translated by Gregory Rabassa

Aramaic: An ancient Semitic language; one of the biblical languages

Bite into the Onion

MARGE PIERCY

Take a big bite and let its jagged fumes pierce
the roof of your mouth and kick your sinuses.
All the fine layers of it intricate as a mosaic,
wrapped like a present, in wine colored silk of the red,
the plain brown wrapper of the pornographic yellow
that will strip and strip for you down to the baby core,
the ivory parchment of the white.

Everyone all day will know what you had for lunch.
They will back off from you with a look of polite
distaste and stand across the room barking like poodles.
You will sneak up on your friends and give them a big
kiss of hostility and affection mixed in a busy palette.
Your own breath will hang around you in a prickly
holly wreath hung with its own internal bells.

Onion, I undress you in your wardrobe of veils,
I enter you room upon room inside each other
like Russian dolls. You sizzle my nose,
healthy, obstinate, loud as a peasant uncle
coming in with his boots dirty and a chicken
with its neck wrung clutched in his fist.
What soup or stew is not empty without you?

Cooked, you change your whole character.
You are suave and unctuous, polite to mushrooms
and the palest fish. You play under the meal
like a well-bred string quartet in a posh restaurant,
pianissimo, legato, just enough to mute cutlery.
You are the ideal lover for every entree.
Animal or vegetable, you tickle them all.

Your cousins are my darlings, the leek—a scallion
taking steroids, the sly magenta shallots, the garlic
that blesses food, the Egyptian onions that go down on
their knees to plant themselves. But many times
nothing but you will do, big as a wrestler's fist,
obvious as a splash of yellow paint in the roadway,
when food must slam a door, roar and shout.

Deportation at Breakfast

LARRY FONDATION

Expect more questions than answers from this example of an increasingly popular genre—"flash fiction."

The signs on the windows lured me inside. For a dollar I could get two eggs, toast, and potatoes. The place looked better than most—family-run and clean. The signs were hand-lettered and neat. The paper had yellowed some, but the black letters remained bold. A green-and-white awning was perched over the door, where the name "Clara's" was stenciled.

Inside, the place had an appealing and old-fashioned look. The air smelled fresh and homey, not greasy. The menu was printed on a chalkboard. It was short and to the point. It listed the kinds of toast you could choose from. One entry was erased from the middle of the list. By deduction, I figured it was rye. I didn't want rye toast anyway.

Because I was alone, I sat at the counter, leaving the empty tables free for other customers that might come in. At the time, business was quiet. Only two tables were occupied; and I was alone at the counter. But it was still early—not yet seven-thirty.

Behind the counter was a short man with dark black hair, a mustache, and a youthful beard, one that never grew much past stubble. He was dressed immaculately, all in chef's white—pants, shirt, and apron, but no hat. He had a thick accent. The name "Javier" was stitched on his shirt.

I ordered coffee, and asked for a minute to choose between the breakfast special for a dollar and the cheese omelette for $1.59. I selected the omelette.

The coffee was hot, strong, and fresh. I spread my newspaper on the counter and sipped at the mug as Javier went to the grill to cook my meal.

The eggs were spread out on the griddle, the bread plunged inside the toaster, when the authorities came in. They grabbed Javier quickly and without a word, forcing his hands behind his back. He, too, said nothing. He did not resist, and they shoved him out the door and into their waiting car.

On the grill, my eggs bubbled. I looked around for another employee—maybe out back somewhere, or in the washroom. I leaned over the counter and called for someone. No one answered. I looked behind me toward the tables. Two elderly men sat at one; two elderly women at the other. The two women were talking. The men were reading the paper. They seemed not to have noticed Javier's exit.

I could smell my eggs starting to burn. I wasn't quite sure what to do about it. I thought about Javier and stared at my eggs. After some hesitation, I got up from my red swivel stool and went behind the counter. I grabbed a spare apron, then picked up the spatula and turned my eggs. My toast had popped up, but it was not browned, so I put it down again. While I was cooking, the two elderly women came to the counter and asked to pay. I asked what they had had. They seemed surprised that I didn't remember. I checked the prices on the chalkboard and rang up their order. They paid slowly, fishing through large purses, and went out, leaving me a dollar tip. I took my eggs off the grill and slid them onto a clean plate. My toast had come up. I buttered it and put it on my plate beside my eggs. I put the plate at my spot at the counter, right next to my newspaper.

As I began to come back from behind the counter to my stool, six new customers came through the door. "Can we pull some tables together?" they asked. "We're all one party." I told them yes. They ordered six coffees, two decaffeinated.

I thought of telling them I didn't work there. But perhaps they were hungry. I poured their coffee. Their order was simple: six breakfast specials, all with scrambled eggs and wheat toast. I got busy at the grill.

Then the elderly men came to pay. More new customers began arriving. By eight-thirty, I had my hands full. With this kind of business, I couldn't understand why Javier hadn't hired a waitress. Maybe I'd take out a help-wanted ad in the paper tomorrow. I had never been in the restaurant business. There was no way I could run this place alone.

A Girl's Story

DAVID ARNASON

This is your invitation to step right up and actually participate in the writing of a story. Have fun!

You've wondered what it would be like to be a character in a story, to sort of slip out of your ordinary self and into some other character. Well, I'm offering you the opportunity. I've been trying to think of a heroine for this story, and frankly, it hasn't been going too well. A writer's life isn't easy, especially if, like me, he's got a tendency sometimes to drink a little bit too much. Yesterday, I went for a beer with Dennis and Ken (they're real-life friends of mine) and we stayed a little longer than we should have. Then I came home and quickly mixed a drink and started drinking it so my wife would think the liquor on my breath came from the drink I was drinking and not from the drinks I had had earlier. I wasn't going to tell her about those drinks. Anyway, Wayne dropped over in the evening and I had some more drinks, and this morning my head isn't working very well.

To be absolutely frank about it, I always have trouble getting characters, even when I'm stone cold sober. I can think of plots; plots are really easy. If you can't think of one, you just pick up a book, and sure enough, there's a plot. You just move a few things around and nobody knows you stole the idea. Characters are the problem. It doesn't matter how good the plot is if your characters are dull. You can steal characters too, and put them into different plots. I've done that. I stole Eustacia Vye from Hardy and gave her another name. The problem was that she turned out a lot sulkier than I remembered and the plot I put her in was a light comedy. Now nobody wants to publish the story. I'm still sending it out, though. If you send a story to enough publishers, no matter how bad it is, somebody will ultimately publish it.

For this story I need a beautiful girl. You probably don't think you're beautiful enough, but I can fix that. I can do all kinds of retouching once I've got the basic material, and if I miss anything, Karl (he's my editor) will find it. So I'm going to make you fairly tall, about five-foot eight and a quarter in your stocking feet. I'm going to give you long blonde hair because long blonde hair is sexy and virtuous. Black hair can be sexy too, but it doesn't go with virtue. I've got to deal with a whole literary tradition where black-haired women are basically evil. If I were feeling better I might be able to do it in an ironic way, then black hair would be OK, but I don't think I'm up to it this morning. If you're going to use irony, then you've got to be really careful about tone. I could make you a redhead, but redheads have a way of turning out pixie-ish, and that would wreck my plot.

So you've got long blonde hair and you're this tall slender girl with amazingly blue eyes. Your face is narrow and your nose is straight and thin. I could have turned up the nose a little, but that would have made you cute, and I really need a beautiful girl. I'm going to put a tiny black mole on your cheek. It's traditional. If you want your character to be really beautiful there has to be some minor defect.

Now, I'm going to sit you on the bank of a river. I'm not much for setting. I've read so many things where you get great long descriptions of the setting, and mostly it's just boring. When my last book came out, one of the reviewers suggested that the reason I don't do settings is that I'm not very good at them. That's just silly. I'm writing a different kind of story, not that old realist stuff. If you think I can't do setting, just watch.

There's a curl in the river just below the old dam where the water seems to make a broad sweep. The flatness is deceptive, though. Under the innocent sheen of the mirroring surface, the current is treacherous. The water swirls, stabs, takes sharp angles and dangerous vectors. The trees that lean from the bank shimmer with the multi-hued greenness of elm, oak, maple and aspen. The leaves turn in the gentle breeze, showing their paler green undersides. The undergrowth, too, is thick and green, hiding the poison ivy, the poison sumac and the thorns. On a patch of grass that slopes gently to the water, the only clear part of the bank on that side of the river, a girl sits, a girl with long blonde hair. She has slipped a ring from her finger and seems to be holding it toward the light.

You see? I could do a lot more of that, but you wouldn't like it. I slipped a lot of details in there and provided all those hints about strange and dangerous things under the surface. That's called foreshadowing.

I put in the ring at the end there so that you'd wonder what was going to happen. That's to create suspense. You're supposed to ask yourself what the ring means. Obviously it has something to do with love, rings always do, and since she's taken it off, obviously something has gone wrong in the love relationship. Now I just have to hold off answering that question for as long as I can, and I've got my story. I've got a friend who's also a writer who says never tell the buggers anything until they absolutely have to know.

I'm going to have trouble with the feminists about this story. I can see that already. I've got that river that's calm on the surface and boiling underneath, and I've got those trees that are gentle and beautiful with poisonous and dangerous undergrowth. Obviously, the girl is going to be like that, calm on the surface but passionate underneath. The feminists are going to say that I'm perpetuating stereotypes, that by giving the impression the girl is full of hidden passion I'm encouraging rapists. That's crazy. I'm just using a literary convention. Most of the world's great books are about the conflict between reason and passion. If you take that away, what's left to write about?

So I've got you sitting on the riverbank, twirling your ring. I forgot the birds. The trees are full of singing birds. There are meadowlarks and vireos and even Blackburnian warblers. I know a lot about birds but I'm not going to put in too many. You've got to be careful not to overdo things. In a minute I'm going to enter your mind and reveal what you're thinking. I'm going to do this in the third person. Using the first person is sometimes more effective, but I'm always afraid to do a female character in the first person. It seems wrong to me, like putting on a woman's dress.

Your name is Linda. I had to be careful not to give you a biblical name like Judith or Rachel. I don't want any symbolism in this story. Symbolism makes me sick, especially biblical symbolism. You always end up with some crazy moral argument that you don't believe and none of the readers believe. Then you lose control of your characters, because they've got to be like the biblical characters. You've got this terrific episode you'd like to use, but you can't because Rachel or Judith or whoever wouldn't do it. I think of stories with a lot of symbolism in them as sticky.

Here goes.

Linda held the ring up toward the light. The diamond flashed rainbow colours. It was a small diamond, and Linda reflected that it was probably a perfect symbol of her relationship with Gregg. Everything Gregg did was on a small scale. He was careful with his money and just as careful with his emotions. In one week they would have a small wedding and then move into a small apartment. She supposed that she ought to be happy. Gregg was very handsome, and she did love him. Why did it seem that she was walking into a trap?

That sounds kind of distant, but it's supposed to be distant. I'm using indirect quotation because the reader has just met Linda, and we don't want to get too intimate right away. Besides, I've got to get a lot of explaining done quickly, and if you can do it with the character's thoughts, then that's best.

Linda twirled the ring again, then with a suddenness that surprised her, she stood up and threw it into the river. She was immediately struck by a feeling of panic. For a moment she almost decided to dive into the river to try to recover it. Then, suddenly, she felt free. It was now impossible to marry Gregg. He would not forgive her for throwing the ring away. Gregg would say he'd had enough of her theatrics for one lifetime. He always accused her of being a romantic. She'd never had the courage to admit that he was correct, and that she intended to continue being a romantic. She was sitting alone by the river in a long blue dress because it was a romantic pose. Anyway, she thought a little wryly, you're only likely to find romance if you look for it in romantic places and dress for the occasion.

Suddenly, she heard a rustling in the bush, the sound of someone coming down the narrow path from the road above.

I had to do that, you see. I'd used up all the potential in the relationship with Gregg, and the plot would have started to flag if I hadn't introduced a new character. The man who is coming down the path is tall and athletic with wavy brown hair. He has dark brown eyes that crinkle when he smiles, and he looks kind. His skin is tanned, as if he spends a lot of time outdoors, and he moves gracefully. He is smoking a pipe. I don't want to give too many details. I'm not absolutely sure what features women find attractive in men these days, but what I've described seems safe enough. I got all of it from stories written by women, and I assume they must know. I could give him a chiselled jaw, but that's about as far as I'll go.

The man stepped into the clearing. He carried an old-fashioned wicker fishing creel and a telescoped fishing rod. Linda remained sitting on the grass, her blue dress spread out around her. The man noticed her and apologized.

"I'm sorry, I always come here to fish on Saturday afternoons and I've never encountered anyone here before." His voice was low with something of an amused tone in it.

"Don't worry," Linda replied. "I'll only be here for a little while. Go ahead and fish. I won't make any noise." In some way she couldn't understand, the man looked familiar to her. She felt she knew him. She thought she might have seen him on television or in a movie, but of course she knew that movie and television stars do not spend every Saturday afternoon fishing on the banks of small, muddy rivers.

"You can make all the noise you want," he told her. "The fish in this river are almost entirely deaf. Besides, I don't care if I catch any. I only like the act of fishing. If I catch them, then I have to take them home and clean them. Then I've got to cook them and eat them. I don't even like fish that much, and the fish you catch here all taste of mud."

"Why do you bother fishing then?" Linda asked him. "Why don't you just come and sit on the riverbank?"

"It's not that easy," he told her. "A beautiful girl in a blue dress may go and sit on a riverbank any time she wants. But a man can only sit on a riverbank if he has a very good reason. Because I fish, I am a man with a hobby. After a hard week of work, I deserve some relaxation. But if I just came and sat on the riverbank, I would be a romantic fool. People would make fun of me. They would think I was irresponsible, and before long I would be a failure." As he spoke, he attached a lure to his line, untelescoped his fishing pole and cast his line into the water.

You may object that this would not have happened in real life, that the conversation would have been awkward, that Linda would have been a bit frightened by the man. Well, why don't you just run out to the grocery store and buy a bottle of milk and a loaf of bread? The grocer will give you your change without even looking at you. That's what happens in real life, and if that's what you're after, why are you reading a book?

I'm sorry. I shouldn't have got upset. But it's not easy you know. Dialogue is about the hardest stuff to write. You've got all those "he saids" and "she saids" and "he replieds." And you've got to remember the quotation marks and whether the comma is inside or outside the quotation marks. Sometimes you can leave out the "he saids" and "she saids" but then the reader gets confused and can't figure out who's talking. Hemingway is bad for that. Sometimes you can read an entire chapter without figuring out who is on what side.

Anyway, something must have been in the air that afternoon. Linda felt free and open.

Did I mention that it was warm and the sun was shining?

She chattered away, telling the stranger all about her life, what she had done when she was a little girl, the time her dad had taken the whole family to Hawaii and she got such a bad sunburn that she was peeling in February, how she was a better water skier than Gregg and how mad he got when she beat him at tennis. The man, whose name was Michael (you can use biblical names for men as long as you avoid Joshua or Isaac), told her he was a doctor, but had always wanted to be a cowboy. He told her about the time he skinned his knee when he fell off his bicycle and had to spend two weeks in the hospital because of infection. In short, they did what people who are falling in love always do. They unfolded their brightest and happiest memories and gave them to each other as gifts.

Then Michael took a bottle of wine and a Klik sandwich out of his wicker creel and invited Linda to join him in a picnic. He had forgotten his corkscrew and he had to push the cork down into the bottle with his filletting knife. They drank wine and laughed and spat out little pieces of cork. Michael reeled in his line, and to his amazement discovered a diamond ring on his hook. Linda didn't dare tell him where the ring had come from. Then Michael took Linda's hand, and slipped the ring onto her finger. In a comic-solemn voice, he asked her to marry him. With the same kind of comic solemnity, she agreed. Then they kissed, a first gentle kiss with their lips barely brushing and without touching each other.

Now I've got to bring this to some kind of ending. You think writers know how stories end before they write them, but that's not true. We're wracked with confusion and guilt about how things are going to end.

And just as you're playing the role of Linda in this story, Michael is my alter ego. He even looks a little like me and he smokes the same kind of pipe. We all want this to end happily. If I were going to be realistic about this, I suppose I'd have to let them make love. Then, shaken with guilt and horror, Linda would go back and marry Gregg, and the doctor would go back to his practice. But I'm not going to do that. In the story from which I stole the plot, Michael turned out not to be a doctor at all, but a returned soldier who had always been in love with Linda. She recognized him as they kissed, because they had kissed as children, and even though they had grown up and changed, she recognized the flavour of wintergreen on his breath. That's no good. It brings in too many unexplained facts at the last minute.

I'm going to end it right here at the moment of the kiss. You can do what you want with the rest of it, except you can't make him a returned soldier, and you can't have them make love then separate forever. I've eliminated those options. In fact, I think I'll eliminate all options. This is where the story ends, at the moment of the kiss. It goes on and on forever while cities burn, nations rise and fall, galaxies are born and die, and the universe snuffs out the stars one by one. It goes on, the story, the brush of a kiss.

Eustacia Vye: a heroine in Thomas Hardy's novel *The Return of the Native*

The Experimental World

PÄR LAGERKVIST

Our earth could be such a wonderful place, but somehow we always
fall short of perfection. Why?

Once upon a time there was a world which was not intended
to be a real, proper world but which was only meant to experiment with this and that, where one could see by trial and
error how everything turned out, what could be made of it. It was to
be like a laboratory, a research station where various suggestions and
ideas could be tried out to see what they were worth. If anything chanced
to give a satisfactory result, proved to be perfect, then it was to be used
elsewhere.

A start was made with a little of everything. Plants and trees were
set out and tended, fertilized with sun. They grew a bit, then they died
out and mouldered away, others had to be started. Many animals were
tried, they did fairly well, they developed; but then all at once they stopped
where they were or crept back almost to where they had begun; everything came to a standstill. But it didn't matter very much; failures were
only to be expected. Some things were not so bad for all that, and much
was learned.

Then it was seen what could be done with human beings. It didn't
go at all well. They grew a bit, but then they slipped back again. They
could be got so that they seemed almost perfect, whole nations, great
and noble, but all at once they slipped back, proved to be nothing but
animals. But it didn't matter very much; failures were only to be expected.
The earth was full of bones from all kinds of human beings who had
turned out badly, from nations that had been a failure. But quite a lot
was learned about how it should not be.

Then came the idea to try just one or two; it was no use with such
a lot of people. A boy- and a girl-child were chosen who were to grow
up in the most beautiful part of the earth. They were allowed to run

about in the woods and romp, play under the trees and take delight in everything. They were allowed to become a young man and woman who loved one another, their happiness was complete, their eyes met as openly as if their love had been but a clear summer's day. Even all the human failures around them saw that there was an unaccountable splendour about them which made them different from everything else in the world. And they rejoiced at it; they could do that at least. Love drew the two lovers together. It could not remain merely a beautiful earthly day; it rose up into a light where the young people felt dizzy, where they had to shut their eyes or be blinded; their hearts thumped, their lips quivered. They lay under the rose trees in the most beautiful part of the earth, in a wonderful night which had been provided for them. And they fell asleep in bliss, in the ecstasy and perfect beauty of love, locked in each other's arms. They awakened no more; they were dead. They were to be used elsewhere.

Translated by Alan Blair

The Vanishing Princess or The Origins of Cubism

JENNY DISKI

To get an idea of Cubism, think of Picasso. Some of his paintings of women, in which parts of the body look like separate, geometrical forms, are among the best known examples of the style.

There was once a Princess who lived in a tower. It is hard to say precisely if she was imprisoned there. Certainly she had always been there, and she had never left the circular room at the top of the long winding staircase. But since she had never tried to leave it, it wouldn't be quite accurate to say that she was imprisoned.

The room had a door, and the door had a keyhole, and there was, on the side of the door that she had never seen, a key that hung from a hook in the lintel. She had been put into the room at birth and a series of people, who called themselves relatives, had come and gone, visiting the turret room, opening and shutting the door from time to time. They maintained the lock on the door very carefully, making sure it was always well oiled, so that the Princess never heard the key turn in the lock, if indeed it did, and therefore never considered the possibility that she was their prisoner.

Since no one ever spoke to her about the world outside the door she came to assume that it was nothing to do with her. She lacked, perhaps, curiosity: but then no one had ever suggested to her that curiosity was a quality to be cultivated. Anyway, she never attempted to open the door from her side, and so never found out if she was a prisoner or not.

After a while the relatives stopped visiting, and there was a long period when no one came to the room at all. The Princess had little sense of time and barely noticed their absence. She spent her days lying on her bed in the circular room reading the books that filled the shelves that covered the walls from floor to ceiling. Apart from the bed and the books there was a narrow window in the room.

Sometimes, when she was replacing a book she had read, or choosing the next, she passed the window. As a child she had seen green fields and woods far off in the distance, and recognised them from the stories she had read. But since her visitors had stopped coming, the land around the tower had grown rampant and it was many years since she had seen anything but vines and creepers covered with briars and merciless thorns. It looked, at the very least, unattractive.

One day, many years after the Princess had been abandoned in the tower, a soldier passed nearby. He was a mercenary returning from the last of many campaigns; world-weary and bored with the sameness of everything. He noticed the tangled growth in the distance and wondered at it, that wild forest in the middle of rolling fields. Pleased to find himself curious about anything after so long a period of lassitude, he decided to investigate, and cutting through the hedges, unworried, soldier that he was, by the merciless thorns, he discovered the tower, and the staircase, and the door to the room where the Princess lay on her bed reading books.

The Princess looked up from her volume as he came through the door, and waited in silence to find out what he wanted. She felt no great excitement at his arrival, for it didn't seem to her that she was lacking anything in her life. She had what she always had, and wanted, so far as she knew, nothing.

The soldier questioned the Princess about her life in the tower and she told him what little there was to tell: about the relatives who had visited but no longer did, about her books, about the view from the window.

"But what about food?" the soldier asked. "When they stopped coming, what did you do for food?"

"Food?" said the Princess.

Which was how the soldier discovered that by some means or other, the Princess, never having had food, had never learned to need it. This was of particular interest to the soldier, because although he had done everything and seen everything and been everywhere, and was tired of it all, there remained one thing that still gave him special pleasure: the sight of a woman eating excited him as nothing else now could. And though the Princess was neither beautiful nor not beautiful, she did have an exceptionally well-formed mouth.

"I'll be back," he said, closing the door behind him. And as he found an oil can above the lintel and oiled the lock, the Princess couldn't tell whether the key had been turned or not.

He returned, although the Princess, having no way of gauging the passing of time, had no idea how long it had been since he first arrived. He opened the door and saw the Princess on her bed reading. She looked up and smiled. The soldier took the book from her hands and laid a small cloth on the bed, on which he placed the food he had brought. She smiled again, and without having to be told, began to pick up this morsel and that, first savouring the smell, then pressing it gently against her lips, and finally tasting. It pleased her, and it pleased him to watch her eat.

Now, at intervals, the soldier came to her with food. Never too often and never with too much. Food remained a pleasure but never became a necessity. Whenever he tired of his wanderings he would visit the tower with small delicacies wrapped in a white cloth; and she was always willing to exchange the pleasure of her book for the pleasure of food. This went on for many years. The Princess came to expect his visits, although, in her timeless world, it couldn't be said that she actually looked forward to them.

Then, one day, a second soldier passed that way. By now rumours had spread abroad about the strange Princess in the tower and the soldier who visited her from time to time with small quantities of delicious food. The second soldier had heard these stories and, one day, being battle-fatigued and lacking anything better to do, set out to see if he couldn't find the Princess.

He recognised the thicket covering the tower from a good way off and found the small path that the first soldier had worn through the undergrowth. When he entered the room at the top of the tower, he found the Princess in her usual pose on the bed. She looked up from her book expecting to see the first soldier and his small bundle.

"Don't be frightened," the second soldier said, although such an emotion had not occurred to her before he said it. "I've been looking for you."

And now she did begin to feel alarmed. She had never thought of herself as known in the outside world, and felt a strange distress at the thought of existing in someone's mind as something to be found. The second soldier was a clever man, and knowing about the first soldier and the food, he knew he needed an edge. He looked carefully about the room and thought for a long time.

"I'll be back," he said, as he closed the door behind him and oiled the lock. And the Princess didn't doubt it.

When he returned he brought with him two objects: a mirror and a calendar with all the days of the week, and the months of the year laid out for years to come. He placed the mirror on the wall in front of the Princess' bed, and nailed the calendar to the door.

"Look," he said, taking the Princess' hand and leading her from the bed to stand in front of the mirror. The second soldier had understood on his first visit that it was not only food the Princess had lacked all her life.

Having no way of seeing herself, she had no precise notion that she existed at all. And having no way to mark the passage of time, lacked any sense of expectation. The first soldier could come and go, but she did not wait or hope that he would come soon, or this week, or tomorrow.

She looked at her reflection in the mirror, and at first it distressed her. She hadn't seen anything quite like it before. But the second soldier stood by her and she watched his reflection standing next to hers and telling her, "That is you."

It took some time, but very gradually she started to think. "Perhaps it is. Perhaps I am here. Perhaps, when people come into this room, they see me." And she looked sideways, out of the corners of her narrowing eyes at the Princess in the mirror.

"When I come to see you," the second soldier said, "that is what I come to see. You."

"Me," the Princess repeated, trying to get used to the idea. It was still very disturbing, and yet, there was something about it that she found very pleasant. Strange, but pleasant.

"I will come again next week," the second soldier said, and led her to the calendar to show her how to mark the days. "On this day, Friday, next week, I will come back to see you." And he looked long and hard into her eyes. For this soldier too had something that gave him particular pleasure. He loved to see in women's eyes a look of expectation, a dawning of new possibilities. And the Princess had eyes that enabled this to show to an extraordinary degree. But that was not all; the look of expectation was only a part of his pleasure. To complete it he wanted to see that gleam fade to a subtler tone of disappointment.

He had returned on the appointed day and watched as the Princess' eyes began to show she had understood the nature of time. When he left he gave her another day, and came then too. But on the third occasion he did not come when he had said, but two days later, and there in her eyes was the completion of his pleasure. When he left saying he would be back on such a date, he saw hope and anxiety mingle in a way he could never have hoped for.

The first soldier did not make a visit during this time, and the second

soldier was careful to check that the Princess was alone when he arrived. But he left the calendar and the mirror in the room, and she let them stay where he had put them.

When the first soldier came again he looked at both the objects, but said nothing. He laid the food before the Princess and watched her lips as she bit off and chewed small mouthfuls. When she had finished he took up the cloth and walked over to the mirror.

"Stand here," he said, pointing to a spot just in front of it. He looked at her reflection for a moment and then took off a diamond ring he wore and, using the edge of one of its facets, he etched the outline of the Princess' reflection on to the glass.

"I'll be back when I can," he said, glancing at the calendar, and left.

When the second soldier returned, the Princess was pleased to see him as he came through the door, looking, as she had now come to feel, at her. But immediately his gaze fell on the mirror, and the outline etched upon it. He looked first at the Princess and then at the glass.

"Stand here," he said, pointing to a spot in front of the mirror, and when she did, he moved her slightly until her reflection exactly filled the outline. The Princess looked at herself, and thought, as she always did, when she caught her reflection as she passed by to return or get a book, "Here I am."

The second soldier eased a ring from his finger, and with the edge of a facet of the diamond, drew around the reflection of her eyes. First one, then the other. He stepped back to look at it for a moment, then filled in the lids, the pupils and the irises. At last, a pair of eyes stared out from the outline of a woman on the glass, fixed in an expression of longing and alarm so poignant that the Princess gasped. She could no longer see her own eyes when she looked into the mirror.

When the first soldier came back he spent at least as much time looking at the eyes in the glass as he did watching the Princess eat. When she had finished, he had her stand in front of the mirror and drew her mouth; the lips full and open, mobile and beautiful. The Princess could no longer see her lips when she looked into the glass.

Now, on each occasion, the portrait in the mirror was added to. Each soldier examined the work of the other, and then etched a new piece on to the mirror. The outline became no more than a frame, as each man added a feature according to his mood. An elbow was matched with the bridge of a nose; a wrist with a knee; a buttock curved beside an anklebone; one ear rested on a fingernail. Neither man noticed anything that had gone before the other man's last sketch.

Eventually the first soldier stopped bringing food, and the second soldier no longer bothered with the calendar. There came a time when the Princess could no longer see herself at all in the mirror. "I'm not here," she said to herself. "Perhaps I never was." And she disappeared.

No one knows exactly how it happened. It could have been that she opened the door one day, discovered that the soldiers had long since stopped locking it, and walked down the winding staircase and vanished forever in the dense, impenetrable forest that surrounded the tower. Or it may have been that, finding herself no longer there, she simply wasn't any more. At any rate, she vanished and no one ever saw or heard of her again.

The two soldiers hardly noticed her absence. They continued to visit the tower, turn by turn, and left their messages for each other on the mirror. The years passed, and although they never met, their contentment and affection deepened. Eventually they grew old and died. One day the first soldier arrived and found that nothing had been added to the glass. It was not long after that he stopped coming too.

And the mirror rusted, the silvering began to flake away, leaving only the scratches on the glass that were indecipherable. When the tower began to crumble, pieces of stone fell and broke the glass itself until there was nothing left of this earliest of examples of Cubist art except rubble greened over with wild vegetation. It was to be many centuries before the form would be revived, but by then, no one had any notion that it wasn't the first time.

Two Sheep

JANET FRAME

Animal fables have a way of sounding simple, but their morals can be very complex. This modern fable is a real mind-teaser.

T wo sheep were travelling to the saleyards. The first sheep knew that after they had been sold their destination was the slaughter-house at the freezing works. The second sheep did not know of their fate. They were being driven with the rest of the flock along a hot dusty valley road where the surrounding hills leaned in a sun-scorched wilderness of rock, tussock and old rabbit warrens. They moved slowly, for the drover in his trap was in no hurry, and had even taken one of the dogs to sit beside him while the other scrambled from side to side of the flock, guiding them.

"I think," said the first sheep who was aware of their approaching death, "that the sun has never shone so warm on my fleece, nor, from what I see with my small sheep's eye, has the sky seemed so flawless, without seams or tucks or cracks or blemishes."

"You are crazy," said the second sheep who did not know of their approaching death. "The sun is warm, yes, but how hot and dusty and heavy my wool feels! It is a burden to go trotting along this oven shelf. It seems our journey will never end."

"How fresh and juicy the grass appears on the hill!" the first sheep exclaimed. "And not a hawk in the sky!"

"I think," replied the second sheep, "that something has blinded you. Just look up in the sky and see those three hawks waiting to swoop and attack us!"

They trotted on further through the valley road. Now and again the second sheep stumbled.

"I feel so tired," he said. "I wonder how much longer we must walk on and on through this hot dusty valley?"

But the first sheep walked nimbly and his wool felt light upon him as if he had just been shorn. He could have gambolled like a lamb in August.

"I still think," he said, "that today is the most wonderful day I have known. I do not feel that the road is hot and dusty. I do not notice the stones and grit that you complain of. To me the hills have never seemed so green and enticing, the sun has never seemed so warm and comforting. I believe that I could walk through this valley forever, and never feel tired or hungry or thirsty."

"Whatever has come over you?" the second sheep asked crossly. "Here we are, trotting along hour after hour, and soon we shall stand in our pens in the saleyards while the sun leans over us with its branding irons and our overcoats are such a burden that they drag us to the floor of our pen where we are almost trampled to death by the so dainty feet of our fellow sheep. A fine life that is. It would not surprise me if after we are sold we are taken in trucks to the freezing works and killed in cold blood. But," he added, comforting himself, "that is not likely to happen. Oh no, that could never happen! I have it on authority that even when they are trampled by their fellows, sheep do not die. The tales we hear from time to time are but malicious rumours, and those vivid dreams which strike us in the night as we sleep on the sheltered hills, they are but illusions. Do you not agree?" he asked the first sheep.

They were turning now from the valley road, and the saleyards were in sight, while drawn up in the siding on the rusty railway lines, the red trucks stood waiting, spattered inside with sheep and cattle dirt and with white chalk marks, in cipher, on the outside. And still the first sheep did not reveal to his companion that they were being driven to certain death.

When they were jostled inside their pen the first sheep gave an exclamation of delight.

"What a pleasant little house they have led us to! I have never seen such smart red-painted bars, and such four-square corners. And look at the elegant stairway which we will climb to enter those red caravans for our seaside holiday!"

"You make me tired," the second sheep said. "We are standing inside a dirty pen, nothing more, and I cannot move my feet in their nicely polished black shoes but I tread upon the dirt left by sheep which have been imprisoned here before us. In fact I have never been so badly treated in all my life!" And the second sheep began to cry. Just then a kind elderly sheep jostled through the flock and began to comfort him.

"You have been frightening your companion, I suppose," she said angrily to the first sheep. "You have been telling horrible tales of our fate. Some sheep never know when to keep things to themselves. There was no need to tell your companion the truth, that we are being led to certain death!"

But the first sheep did not answer. He was thinking that the sun had never blessed him with so much warmth, that no crowded pen had ever seemed so comfortable and luxurious. Then suddenly he was taken by surprise and hustled out of a little gate and up the ramp into the waiting truck, and suddenly too the sun shone in its true colours, battering him about the head with gigantic burning bars, while the hawks congregated above, sizzling the sky with their wings, and a pall of dust clung to the barren used-up hills, and everywhere was commotion, pushing, struggling, bleating, trampling.

"This must be death," he thought, and he began to struggle and cry out.

The second sheep, having at last learned that he would meet his fate at the freezing works, stood unperturbed now in the truck with his nose against the wall and his eyes looking through the slits.

"You are right," he said to the first sheep. "The hill has never seemed so green, the sun has never been warmer, and this truck with its neat red walls is a mansion where I would happily spend the rest of my days."

But the first sheep did not answer. He had seen the approach of death. He could hide from it no longer. He had given up the struggle and was lying exhausted in a corner of the truck. And when the truck arrived at its destination, the freezing works, the man whose duty it was to unload the sheep noticed the first lying so still in the corner that he believed it was dead.

"We can't have dead sheep," he said. "How can you kill a dead sheep?"

So he heaved the first sheep out of the door of the truck onto the rusty railway line.

"I'll move it away later," he said to himself. "Meanwhile here goes with this lot."

And while he was so busy moving the flock, the first sheep, recovering, sprang up and trotted away along the line, out the gate of the freezing works, up the road, along another road, until he saw a flock being driven before him.

"I will join the flock," he said. "No one will notice, and I shall be safe."

While the drover was not looking, the first sheep hurried in among the flock and was soon trotting along with them until they came to a hot dusty road through a valley where the hills leaned in a sun-scorched wilderness of rock, tussock, and old rabbit warrens.

By now he was feeling very tired. He spoke for the first time to his new companions.

"What a hot dusty road," he said. "How uncomfortable the heat is, and the sun seems to be striking me for its own burning purposes."

The sheep walking beside him looked surprised.

"It is a wonderful day," he exclaimed. "The sun is warmer than I have ever known it, the hills glow green with luscious grass, and there is not a hawk in the sky to threaten us!"

"You mean," the first sheep replied slyly, that you are on your way to the saleyards, and then to the freezing works to be killed."

The other sheep gave a bleat of surprise.

"How did you guess?" he asked.

"Oh," said the first sheep wisely, "I know the code. And because I know the code I shall go around in circles all my life, not knowing whether to think that the hills are bare or whether they are green, whether the hawks are scarce or plentiful, whether the sun is friend or foe. For the rest of my life I shall not speak another word. I shall trot along the hot dusty valleys where the hills are both barren and lush with spring grass.

"What shall I do but keep silent?"

And so it happened, and over and over again the first sheep escaped death, and rejoined the flock of sheep who were travelling to the freezing works. He is still alive today. If you notice him in a flock, being driven along a hot dusty road, you will be able to distinguish him by his timidity, his uncertainty, the frenzied expression in his eyes when he tries, in his condemned silence, to discover whether the sky is at last free from hawks, or whether they circle in twos and threes above him, waiting to kill him.

Fire

ISAAC BASHEVIS SINGER

*"Anger won't make a house burn." Perhaps not, but poor Leibus has
reason to believe it did!*

I want to tell you a story. It isn't from a book—it happened to me
personally. I've kept it secret all these years, but I know now I'll
never leave this poorhouse alive. I'll be carried straight from here
to the morgue. So I want the truth known. I'd have had the rabbi and
the town elders here, and got them to record it in the community book,
but why embarrass my brother's children and grandchildren? Here is
my story.

I come from Janow near Zomosc. The place is called Poorman's Kingdom, for obvious reasons. My father, God bless his memory, had seven
children, but lost five of them. They grew up strong as oaks and then
down they fell. Three boys and two girls! No one knew what was wrong.
The fever got them one after the other. When Chaim Jonah, the youngest,
died, my mother—may she intercede for me in heaven—went out like
a candle. She wasn't ill, she just stopped eating and stayed in bed. Neighbors dripped in and asked, "Beile Rivke, what's wrong?" and she answered, "Nothing. I'm just going to die." The doctor came and she was
bled; they applied cups and leeches, exorcised the evil eye, washed her
with urine, but nothing worked. She shriveled up until she was nothing
but a bag of bones. When she had said her Confession of Sins she called
me to her side. "Your brother Lippe will make his way in the world,"
she said, "but you, Leibus, I pity."

Father never liked me. I don't know why. Lippe was taller than me,
he took after Mother's family. He was smart in school though he didn't
study. I studied, but it didn't help. What I heard went in one ear and

out the other. Even so I can find my way around in the Bible. I was soon taken out of *cheder.*

My brother Lippe was, as the saying goes, the apple of Father's eye. When my brother did something wrong, Father looked the other way, but God forbid that I should make a mistake. He had a weighty hand; every time he smacked me I saw my dead grandmother. As far back as I can remember it was like that. The slightest thing and off came his belt. He beat me black and blue. It was always, "Don't go here, don't go there." In the synagogue, for example, all the other boys fooled around during the services, but if I left out a single "Amen," I got my "reward." At home I did all the work. We had a handmill, and all day long I ground buckwheat; I was also water-carrier and wood-chopper; I made the fire and cleaned the outhouse. Mother protected me while she was alive, but after she was gone, I was a stepchild. Don't think it didn't eat into me, but what could I do? My brother Lippe shoved me around too.— "Leibus, do this. Leibus, do that."—Lippe had his friends; he liked to drink; he hung around the tavern.

There was a pretty girl in our town, Havele. Her father owned a drygoods store. He was well fixed, and he had his ideas about a son-in-law. My brother had other ideas. He set his trap carefully. He paid the matchmakers not to bring her proposals. He spread a rumor that someone in her family had hanged himself. His friends helped out, and in return they got their share of brandy and poppy seed cake. Money was no problem for him. He just opened Father's drawer and took what he pleased. In the end Havele's father was beaten down, and gave consent to the marriage to Lippe.

The whole town celebrated the engagement. The bridegroom does not usually bring a dowry, but Lippe persuaded Father to give him two hundred gulden. He also got a wardrobe fit for a landlord. At the wedding there were two bands, one from Janow and one from Bilgorai. That is how he started on his way up. But it was different for the younger brother; he didn't even get a new pair of pants. Father had promised me clothes, but he put off ordering from day to day, and by the time he had bought the material it was too late to have it made up. I went to the wedding in rags. The girls laughed at me. Such was my luck.

I thought I would go the way of my other brothers and sisters. But I was not fated to die. Lippe got married; as the saying goes, he started off on the right foot. He became a successful dealer in grain. Near Janow there was a watermill belonging to Reb Israel David, son of Malka, a fine man. Israel David took a liking to my brother and sold him the mill for a song. I don't know why he sold it; some said that he wanted to go to the Holy Land, others that he had relatives in Hungary. Whatever the reason, shortly after selling the mill, he died.

Havele had one child after another, each prettier than the last; they were such marvels, people came just to look at them. The dowry Father had given Lippe undermined his own business; he was left without a cent. The business collapsed, as well as his strength, but if you think that my brother Lippe gave him a helping hand, you're very much mistaken. Lippe neither saw nor heard anything, and Father took his bitterness out on me. What he had against me I don't know; sometimes a man conceives such a hatred for his child. No matter what I said, it was wrong, and no matter how much I did, it was not enough.

Then father fell ill, and everyone could see he would not last long. My brother Lippe was busy making money. I took care of Father. It was I who carried the bedpan; it was I who washed, bathed, combed him. He couldn't digest anything; he kept spitting up whatever he ate. The disease spread to his legs too, so he couldn't walk. I had to bring him everything, and whenever he saw me he looked at me as though I were dirt. Sometimes he wore me out so that I wanted to run from him to the end of the world, but how can you leave your own father? And so I suffered in silence. The final weeks were just hell: Father swearing and groaning. I have never heard more horrible curses. My brother Lippe would drop in twice a week and ask with a smile, "Well, how are you, Father? No better?" and the moment Father saw him, his eyes brightened. I have forgiven him, and may God forgive him too: does a man know what he is doing?

It took him two weeks to die and I can't begin to describe his agony. Every time he opened his eyes he stared at me in rage. After the funeral his will was found under a pillow; I was dispossessed. Everything was left to Lippe—the house, the handmill, the cupboard, the chest of drawers, even the dishes. The town was shocked; such a will, people said, was illegal. There was even a precedent to this effect in the Talmud. It was suggested that Lippe give me the house, but he merely laughed. Instead he sold it immediately, and moved the handmill and the furniture to his own place. I was left the pillow. This is the truth pure and simple. May I be no less pure when I come before God!

I began to work for a carpenter and I could scarcely earn a living. I slept in a shed; Lippe forgot that he had a brother. But who do you suppose said *kaddish* for Father? There was always some reason why it couldn't be Lippe: I lived in town, there weren't enough men at the mill for the service, it was too far away for him to get to *shul* on Saturday.

At first they gossiped about his treatment of me, but then people began to say he must have his reasons. When a man is down, everyone likes to walk on him.

I was now no longer young and still unmarried. I had grown a beard but no one thought of a match for me. If a matchmaker did come, what he offered was the dregs of the dregs. But why should I deny it, I did fall in love. The girl was the cobbler's daughter and I used to watch her emptying slops. But she became engaged to a cooper. Who wants an orphan? I was no fool; it hurt. Sometimes I couldn't sleep at night. I would toss about in my bed as if I had a fever. Why? What had I done to my father? I decided that I would stop saying *kaddish*, but a year had almost gone by. Besides how can you take revenge on the dead?

And now let me tell you what happened.

One Friday night I lay in my shed on a pile of shavings. I had worked hard; in those days one began at dawn, and the price of the candle was deducted from one's wages. I hadn't even had time to go to the bathhouse. On Fridays we got no lunch, so we should have a keener appetite for the Sabbath dinner, but at dinner the carpenter's wife always dished out less to me than to the others. Everyone else got a nice piece of fish, I got the tail. I would choke on the first mouthful of bone. The soup was watery, and my portion of meat was the chicken legs, along with some strings of muscle. It was not only that you couldn't chew it, but if you swallowed it, according to the Talmud, it weakened your memory. I didn't even get enough *challah*, and as for any of the sweets, I never got a taste. So I had gone to sleep hungry.

It was winter, and bitter cold in my shed. There was an awful racket— the mice. I lay on my pile of shavings, with rags for covers, burning with rage. What I wanted was to get my hands on my brother Lippe. Havele also came into my mind; you might expect a sister-in-law to be kinder than a brother, but she had time only for herself and her little dolls. The way she dressed you would have thought she was a great lady; the few times she came to *shul* to attend a wedding, she wore a plumed hat. Wherever I went I would hear told how Lippe had bought this, Havele had bought that; their main business, it seemed, was adorning themselves. She treated herself to a skunk coat, and then to a fox fur; she paraded herself in flounces while I lay like a dog, my belly growling with hunger. I cursed them both. I prayed that God would send them plagues, and everything else I could think of. Gradually I fell asleep.

But then I awoke; it was the middle of the night and I felt that

I must take revenge. It was as if some devil had seized me by the hair and shouted, "Leibus, it is time for revenge!" I got up; in the darkness I found a bag which I filled with shavings. Such things are forbidden on the Sabbath, but I had forgotten my religion: surely there was a *dybbuk* in me. I dressed quietly, took the bag with the shavings, two flints and a wick, and sneaked out. I would set fire to my brother's house, the mill, the granary, everything.

It was pitch dark out and I had a long way to go. I kept away from the town. I cut across swampy pastures, over fields and meadows. I knew that I would lose everything—this world and the next. I even thought of my mother lying in her grave: what would she say? But when you're mad you can't stop. You bite off your tongue to spite your face, as the saying goes. I wasn't even worried about running into someone I knew. I just wasn't myself.

I walked and walked, and the wind blew; the cold cut into me. I sank into snow over my knees, and climbed out of one ditch only to fall into another. As I passed by the hamlet known as "The Pines," dogs attacked me. You know how it is: when one dog barks, all the rest join in. I was pursued by a pack, and I thought I would be torn to pieces. It was a miracle that the peasants didn't wake and take me for a horse thief; they would have done away with me on the spot. I was on the verge of giving up the whole thing; I wanted to drop the bag and hurry back to bed. Or I thought of simply wandering away, but my *dybbuk* kept inciting me: "Now or never!" I trudged on and on. Wood shavings aren't heavy, but if you carry a bagful long enough you feel it. I began to sweat, but I kept on going at the risk of my life.

And now listen to this coincidence.

As I walked I suddenly saw a red glow in the sky. Could it be dawn? No, that didn't seem possible. It was early winter; the nights were long. I was very close to the mill and I walked faster. I almost ran. Well, to make a long story short, I arrived at the mill to find it on fire. Can you imagine that? I had come to set a building on fire and it was already burning. I stood as though paralyzed, with my head spinning; it seemed to me that I was losing my mind. Maybe I was: for the very next moment I threw down my bag of shavings and began to scream for help. I was about to run to the mill when I remembered Lippe and his family, and so I rushed to the house; it was a blazing inferno. It seemed they had all been overcome by smoke. Beams were burning; it was as bright as on Simchas Torah. Inside it felt like an oven, but I ran to the bedroom, smashed open a window, seized my brother, and threw him into the

snow. I did the same with his wife and children. I almost choked to death but I rescued them all. No sooner had I finished, than the roof collapsed. My screams had awakened the peasants and now they came running. They revived my brother and his family. The chimney and a pile of ashes were all that was left of the house but the peasants managed to put out the fire in the mill. I caught sight of the bag of shavings and threw it into the fire. My brother and his family found shelter with some neighbors. By this time it was daylight.

My brother's first question was, "How did it happen? How come you're here?" My sister-in-law rushed at me to scratch my eyes out. "He did it! He set the fire!" The peasants also questioned me, "What devil brought you here?" I didn't know what to say. They began to club me. Just before I was battered to a pulp, my brother held up his hand, "No more, neighbors. There is a God and He'll punish him," and with that he spat in my face.

Somehow or other I managed to get home; I didn't walk, I dragged myself. Like a crippled animal I pulled myself along on all fours. A few times I paused to cool my wounds in the snow. But when I got home my real troubles began. Everyone asked, "Where were you? How come you knew your brother's house was on fire?" Then they learned that I was suspected. The man I worked for came to my shed and raised the roof when he found that one of his bags was missing. All Janow said that I had set my brother's house on fire, and on the Sabbath no less.

Things couldn't have been worse. I was in danger of being jailed, or pilloried in the synagogue yard. I didn't wait, I made myself scarce.

A carter took pity on me and drove me to Zamosc that Saturday night. He carried no passengers, only freight, and he squeezed me in among the barrels. When the story of the fire reached Zamosc, I left for Lublin. There I became a carpenter and married. My wife bore me no children; I worked hard but I had no luck. My brother Lippe became a millionaire— he owned half of Janow—but I never had a line from him. His children married rabbis and wealthy businessmen. He is no longer alive—he died weighted down with riches and honors.

Until now I have told this story to no one. Who would have believed it? I even kept it a secret that I was from Janow. I always said that I was from Shebreshin. But now that I'm on my deathbed, why should I lie? What I've told is the truth, the whole whole truth. There's only one thing I don't understand and won't understand it until I'm in my grave: why did a fire have to break out in my brother's house on just that night? Some time ago it occurred to me that it was my anger that started the fire. What do you think?

"Anger won't make a house burn."

"I know. . . . Still there's that expression, 'burning anger!' "

"Oh, that's just a way of talking."

Well, when I saw that fire I forgot everything and rushed to save them. Without me they would have all been ashes. Now that I'm about to die, I want the truth known.

Translated by Norbert Guterman

---

challah: braided eggbread

cheder: elementary religious classes

dybbuk: the body of a living person occupied by the wandering soul of a dead person

Kaddish: a prayer recited after the death of a close relative

shul: a synagogue

Simchas Torah: a Jewish festival celebrating the Law of Moses

Talmud: a body of Jewish ceremonial law and legend dating from the 5th century B.C.

The Ghost

RAFAEL ALBERTI

It appears to me white in the morning.
It looks at me and deeply lost in thought
goes round and round the house.

Later, in the woods, I come upon it green.
It looks at me, pricking up its ears.
The air echoes the sea. It inhales it and slowly
goes round and round the house.

It appears to me red in the afternoon,
lost in the sands of the beach.
The waves burn, it studies them and sadly
goes round and round the house.

It appears to me black at night,
staring, its mane bristling.
The moon rises. It neighs at it and alone
goes round and round the house.

Translated by José A. Elgorriaga
and Martin Paul

Immortality

YASUNARI KAWABATA

If their love is true, surely lovers can meet beyond the grave?

An old man and a girl were walking.

The pair looked odd in several respects. There was probably sixty years' difference in their ages, but they did not seem to mind it in the least and walked close together like sweethearts. The old man was deaf. He could hardly catch what the girl said. She wore a purple kimono showing a pattern of small white arrows, although the lower part of it was hidden under a *hakama* of reddish purple. Her sleeves were a little too long. The old man was dressed in something like what a peasant woman would wear to go weeding in rice paddies. He did not wear working gloves or leggings, but his cotton shirt and pants looked like a woman's. The pants were too large around his puny waist.

On the lawn, and a short distance ahead of the pair, there stood a high fence of netted wires. Although it blocked their way, they seemed to pay no attention. Without even slowing down, they walked straight through the fence, moving like a breeze.

The girl seemed to notice the fence after they were on the other side.

"My!" She stared at the old man with inquisitive eyes. "You were able to walk through the fence, too, weren't you, Shintarō?"

The old man did not hear. But he grabbed the wire netting and began to shake it.

"This damned thing! This damned thing!" he yelled.

He pushed the fence so hard that, to his surprise, it began to move away from him. He staggered and clung to the fence, his body leaning forward.

"Careful, Shintarō! What has happened?" cried the girl, dashing to hold his upper body from behind. "You can take your hands off the fence now." Then she added, "How light you've become!"

At last the old man was able to stand straight again. As he panted, his shoulders rose and fell.

"Thank you," he said and clasped the netting again, this time lightly with one hand. He then continued to speak in the loud voice characteristic of a deaf man. "Day in and day out I used to pick up golf balls on the other side of this fence. It was my job for seventeen long years."

"Only for seventeen years? That's not so very long!"

"They would hit balls any way they wanted. The balls made a sound when they hit the net. At each sound I ducked my head, until I got used to it. It was because of the sound that I lost my hearing. This damned thing!"

The wire fence, designed to protect caddies, had casters at its base and could be moved in any direction on the practice field. The field and the golf course were separated by a line of trees. The trees stood in an irregular line because they had grown there naturally and were left uncut when the big grove was developed into a golf course.

The old man and the girl began to walk away from the fence. "You can hear the same dear sound of the waves," the girl said. Wanting to make sure that the man heard her, she put her mouth to his ear and repeated, "You can hear the same dear sound of the waves."

"What?" The old man closed his eyes. "Such sweet breath from Misako. It's just as it was in the old days."

"Can't you hear the same dear sound of the waves?"

"The waves? Did you say the waves? And dear? How could the waves sound dear to you after you drowned yourself in them?"

"It's all so dear. I've come back to my old home after fifty-five years and found that you've come home, too. It's all so romantic." Although the words no longer reached him, she continued on. "It was right for me to throw myself into the sea. Because of that, I have been and will be able to love you always, in the same way I loved you at the time I died. Besides, all my memories and recollections ended at the age of seventeen. As far as I'm concerned, you will be a young man forever. It's the same for you, too, Shintarō. If I hadn't killed myself at seventeen and if you had come back here to see me, you would have found an ugly old woman. How dreadful! I wouldn't have dared to see you."

"I went up to Tokyo," the old man began to speak in the typical way a deaf person mumbles to himself. "But I couldn't make a go of it. I came home as a frustrated old man. I got a job at a golf course. It was the course overlooking the sea, where a grief-stricken girl had drowned herself after being forcibly separated from me. I pleaded with them to hire me there, and they took pity."

"We are now on the land that used to belong to your family, Shintarō."

"To pick up golf balls at the practice field—that was about all I could do. My back ached, but I carried on. There was one girl who threw herself into the sea, all on account of me. The rocky cliff where she jumped off is nearby, so even a senile old man like myself can get there and jump—so I kept thinking."

"Don't do it, Shintarō. Be sure to live on. When you are gone, there won't be a single person in this world to remember me. I'll truly be dead then." The girl clung to the old man as she said so, but he did not hear.

Just the same, he took her in his arms.

"Yes," he said. "Let's die together. You and me this time. You've come to take me with you, haven't you?"

"Together? No, you keep living on, please. Live for my sake." The girl raised her head from the man's shoulders and looked straight ahead. Her voice became animated. "Look! Those big trees are still there. All three of them look just as they did in the old days. They make me nostalgic."

The old man turned his eyes toward the three big trees, too, as the girl pointed at them.

"Golfers are afraid of those trees," he said. "They want to cut them down. They say their balls always turn right, as if those trees were pulling them in with some magic power."

"Those golfers will die soon. Sooner than those trees, which have been standing there for centuries. They say those things because they don't know how short a human life is."

"My ancestors had taken good care of those trees for hundreds of years, so when I sold the land I got a promise that the three trees would not be cut down."

"Let's go over there," the girl urged and led the staggering old man by the hand toward the trees.

She passed through the trunk of one of the trees. So did the old man.

"Oh!" She gazed at the old man in amazement. "Are you dead, too? Are you, Shintarō? When did you die?"

He did not answer.

"You're dead. You're really dead, aren't you? I wonder why we didn't meet in the land of the dead. Now let's see if you are truly alive or dead. If you are dead, I'll enter the tree with you."

The old man and the girl disappeared into the tree trunk. They never came out of it.

The color of evening began to show over the bushes behind the three big trees. The far sky, from which the sound of the sea came, was hazed in faint red.

Translated by Makoto Ueda

---

hakama: a type of divided skirt

Bears Discover Fire

TERRY BISSON

What do people think about when they gaze into campfire flames?
Would bears think the same thing if they sat around a campfire?

I was driving with my brother, the preacher, and my nephew, the preacher's son, on I-65 just north of Bowling Green when we got a flat. It was Sunday night and we had been to visit Mother at the Home. We were in my car. The flat caused what you might call knowing groans since, as the old-fashioned one in my family (so they tell me), I fix my own tires, and my brother is always telling me to get radials and quit buying old tires.

But if you know how to mount and fix tires yourself, you can pick them up for almost nothing.

Since it was a left rear tire, I pulled over left, onto the median grass. The way my Caddy stumbled to a stop, I figured the tire was ruined. "I guess there's no need asking if you have any of the *FlatFix* in the trunk," said Wallace.

"Here, son, hold the light," I said to Wallace Jr. He's old enough to want to help and not old enough (yet) to think he knows it all. If I'd married and had kids, he's the kind I'd have wanted.

An old Caddy has a big trunk that tends to fill up like a shed. Mine's a '56. Wallace was wearing his Sunday shirt, so he didn't offer to help while I pulled magazines, fishing tackle, a wooden tool box, some old clothes, a comealong wrapped in a grass sack, and a tobacco sprayer out of the way, looking for my jack. The spare looked a little soft.

The light went out. "Shake it, son," I said.

It went back on. The bumper jack was long gone, but I carry a little 1/4 ton hydraulic. I finally found it under Mother's old *Southern Livings*, 1978-1986. I had been meaning to drop them at the dump.

313

If Wallace hadn't been along, I'd have let Wallace Jr. position the jack under the axle, but I got on my knees and did it myself. There's nothing wrong with a boy learning to change a tire. Even if you're not going to fix and mount them, you're still going to have to change a few in this life. The light went off again before I had the wheel off the ground. I was surprised at how dark the night was already. It was late October and beginning to get cool. "Shake it again, son," I said.

It went back on but it was weak. Flickery.

"With radials you just don't *have* flats," Wallace explained in that voice he uses when he's talking to a number of people at once; in this case, Wallace Jr. and myself. "And even when you do, you just squirt them with this stuff called *FlatFix* and you just drive on. $3.95 the can."

"Uncle Bobby can fix a tire hisself," said Wallace Jr., out of loyalty I presume.

"Himself," I said from halfway under the car. If it was up to Wallace, the boy would talk like what Mother used to call "a helock from the gorges of the mountains." But drive on radials.

"Shake that light again," I said. It was about gone. I spun the lugs off into the hubcap and pulled the wheel. The tire had blown out along the sidewall. "Won't be fixing this one," I said. Not that I cared. I have a pile as tall as a man out by the barn.

The light went out again, then came back better than ever as I was fitting the spare over the lugs. "Much better," I said. There was a flood of dim orange flickery light. But when I turned to find the lug nuts, I was surprised to see that the flashlight the boy was holding was dead. The light was coming from two bears at the edge of the trees, holding torches. They were big, three-hundred-pounders, standing about five feet tall. Wallace Jr. and his father had seen them and were standing perfectly still. It's best not to alarm bears.

I fished the lug nuts out of the hubcap and spun them on. I usually like to put a little oil on them, but this time I let it go. I reached under the car and let the jack down and pulled it out. I was relieved to see that the spare was high enough to drive on. I put the jack and the lug wrench and the flat into the trunk. Instead of replacing the hubcap, I put it in there too. All this time, the bears never made a move. They just held the torches up, whether out of curiosity or helpfulness, there was no way of knowing. It looked like there may have been more bears behind them, in the trees.

Opening three doors at once, we got into the car and drove off. Wallace was the first to speak. "Looks like bears have discovered fire," he said.

When we first took Mother to the Home, almost four years (forty-seven months) ago, she told Wallace and me she was ready to die. "Don't worry about me, boys," she whispered, pulling us both down so the nurse wouldn't hear. "I've drove a million miles and I'm ready to pass over to the other shore. I won't have long to linger here." She drove a consolidated school bus for thirty-nine years. Later, after Wallace left, she told me about her dream. A bunch of doctors were sitting around in a circle discussing her case. One said, "We've done all we can for her, boys, let's let her go." They all turned their hands up and smiled. When she didn't die that fall, she seemed disappointed, though as spring came she forgot about it, as old people will.

In addition to taking Wallace and Wallace Jr. to see Mother on Sunday nights, I go myself on Tuesdays and Thursdays. I usually find her sitting in front of the TV, even though she doesn't watch it. The nurses keep it on all the time. They say the old folks like the flickering. It soothes them down.

"What's this I hear about bears discovering fire?" she said on Tuesday. "It's true," I told her as I combed her long white hair with the shell comb Wallace had bought her from Florida. Monday there had been a story in the Louisville *Courier-Journal*, and Tuesday one on NBC or CBS Nightly News. People were seeing bears all over the state, and in Virginia as well. They had quit hibernating, and were apparently planning to spend the winter in the medians of the interstates. There have always been bears in the mountains of Virginia, but not here in western Kentucky, not for almost a hundred years. The last one was killed when Mother was a girl. The theory in the *Courier-Journal* was that they were following I-65 down from the forests of Michigan and Canada, but one old man from Allen County (interviewed on nationwide TV) said that there had always been a few bears left back in the hills, and they had come out to join the others now that they had discovered fire.

"They don't hibernate any more," I said. "They make a fire and keep it going all winter."

"I declare," Mother said. "What'll they think of next!" The nurse came to take her tobacco away, which is the signal for bedtime.

Every October, Wallace Jr. stays with me while his parents go to camp. I realize how backward that sounds, but there it is. My brother is a minister (House of the Righteous Way, Reformed), but he makes two thirds of his living in real estate. He and Elizabeth go to a Christian Success Retreat in South Carolina, where people from all over the country practise selling things to one another. I know what it's like not because they've ever bothered to tell me, but because I've seen the Revolving Equity Success Plan ads late at night on TV.

The schoolbus let Wallace Jr. off at my house on Wednesday, the day they left. The boy doesn't have to pack much of a bag when he stays with me. He has his own room here. As the eldest of our family, I hung onto the old home place near Smiths Grove. It's getting run down, but Wallace Jr. and I don't mind. He has his own room in Bowling Green, too, but since Wallace and Elizabeth move to a different house every three months (part of the Plan), he keeps his .22 and his comics, the stuff that's important to a boy his age, in his room here at the home place. It's the room his dad and I used to share.

Wallace Jr. is twelve. I found him sitting on the back porch that overlooks the interstate when I got home from work. I sell crop insurance.

After I changed clothes, I showed him how to break the bead on a tire two ways, with a hammer and by backing a car over it. Like making sorghum, fixing tires by hand is a dying art. The boy caught on fast, though. "Tomorrow I'll show you how to mount your tire with the hammer and a tire iron," I said.

"What I wish is I could see the bears," he said. He was looking across the field to I-65, where the northbound lanes cut off the corner of our field. From the house at night, sometimes the traffic sounds like a waterfall.

"Can't see their fire in the daytime," I said. "But wait till tonight." That night CBS or NBC (I forget which is which) did a special on the bears, which were becoming a story of nationwide interest. They were seen in Kentucky, West Virginia, Missouri, Illinois (southern), and, of course, Virginia. There have always been bears in Virginia. Some characters there were even talking about hunting them. A scientist said they were heading into the states where there is some snow but not too much, and where there is enough timber in the medians for firewood. He had gone in with a video camera, but his shots were just blurry figures sitting around a fire. Another scientist said the bears were attracted by the berries on a new bush that grew only in the medians of the interstates. He claimed this berry was the first new species in recent history, brought about by the mixing of seeds along the highway. He ate one on TV, making a face, and called it a "newberry." A climatic ecologist said that the warm winters (there was no snow last winter in Nashville, and only one flurry in Louisville) had changed the bears' hibernation cycle, and now they were able to remember things from year to year. "Bears may have discovered fire centuries ago," he said, "but forgot it." Another theory was that they had discovered (or remembered) fire when Yellowstone burned, several years ago.

The TV showed more guys talking about bears than it showed bears, and Wallace Jr. and I lost interest. After the supper dishes were done I took the boy out behind the house and down to our fence. Across the interstate and through the trees, we could see the light of the bears' fire. Wallace Jr. wanted to go back to the house and get his .22 and go shoot one, and I explained why that would be wrong. "Besides," I said, "a .22 wouldn't do much more to a bear than make it mad."

"Besides," I added, "it's illegal to hunt in the medians."

The only trick to mounting a tire by hand, once you have beaten or pried it onto the rim, is setting the bed. You do this by setting the tire upright, sitting on it, and bouncing it up and down between your legs while the air goes in. When the bead sets on the rim, it makes a satisfying "pop." On Thursday, I kept Wallace Jr. home from school and showed him how to do this until he got it right. Then we climbed our fence and crossed the field to get a look at the bears.

In northern Virginia, according to "Good Morning America," the bears were keeping their fires going all day long. Here in western Kentucky, though, it was still warm for late October and they only stayed around the fires at night. Where they went and what they did in the daytime, I don't know. Maybe they were watching from the newberry bushes as Wallace Jr. and I climbed the government fence and crossed the northbound lanes. I carried an axe and Wallace Jr. brought his .22, not because he wanted to kill a bear but because a boy likes to carry some kind of a gun. The median was all tangled with brush and vines under maples, oaks, and sycamores. Even though we were only a hundred yards from the house, I had never been there, and neither had anyone else that I knew of. It was like a created country. We found a path in the center and followed it down across a slow, short stream that flowed out of one grate and into another. The tracks in the gray mud were the first bear signs we saw. There was a musty but not really unpleasant smell. In a clearing under a big hollow beech, where the fire had been, we found nothing but ashes. Logs were drawn up in a rough circle and the smell was stronger. I stirred the ashes and found enough coals left to start a new flame, so I banked them back the way they had been left.

I cut a little firewood and stacked it to one side, just to be neighborly. Maybe the bears were watching us from the bushes even then.

There's no way to know. I tasted one of the newberries and spit it out. It was so sweet it was sour, just the sort of thing you would imagine a bear would like.

That evening after supper, I asked Wallace Jr. if he might want to go with me to visit Mother. I wasn't surprised when he said "yes." Kids have more consideration than folks give them credit for. We found her sitting on the concrete front porch of the Home, watching the cars go by on I-65. The nurse said she had been agitated all day. I wasn't surprised by that, either. Every fall as the leaves change, she gets restless, maybe the word is hopeful, again. I brought her into the dayroom and combed her long white hair. "Nothing but bears on TV anymore," the nurse complained, flipping the channels. Wallace Jr. picked up the remote after the nurse left, and we watched a CBS or NBC Special Report about some hunters in Virginia who had gotten their houses torched. The TV interviewed a hunter and his wife whose $117,500 Shenandoah Valley home had burned. She blamed the bears. He didn't blame the bears, but he was suing for compensation from the state since he had a valid hunting licence. The state hunting commissioner came on and said that possession of a hunting licence didn't prohibit (enjoin, I think, was the word he used) *the hunted* from striking back. I thought that was a pretty liberal view for a state commissioner. Of course, he had a vested interest in not paying off. I'm not a hunter myself.

"Don't bother coming on Sunday," Mother told Wallace Jr. with a wink. "I've drove a million miles and I've got one hand on the gate." I'm used to her saying stuff like that, especially in the fall, but I was afraid it would upset the boy. In fact, he looked worried after we left and I asked him what was wrong.

"How could she have drove a million miles?" he asked. She had told him 48 miles a day for 39 years, and he had worked it out on his calculator to be 336,960 miles.

"Have *driven*," I said. "And it's forty-eight in the morning and forty-eight in the afternoon. Plus there were the football trips. Plus, old folks exaggerate a little." Mother was the first woman school bus driver in the state. She did it every day and raised a family, too. Dad just farmed.

I usually get off the interstate at Smiths Grove, but that night I drove north all the way to Horse Cave and doubled back so Wallace Jr. and I could see the bears' fires. There were not as many as you would think from the TV—one every six or seven miles, hidden back in a clump of trees or under a rocky ledge. Probably they look for water as well as wood. Wallace Jr. wanted to stop, but it's against the law to stop on the interstate and I was afraid the state police would run us off.

There was a card from Wallace in the mailbox. He and Elizabeth were doing fine and having a wonderful time. Not a word about Wallace Jr., but the boy didn't seem to mind. Like most kids his age, he doesn't really enjoy going places with his parents.

On Saturday afternoon, the Home called my office (Burley Belt Drought & Hail) and left word that Mother was gone. I was on the road. I work Saturdays. It's the only day a lot of part-time farmers are home. My heart literally skipped a beat when I called in and got the message, but only a beat. I had long been prepared. "It's a blessing," I said when I got the nurse on the phone.

"You don't understand," the nurse said. "Not *passed* away, gone. *Ran* away, gone. Your mother has escaped." Mother had gone through the door at the end of the corridor when no one was looking, wedging the door with her comb and taking a bedspread which belonged to the Home. What about her tobacco? I asked. It was gone. That was a sure sign she was planning to stay away. I was in Franklin, and it took me less than an hour to get to the Home on I-65. The nurse told me that Mother had been acting more and more confused lately. Of course they are going to say that. We looked around the grounds, which is only an acre with no trees between the interstate and a soybean field. Then they had me leave a message at the Sheriff's office. I would have to keep paying for her care until she was officially listed as Missing, which would be Monday.

It was dark by the time I got back to the house, and Wallace Jr. was fixing supper. This just involves opening a few cans, already selected and grouped together with a rubber band. I told him his grandmother had gone, and he nodded, saying, "She told us she would be." I called Florida and left a message. There was nothing more to be done. I sat down and tried to watch TV, but there was nothing on. Then, I looked out the back door, and saw the firelight twinkling through the trees across the northbound lane of I-65, and realized I just might know where to find her.

It was definitely getting colder, so I got my jacket. I told the boy to wait by the phone in case the Sheriff called, but when I looked back, halfway across the field, there he was behind me. He didn't have a jacket. I let him catch up. He was carrying his .22, and I made him leave it leaning against our fence. It was harder climbing the government fence in the dark, at my age, than it had been in the daylight. I am sixty-one. The highway was busy with cars heading south and trucks heading north.

Crossing the shoulder, I got my pants cuffs wet on the long grass, already wet with dew. It is actually bluegrass.

The first few feet into the trees it was pitch black and the boy grabbed my hand. Then it got lighter. At first I thought it was the moon, but it was the high beams shining like moonlight into the treetops, allowing Wallace Jr. and me to pick our way through the brush. We soon found the path and its familiar bear smell.

I was wary of approaching the bears at night. If we stayed on the path we might run into one in the dark, but if we went through the bushes we might be seen as intruders. I wondered if maybe we shouldn't have brought the gun.

We stayed on the path. The light seemed to drip down from the canopy of the woods like rain. The going was easy, especially if we didn't try to look at the path but let our feet find their own way.

Then through the trees I saw their fire.

The fire was mostly of sycamore and beech branches, the kind of fire that puts out very little heat or light and lots of smoke. The bears hadn't learned the ins and outs of wood yet. They did okay at tending it, though. A large cinnamon brown northern-looking bear was poking the fire with a stick, adding a branch now and then from a pile at his side. The others sat around in a loose circle on the logs. Most were smaller black or honey bears, one was a mother with cubs. Some were eating berries from a hubcap. Not eating, but just watching the fire, my mother sat among them with the bedspread from the Home around her shoulders.

If the bears noticed us, they didn't let on. Mother patted a spot right next to her on the log and I sat down. A bear moved over to let Wallace Jr. sit on her other side.

The bear smell is rank but not unpleasant, once you get used to it. It's not like a barn smell, but wilder. I leaned over to whisper something to Mother and she shook her head. *It would be rude to whisper around these creatures that don't possess the power of speech*, she let me know without speaking. Wallace Jr. was silent too. Mother shared the bedspread with us and we sat for what seemed hours, looking into the fire.

The big bear tended the fire, breaking up the dry branches by holding one end and stepping on them, like people do. He was good at keeping it going at the same level. Another bear poked the fire from time to

time, but the others left it alone. It looked like only a few of the bears knew how to use fire, and were carrying the others along. But isn't that how it is with everything? Every once in a while, a smaller bear walked into the circle of firelight with an armload of wood and dropped it onto the pile. Median wood has a silvery cast, like driftwood.

Wallace Jr. isn't fidgety like a lot of kids. I found it pleasant to sit and stare into the fire. I took a little piece of Mother's *Red Man*, though I don't generally chew. It was no different from visiting her at the Home, only more interesting, because of the bears. There were about eight or ten of them. Inside the fire itself, things weren't so dull, either: little dramas were being played out as fiery chambers were created and then destroyed in a crashing of sparks. My imagination ran wild. I looked around the circle at the bears and wondered what *they* saw. Some had their eyes closed. Though they were gathered together, their spirits still seemed solitary, as if each bear was sitting alone in front of its own fire.

The hubcap came around and we all took some newberries. I don't know about Mother, but I just pretended to eat mine. Wallace Jr. made a face and spit his out. When he went to sleep, I wrapped the bedspread around all three of us. It was getting colder and we were not provided, like the bears, with fur. I was ready to go home, but not Mother. She pointed up toward the canopy of trees, where a light was spreading, and then pointed to herself. Did she think it was angels approaching from on high? It was only the high beams of some southbound truck, but she seemed mighty pleased. Holding her hand, I felt it grow colder and colder in mine.

Wallace Jr. woke me up by tapping on my knee. It was past dawn, and his grandmother had died sitting on the log between us. The fire was banked up and the bears were gone and someone was crashing straight through the woods, ignoring the path. It was Wallace. Two state troopers were right behind him. He was wearing a white shirt, and I realized it was Sunday morning. Underneath his sadness on learning of Mother's death, he looked peeved.

The troopers were sniffing the air and nodding. The bear smell was still strong. Wallace and I wrapped Mother in the bedspread and started with her body back out to the highway. The troopers stayed behind and scattered the bears' fire ashes and flung their firewood away into the bushes. It seemed a petty thing to do. They were like bears themselves, each one solitary in his own uniform.

There was Wallace's Olds 98 on the median, with its radial tires looking squashed on the grass. In front of it there was a police car with a trooper standing beside it, and behind it a funeral home hearse, also an Olds 98.

"First report we've had of them bothering old folks," the trooper said to Wallace. "That's not hardly what happened at all," I said, but nobody asked me to explain. They have their own procedures. Two men in suits got out of the hearse and opened the rear door. That to me was the point at which Mother departed this life. After we put her in, I put my arms around the boy. He was shivering even though it wasn't that cold. Sometimes death will do that, especially at dawn, with the police around and the grass wet, even when it comes as a friend.

We stood for a minute watching the cars pass. "It's a blessing," Wallace said. It's surprising how much traffic there is at 6:22 A.M.

That afternoon, I went back to the median and cut a little firewood to replace what the troopers had flung away. I could see the fire through the trees that night.

I went back two nights later, after the funeral. The fire was going and it was the same bunch of bears, as far as I could tell. I sat around with them a while but it seemed to make them nervous, so I went home. I had taken a handful of newberries from the hubcap, and on Sunday I went with the boy and arranged them on Mother's grave. I tried again, but it's no use, you can't eat them.

Unless you're a bear.

Author Biographies

CHINUA ACHEBE is one of Africa's most important writers and social commentators. He was born in Nigeria in 1930, studied at the University of Ibadan, and was the first director of the Nigerian Broadcasting Corporation. His first novel, *Things Fall Apart* (1958), made him famous. In it he dramatized the fatal encounter between the people of a traditional Ibo village and the first white missionaries and colonialists. Achebe's novels and short stories are now studied at universities in many countries. As the editor of several anthologies, he has helped to spread African literature throughout the world. He believes writers have the responsibility of using language as a tool to undo or go beyond the deceitful and manipulative language of politics. He has also written poetry and children's stories.

"The Novelist as Teacher", written in 1965, comes from his book *Hopes and Impediments: Selected Essays*. In it he deals with the role a writer plays in a society which is just beginning to emerge from its colonial past. "The Sacrificial Egg" was published in *The Sacrificial Egg and Other Stories* in 1962.

JOHN AGARD is a poet, performer, and anthologist from Guyana who now lives in England. He has been described as a West Indian-British troubadour, "hilarious and moving by turns, with sharply satiric intelligence conjuring delighted audiences to join in." His first collection of poetry was self-published. He went on to publish books for children, and joined a "mobile group" of actors and storytellers. He migrated to England in 1977, where he became part of the resurgence of oral poetry, also called jazzoetry, dub poetry, and rapso poetry by black poets.

Of the poems in his book *Limbo Dancer in Dark Glasses* Agard writes, "The Limbo Dancer sequence took off from a traditional view that limbo dancing was born in the cramped conditions of the slave ship—a far cry from the tourist image."

ANNA AKHMATOVA has been acclaimed as Russia's greatest woman poet. She was born in Odessa in 1889. Before 1918, she was part of the

St. Petersburg literary circle, a friend of Boris Pasternak and others, and a writer of lyrical love poetry. Her life changed completely through the course of the Russian Revolution (1917), two world wars, and the Stalinist Terror of the 1930s, during which she was publicly humiliated and her son imprisoned. She was expelled from the Writers' Union, but was later readmitted and became its president. She died in 1966, after completing her long work, *Poem Without a Hero*.

Akhmatova's remarkable poems are a record of the 20th century's upheavals. They are also spare, personal, and deeply moving. "Everything Is Plundered . . ." (1921) dates from the post-Revolutionary years, and reveals her amazing ability to overcome despair with hope.

RAFAEL ALBERTI was born in Andalusia, Spain in 1902. He became a member of a highly inventive group of Spanish poets called the "Generation of 1927," which included Federico García Lorca. In 1936, the Spanish Civil War broke out, and Alberti quickly joined the Republican cause to fight against Franco. Three years later the Republican side was defeated, and he left for France, where he lived in exile for almost four decades. In April 1977, with Franco the dictator dead, and a new beginning for democracy in Spain, Alberti finally returned to his homeland.

Alberti claims that his childhood in Andalusia influenced all of his later poetic development. "I owe the full substance of my poetry to the sea of Cadiz," he wrote. We can be sure that is where the apparition in "The Ghost" is wandering.

DAVID ARNASON, whose roots are Icelandic, was born in the Interlake region of Manitoba in 1940. He is a professor at the University of Manitoba. Arnason has published several books of poetry; collections of short stories, including *The Happiest Man in the World* (1989), from which "A Girl's Story" is taken; and other books. His stories feature a lively wit and humour, a strong sense of place, and a concern for contemporary issues. Arnason is also well known as a literary editor and critic.

"A Girl's Story" is a good introduction to Arnason's accessible and engaging voice. The story takes an ironic look at the "postmodern" narrative technique, in which the author consciously exposes his or her own writing process.

MARGARET ATWOOD is internationally known as a novelist and poet. Born in Ottawa in 1939, she grew up in northern Québec and Ontario, and in Toronto. She has lived in many other cities, including Berlin, Edinburgh, and London. She has worked actively for Amnesty International and other causes. Her novels deal with such significant themes as issues in women's lives, Canadian-American relations, and societies of the future. Among her best-known titles are *The Edible Woman, Surfacing, The Handmaid's Tale, Cat's Eye,* and *Wilderness Tips* (a collection of short stories). Her books have been translated into more than twenty languages. Atwood lives in Toronto.

When Atwood reads her own work, her sense of humour emerges strongly. "Epaulettes," a piece of pure satire, is a fine example of her acerbic wit—but the points she makes are serious. It comes from a collection of parables, monologues, mini-romances, mini-biographies, and speculative fictions entitled *Good Bones*.

JAMES BALDWIN's novels about African-Americans exploded onto the scene before and during the civil-rights movement of the 1960s in the United States. Baldwin was born in Harlem, New York City, in 1924. After leaving high school, he spent six years doing a variety of jobs. In 1948 he went to Paris, and lived there until 1957, when he returned to the United States. He soon established a reputation as one of the most able and articulate supporters of the rights of African-Americans. Among his best-known novels are *Another Country* and *Go Tell It on the Mountain*. He died in 1987.

The anthology selection, in which he describes his first searing encounters with racism, is an excerpt from his autobiography, *Notes of a Native Son*.

FIONA BARR was born in Derry, Northern Ireland, in 1952. A mother of four children, she works as a television critic and writes short stories and articles. Her story "The Wall-Reader" won a writing competition in 1978 and was published with the other competition stories in an anthology called *The Wall-Reader*. Another of her stories, "The Sisters," has also been anthologized and was adapted for British television.

In "The Wall-Reader," Barr creates suspense with the ever-lurking potential for violent incident in her strife-torn country, and raises fascinating questions about whether innocence is possible in such a situation.

JOHN BERGER is known chiefly for his art criticism, but he is also a painter, novelist, and poet. Born in London in 1926, he served in the British army at the end of the Second World War, then attended art school in London. He developed a Marxist view of art in which he examined painting in relation to society and history. His television series about art, *Ways of Seeing*, popularized his ideas. His novel *G* won the Booker Prize in 1972.

"Mother" is an autobiographical essay that reveals a more personal side of John Berger.

TERRY BISSON was born in Kentucky in 1942 and educated there. He became a magazine writer and a book editor for a New York publisher, while pursuing his love for fantasy and science-fiction writing. He now lives in Brooklyn, New York. Among Bisson's novels are *Talking Man* (1986), which was a finalist for the World Fantasy Award, *Fire on the Mountain* (1987), and *Voyage to the Red Planet* (1990). He has also written many short stories.

"Bears Discover Fire" is an example of the storyteller's dictum, "a good story is a story well told." Written with whimsy and imagination, this delightful tale first appeared in *The Year's Best Science Fiction: Eighth Annual Collection* (1991).

JORGE LUIS BORGES is one of the twentieth century's most distinguished writers. Born in Argentina in 1899, he grew up in Buenos Aires and Switzerland. A few of his best-known works are *Fictions*, *The Aleph*, *Dreamtigers*, and *Labyrinths*. He served as Director of the National Library of Argentina until the dictator Juan Perón removed him for political reasons, and was professor of English Literature at the University of Buenos Aires. Borges received at least twenty-five major awards, and his work has been translated into many languages around the world. He died in Switzerland in 1986.

Illusion is an important part of Borges' fictional world. His short stories (his favourite form) constantly question our notions of what is real. A number of his stories, like "The Meeting," focus on knife fights and violent death, perhaps because these subjects involve questions of personal identity, courage, and the value of success and fame.

EDWARD KAMAU BRATHWAITE's poetry draws its strength from folk forms and rhythms as well as from the English literary tradition. Brathwaite was born in Barbados in 1930, and educated there and at Cambridge University. He taught for some years in Ghana before returning to become a lecturer at the University of the West Indies in Jamaica. He frequently recites his own work at poetry festivals, emphasizing the Caribbean heritage of spoken and performed poetry. His most important work is the trilogy *The Arrivants*, which explores the experience of African-Caribbean people through history.

"Dives" makes a powerful statement based on a childhood memory.

SHARON BUTALA lives on a ranch near Eastend in southwestern Saskatchewan, where she combines her writing with the job of ranching. She is the author of several novels, including a trilogy that was concluded with *The Fourth Archangel*. Her short story collection, *Queen of the Headaches*, was shortlisted for the Governor General's Award for fiction in 1986.

Butala's fiction is realistic and uncompromising in its examination of contemporary human relationships. As we see in the anthology story, her work reflects a very strong sense of place, rooted as it is in the Saskatchewan prairie.

ITALO CALVINO has delighted and challenged readers around the world with his lively storytelling and his experiments with fictional forms. He was born in Cuba in 1923, but his parents were Italian. He lived in Italy—in San Remo and Rome—and in Paris. Among his best-known works are the trilogy *The Cloven Viscount, The Baron in the Trees*, and *The Nonexistent Knight; Cosmicomics; Invisible Cities; The Castle of Crossed Destinies;* and *If on a Winter's Night a Traveller*. Calvino has also written many essays on the art of storytelling and writing, published in such collections as *The Uses of Literature*. He died in 1985.

"Last Comes the Raven" is an early wartime story. In a few action-packed scenes, Calvino paints a chilling portrait of the central character, a boy who uses violence to take possession of the world outside himself.

PETER CAREY was born in Bacchus Marsh, Australia, in 1943. His novels include *Bliss, Illywhacker*, and *Oscar and Lucinda*, for which he won the Booker Prize in 1988. He has two short-story collections, *The Fat Man in History* and *War Crimes*.

The story "American Dreams," set in the postwar 1950s, probes the psychology of a poorer country dominated from afar by the luxurious images beamed abroad by Hollywood movies.

NINA CASSIAN was born in Romania in 1924, and was a leading literary figure there for over forty years. She has published more than fifty books, including works of fiction and children's books. Her poetry has been translated into many languages. She is a composer of music, a journalist, a film critic, and a translator, as well as a writer.

In 1985, while she was teaching creative writing at New York University, a friend of hers was arrested in Romania. In his diary, the police discovered Cassian's satirical verses on the Romanian dictator Ceausescu, and as a result he was tortured to death. Cassian had no choice but to seek asylum in New York, where she has lived ever since.

Her poem "A Man" affirms her belief in human potential.

ANTONIO CISNEROS was born in Lima, Peru, in 1942. He broadened his experiences by travelling and by teaching literature at universities in England, France, and Hungary. Cisneros is internationally acclaimed for his satirical works, which challenge the established myths, history, and culture of his native country.

His latest collection (a bilingual book in Spanish and English) is *At Night the Cats*, 1985. Of this book the *Los Angeles Times Book Review* wrote: "Cisneros . . . is today one of the major poets of all Spanish America. . . . His early poems, characterized by their epigrammatic brevity, are lean and taut, precise in language and ironic in tone." "From a Mother" is one of these poems.

DENNIS CRAIG was born in Guyana in 1929 but has lived for many years in Jamaica. He studied at universities in England and the United States, completing his doctorate at London University. An expert in linguistics, his research has thrown light on many aspects of Jamaican English and Creole languages. Poetry writing is only one of Craig's many talents: he is also known as a teacher and a storyteller.

RIENZI CRUSZ was born in Ceylon (now Sri Lanka), and came to Canada in 1965. He studied at the universities of Ceylon, London (England), Toronto and Waterloo, Ontario. At present, he is a librarian at the University of Waterloo. Among his published poetry books are *Flesh and Thorn, Elephant and Ice*, and *Singing Against the Wind*. Sharp contrast is important in Crusz's poetry; the tropical sun, elephants, and warm childhood memories of Ceylon are set against the snow, Arctic ice, and adult alienation of Canada.

In "Roots," the poet looks back more than four hundred years to a time when his ancestors merged two civilizations, Sinhalese (the majority of the population of Ceylon) and Portuguese, the intrepid sailors and explorers of the sixteenth century.

JENNY DISKI is at the forefront of younger British writers today. She was born in London in 1947, where she still lives with her daughter. She is the author of three novels, *Rainforest, Like Mother*, and *Nothing Natural*. Critics have called her original, challenging novels "powerful, honest, frightening . . ." and "chillingly clever . . ."

Diski's short story "The Vanishing Princess" is an intriguing example of the contemporary fairy tale, a surprisingly widespread genre in recent fiction.

SLAVENKA DRAKULIĆ is a Croatian writer who witnessed the horrors of war at first hand during the breakup of the former Yugoslavia. In her book *Balkan Express*, written between 1991 and 1992, she looks at war from the victims' point of view. In a series of short pieces, she describes what it feels like to see young men who have grown up side by side coolly killing their childhood friends, or to watch villagers who have lived in harmony for forty years become too frightened to speak to their neighbours. In other words, she tries to convey how war can contaminate a whole culture, and how, amazingly, people continue trying to live ordinary lives.

LOUISE ERDRICH, according to London's *Sunday Times*, "has given the Chippewas of North Dakota a lasting place in fiction." Born in Little Falls, Minnesota in 1954, Erdrich grew up in Wahpeton, North Dakota. Her Chippewa (Ojibwa) grandfather was the tribal chairman of the Turtle Mountain Reservation, near the Manitoba border. Her parents encouraged her to write from a very early age, giving her nickels and "publishing" her stories with construction paper covers. Among her adult novels are *Tracks, Love Medicine*, and *The Beet Queen*, all dealing with Native American life and mythology.

"A Wedge of Shade" presents reservation life from several different viewpoints: the mother's trust in tradition and family; the take-charge, businesslike attitude of the aunt; the activist stance of the young husband; and the proud optimism of the narrator.

TIMOTHY FINDLEY, one of Canada's best-known writers, was born in Toronto in 1930, and now lives in the country near that city. His novel, *The Wars* (1977), won the Governor General's Award for fiction and was made into a feature film. Its success also led to the re-publication of his earlier novels. Among his newer novels are *Famous Last Words, Not Wanted on the Voyage* (which gives an entirely new perspective to the story of Noah and the Flood), and *The Telling of Lies*, a mystery novel.

"War," the short story in this anthology, was first read on CBC's Anthology, then published in *Dinner Along the Amazon*. It is among his earliest stories, dating from the 1950s. In putting the collection together, Findley noted "with some embarrassment" that over the years his stories and novels have turned again and again to the same sounds and images.

LARRY FONDATION is an organizer for the Industrial Areas Foundation in East Los Angeles which works to build affordable housing for low-income families. His stories have appeared in *Five Fingers Review, Fiction International, Asylum*, and *Black Ice*.

"Deportation at Breakfast" was reprinted in *Flash Fiction: Very Short Stories*. In the story, events "flash" by with inexorable logic toward a totally absurd—or is it?—conclusion.

JANET FRAME was born in New Zealand in 1924. One of that country's most important writers, she is the author of more than twenty novels and short-story collections. Her life was marked by personal tragedy. She was hospitalized for years and treated (probably erroneously) for schizophrenia. Her terrible experiences have become an important part of her fiction—for example, in her first novel, *Owls Do Cry*. One writer even described her as being "obsessed with the mysteries of madness and death."

"Two Sheep" is a contemporary fable in the tradition of Aesop and LaFontaine. Sad but fascinating and speculative, it comes from Frame's collection *The Reservoir and Other Stories*.

GABRIEL GARCÍA MÁRQUEZ, one of the world's most influential writers, was born into a poor family on the Caribbean coast of Colombia in 1928. He was reared by his grandparents, then studied journalism and law and worked as an international journalist. In 1965 he became a full-time writer. He credits his grandmother, her wonderful stories and Caribbean folklore, for the exuberance and sense of wonder that infuses his fiction. His best-known novel, *One Hundred Years of Solitude*, has sold over ten million copies and is responsible for a growing awareness of Latin American writers. García Márquez constantly surprises his readers with his remarkable manipulation of time and reality. Indeed, the term "magic realism" originated largely to describe his fiction. In 1982 he won the Nobel Prize for Literature.

"A Very Old Man With Enormous Wings" is an example of the way García Márquez brings the marvellous and the magical into the everyday world.

ZULFIKAR GHOSE's poems express the uprootedness of someone who is a product of at least two cultures. Born in Sialkot (in what is now Pakistan) in 1935, he went to England to study in 1952. He worked as a cricket correspondent and teacher before publishing his first volume of poetry in 1964. More recently he has lived in the United States and South America. In 1969 he became a professor of English literature in Texas.

Many of Ghose's poems describe his memories of childhood and family life in Pakistan, while others deal with the feelings of an immigrant in England. His view of the world has been described as "sharp and clinical, without sentimentality," and his poems often contain a wry humour.

PATRICIA GRACE was the first Maori woman writer to publish a collection of stories. Born in Wellington, New Zealand in 1937, she is the author of two short-story collections as well as several novels, including *Mutuwhenua, The Moon Sleeps*, and *Potiki*. Her subject is the Maori people themselves, and their struggle to maintain their traditional Native culture in the modern world. She also writes children's books in both English and the Maori language. About her writing she says, "I write from my own background and experience. I guess one's environment, relationships, ancestry, thoughts, feelings, imaginings, culture, spirituality, etc., are all part of one's background and experience. So what I am is what has been 'gifted' to me. I try to draw my stories out of myself."

Patricia Grace's life experiences and unique literary voice are well illustrated in the sad but beautiful story, "At the River." The grandmother's dream of death, her fear of the bird of omen, the excitement of eel-fishing camp—all are a part of the Maori way of life.

MARIE LUISE KASCHNITZ was shaped by the political events of her time and place. Born in 1901 in Karlsruhe, Germany, she began to write during the 1930s. The Second World War, however, was the crisis that led to her most important work. With other Germans of her generation, she shared feelings of guilt about the atrocities committed by the Nazis. Her response was to write about the postwar world of chaos and isolation. Besides writing poetry, she was successful with fiction, essays, and radio drama. Then in 1958 her husband died. This personal crisis led her to write about loneliness and loss. Yet she was always able to express her compassion for others and her hopefulness for the future. She died in 1974.

In the poem *"from* Return to Frankfurt," Kaschnitz recaptures the happiness of youth and the eternal optimism of young lovers.

YASUNARI KAWABATA was the first Japanese writer to win the Nobel Prize for Literature (1968). Born in Osaka in 1899, he suffered a lonely childhood after the deaths of his father, mother, grandmother, and sister before he reached the age of ten. At fifteen he decided to become a novelist. He kept a diary during his grandfather's last days, and published it eleven years later as "Diary of a Sixteen-Year-Old." Among his best-known novels are *The Snow Country* (1937) and *The Sound of the Mountain* (1952), considered to be his masterpiece. He committed suicide in 1972 for unknown reasons.

The sparse yet lyrical style of "Immortality" illustrates how Kawabata combines ancient and modern Japanese traditions. The ghostly lovers could almost be characters in a Japanese Noh play (a traditional form of drama), but the golf-course setting places them firmly in the present.

BARBARA KIMENYE was born in Uganda in 1940 and worked as a journalist there until 1974, when she moved to England. She has published two short-story collections dealing with the everyday lives and problems of rural Uganda and its people. She is also a prolific writer of juvenile novels, among which are the popular *Smugglers* and the *Moses* series.

Kimenye tends to deal sympathetically with her characters, and to reflect an optimistic view of life. "The Winner" is both gentle and humorous in its portrayal of human strengths and failings.

JAMAICA KINCAID is a challenging voice from the Caribbean islands. She was born in St. John's, the capital of Antigua, in 1949. She grew up there, but now lives in the United States. She has written a volume of short stories called *At the Bottom of the River*, and a novel, *Annie John*. Her non-fiction book, *A Small Place*, has been called "a brilliant critique of post-colonial 'realities' in the Caribbean." In it she describes the irony of white tourists who visit the islands in a holiday mood, shutting their eyes to the poverty and degradation of the native residents.

"Girl" reveals another side of Jamaica Kincaid—the observer of folk wisdom. It should be read aloud so that the catchy vocal rhythms and satirical humour can be appreciated.

THOMAS KING is a North American writer of Cherokee, Greek, and German background. He was born in Sacramento, California, in 1943. He has taught at the University of Lethbridge, Alberta, and the University of Minnesota. He currently lives in Toronto. His widely acclaimed first novel, *Medicine River*, was published in 1990, and his stories have appeared in anthologies and literary magazines across North America. King is very instrumental in encouraging Native writers, and has edited an anthology of contemporary Canadian Native fiction, *All My Relations*.

King's stories, such as "Trap Lines," resonate with the qualities of oral storytelling. His use of humour and his memorable characters make his fiction lively and accessible.

JOY KOGAWA is an influential Japanese-Canadian writer. She was born in Vancouver in 1935. During the Second World War, she and her family, like other Japanese Canadians, lost their property and were removed to internment camps in the interior of British Columbia. This experience formed the basis of her first novel, *Obasan* (1981), in which Naomi's childhood is torn apart during the war. Her second novel, *Itsuka* (1992), picks up Naomi's story during her adult years. Kogawa has also written four volumes of poetry, and has received many awards. She now lives in Toronto and Vancouver.

Her short story "Obasan" was first published in *Canadian Forum* magazine in 1978.

PÄR LAGERKVIST was born in Sweden in 1891. He spent long periods of time studying and writing in Denmark, France, and Italy. In 1930 he returned to Sweden, where he was elected to the Swedish Academy in 1940. Shocked by the two world wars, he became an eloquent critic of totalitarianism. Author of over thirty-five books of drama, poetry, essays, and fiction, he was awarded the Nobel Prize for Literature in 1951. He died in 1974.

In his writing, Lagerkvist explores such major themes as the meaning of life, the conflict between good and evil, and the individual's relationship to God. As in "The Experimental World," he often uses the ancient forms of fairy tale, parable, legend, and myth to search for truths in the contemporary world.

HERNÁN LARA ZAVALA was born in Mexico City in 1946, but his parents came from the Yucatan, a beautiful peninsula where he spent much of his childhood. Many of his stories, including the anthology selection, are set there. He currently teaches literature at the University of Mexico and conducts writing workshops in Cuernavaca, where he lives with his wife and son.

"Iguana Hunting" was one of the first stories he ever wrote. "In a sense," he says, "it was dictated to me by the Muses, or rather from the unconsciousness of childhood, which included the Mayan myths, the awakening of sexual life, and the power words have in the minds of young people to evoke sensations yet to be known."

MARGARET LAURENCE is widely regarded as a major Canadian novelist. She was born in Manitoba in 1926, and many of her novels are set in the fictional prairie town of Manawaka. However, she lived many years outside Canada. As a young woman she lived in Ghana, with her husband. Here she saw at first hand the problems of emergent nations. When her marriage broke up, she moved to England with her two children. Ten years later, in the early 1970s, she returned to Canada. She lived the last years of her life in the small Ontario town of Lakefield, actively working for the cause of world peace. She died there in 1987.

Among Laurence's best-known novels are *The Stone Angel*, the story of Hagar Shipley's last journey toward love and death; and *The Diviners*, the story of writer Morag Dunn and her love for a Métis man, Jules Tonnerre. In 1976 her essays were published under the title *Heart of a Stranger*.

KATHLEEN ROCKWELL LAWRENCE has earned acclaim for her light-hearted, timely novels. She was born in New York in 1945, and has made that city the setting for her writing. Her second novel, *The Last Room in Manhattan*, is about a thirty-three-year-old woman who is suddenly without employment or home in New York City. She finds temporary quarters at a women's shelter, where she meets Martha, a woman who is searching for her missing son. Both women eventually turn their lives around. Of her writing Lawrence says, "Someone told me my work was funny, but with a dark side. I was pleased. You want art to mirror life. Life is funny, with a dark side."

The Boys I Didn't Kiss, from which the anthology selection was taken, is a collection of her columns written for the *New York Times Magazine*.

DORIS LESSING is a world-famous fiction writer. Born in Persia (now Iran) in 1919, she grew up and was educated in Southern Rhodesia (now Zimbabwe). Of Africa she has said that it "gives you the knowledge that man is a small creature among other creatures in a large landscape." Her first novel, *The Grass Is Singing*, and her first collection of short stories, *This Was the Old Chief's Country*, are both set there. Her belief in racial justice led her to join the Communist party for a time. In 1949, she moved to England as a political exile. Best known for her feminist novel, *The Golden Notebook*, she continues to write many other works, including science-fiction novels.

"No Witchcraft for Sale" reflects Lessing's passionate interest in equality for black Africans. Among its strengths are the detailed, well-rounded portraits of both black and white characters, and the strong sense of place.

LI PO, according to legend, was almost three metres tall. Born in China in 701, he may have been either a knight or a robber as a young man. Later he became a poet, but a poet who drank, rode to the hunt with princes, and only sometimes obeyed the emperor's command to dash off a masterpiece. He was forced into exile twice for disrespect of various superiors. In 762, he was drowned while drunk, when he tried to embrace the image of the moon in the water. In fact (perhaps?), he was a writer of heroic poems, humorous poems, and personal lyrics—some say, the spirit of poetry incarnate.

Li Po's translator, EZRA POUND, was immensely influential in the early 20th century both as a poet and as a champion of then-unknown writers such as T. S. Eliot. Born in Idaho, in 1885, he became extremely controversial for his anti-Semitic views (which he later acknowledged as foolish) and for radio broadcasts from Italy in which he tried to stop the United States from fighting in the Second World War. He was arrested in 1945 and charged with treason, then judged insane and sent to an asylum. He died in Italy in 1972.

Pound's early poems were famous for their striking imagery. Some of his best poems, like "The River-Merchant's Wife: A Letter," are translations from the Chinese. His methods of translating poetry have also been influential.

CATHERINE LIM was born in the prosperous city-state of Singapore. She graduated from the University of Malaysia, and is now a teacher of English language and literature as well as a writer. Her stories, which often deal with the darker side of Singapore life, are notable for their criticisms of injustice and materialism.

"The Chosen One" illustrates another common theme in Lim's stories, the effect of changing folk-ways on the older generation, whose capacity to adapt is limited. In this story, however, the seemingly guileless old woman achieves satisfaction at the end.

IAN McDONALD was born in Trinidad, in 1933, and was educated there and at Cambridge University. He has lived in Guyana for most of his working life, where he is a director of a large sugar company. A man of wide literary talents, he published a novel of Caribbean childhood, *The Hummingbird Tree*, in 1966. He brought out a much-admired collection of poems, *Mercy Ward*, in 1988, and he edits the Guyanese cultural journal *Kyk-Over-Al*. He has also published plays and short stories and he writes regular radio commentaries.

"The Duel in Mercy Ward" deals sensitively and humorously with the fierce competitiveness of two old men approaching death. The language is colloquial, direct, and uncompromising, thereby giving the story its strength.

WILLIAM McILVANNEY is a Scottish novelist and poet who chronicles the lives of people on the margins of society. Many of his stories are set in a mining community in the fictional town of Graithnock, including *The Big Man*, which was made into a film in 1990. He also writes crime fiction. *Walking Wounded*, the collection from which "The Prisoner" was selected, won the *Glasgow Herald's* People's Prize, chosen by the general public. The book's final story, "Dreaming," was dramatized for BBC Television.

The *Sunday Times* described McIlvanney's writing thus: "His triumph is to find the consolation of hope in the face of apparently fatalistic despair, to find poetry in the cadences of common speech and the inner sadness of his subjects' lives, while always reaffirming their fortitude and resilience." That he also has a sense of humour is demonstrated in "The Prisoner."

BERNARD MacLAVERTY was born in Belfast, Northern Ireland, in 1942. He lives and teaches on the Scottish Isle of Islay. *Secrets* (1977) was his first collection of short stories. He has also published well-received novels, *Lamb* (1980) and *Cal* (1983), both of which have been turned into movies.

"Secrets" deals with the universal theme of guilt, which is also a recurring theme in Irish literature. MacLaverty employs the device of the "story within a story," the aunt's letters, to reveal the untold story—the secrets.

NAGUIB MAHFOUZ was born in Cairo in 1911 and began writing when he was seventeen. Since then he has become one of the world's best-known Arabic novelists. A student of philosophy and an avid reader, he says he has been influenced by many Western writers, including Dostoevsky and Proust. Mahfouz has written more than thirty novels, of which *The Cairo Trilogy* is the most famous. He was awarded the Nobel Prize for Literature in 1988. He lives in a Cairo suburb with his wife and two daughters.

"Half a Day" captures the paradoxical way in which time seems to move both slowly and swiftly; slowly in childhood, more and more swiftly as we get older. Its form—a "short short story" with a sudden twist at the end—nicely reflects its theme.

SHIINA MAKOTO, one of Japan's newer writers, was born in Tokyo in 1944. He graduated from Tokyo University of Photography and became a magazine editor. In 1976, he founded *Hon no Zasshi (The Magazine of Books)*, and he has been its editor ever since. In 1989, Makoto's book *Ino no Keifu (The Pedigree of a Dog)* won him a prestigious literary award for new writers. He has written many other literary works, and his photographs have been exhibited widely. Makoto enjoys travelling in remote regions of the world, and has visited the Strait of Magellan and Cape Horn, the central desert of Australia, and Mongolia.

The story "Swallowtails" provides glimpses of personal lives in modern, urban Japan, but also illuminates the kinds of problems parents deal with around the world.

MAO TSE-TUNG (now spelled MAO ZEDONG) was born in Hunan province, China, in 1893, and became the leader of the Communist revolution in China. He defeated both the Japanese invaders and the opposition nationalist forces to become head of the new People's Republic of China in 1949. In 1966 he launched the Cultural Revolution, which mobilized youth (red guards), workers, and peasants against party leaders who had "taken the capitalist road." The upheaval soon became chaotic, and before it ended many people's lives, especially those of artists and intellectuals, had been ruined. Mao's views were still dominant when he died in 1976.

Mao wrote poetry all his life, and was perhaps a better poet than a politician. He had studied the classics, and wrote about contemporary events using traditional forms and symbolism.

RIGOBERTA MENCHÚ, although not herself a writer, became world-famous because of her book, *I, Rigoberta Menchú*, first published in English in 1984. At that time Menchú was a young Native Indian woman already famous in Guatemala as a leader in the fight against oppression. Six years earlier, her brother, father, and mother had all been brutally killed by the army. She learned Spanish, the language of the ruling class, in order to speak out against injustice. A fervent Catholic, she also turned to religious activity as an expression of social revolt.

Anthropologist Elisabeth Burgos-Debray, herself a Latin American woman, conducted a series of interviews with Rigoberta Menchú. The result was a book which tells Menchú's personal story and explains her views on the oppression of Native people, religion, the role of women, and the environment. It also serves as an invaluable record of everyday life in a Gauatemalan Indian community. Menchú was awarded the Nobel Prize for Peace in 1992.

CZESLAW MILOSZ is a Polish poet now living in the United States. Several of his books of poetry have been translated into English, including *The Collected Poems 1931-1987*. Milosz was awarded the Nobel Prize for Literature in 1980 and is a member of the American Academy of Arts and Letters.

In the poem "In Music," Milosz describes a pastoral wedding pageant from rural Poland. The images, and the warm emotions they evoke, are brought to his mind from the distant past while he listens to music.

R.K. NARAYAN, who writes in English, is India's most famous novelist. Born in Madras in 1906, he has written fourteen novels and five collections of short stories, as well as retellings of Indian legends. His greatest novel, *The Guide* (1958), won India's highest literary prize. Two more recent works are a collection of short stories, *Under the Banyan Tree* (1985), and *The World of Nagaraj* (1990). He has been praised by critics for his acute observations, his gentle humour, and his abiding sense of humanity.

"A Horse and Two Goats" illustrates how Narayan's writing grows out of the oral storytelling tradition. The two separate yet parallel tracks of conversation represent the vast gulf between the two cultures of the protagonists.

NIE JIAN-GUO was born in China in 1955, the son of an army general. At age 14 he joined the People's Liberation Army and served for five years. Unlike the rest of his family, however, he never joined the Communist Party. After leaving the Army, Nie became a journalist. He was in Beijing at the time of the Tienanmen Square demonstrations and the subsequent crushing of the protest by the PLA. His time in the Army made the clash between citizens and soldiers particularly painful. He says, "I stood with the students. For that, I had to escape from my home country." Nie currently lives in exile in the United States.

"Tienanmen Square: A Soldier's Story" is an excerpt from his autobiography, as yet unpublished, to be titled *From Little Red Guard to Exile.*

BEN OKRI is one of a growing number of non-British, non-North American writers who are enriching English-language literature while remaining rooted in and inspired by the culture of their home countries. Okri is a Nigerian who now lives in London, England. He produces short stories and novels as well as poetry. His novel *The Famished Road* won Britain's Booker Prize in 1991. One of the judges writes that the novel "combines fantasy and the vision of a child, the supernatural and the here-and-now, to convey Nigerian peasant life in a changing world."

"You Walked Gently towards Me" comes from a volume of bitter-sweet poetry entitled *An African Elegy.*

338

NIYI OSUNDARE is a young Nigerian poet who writes in English. His collection *The Eye of the Earth* was joint winner of the 1986 Commonwealth Poetry Prize. Other works include *Songs of the Marketplace, Village Voices, A Nib in the Pond, Moonsongs,* and *Waiting Laughters.* He is currently a lecturer in English at the University of Ibadan, Nigeria.

The debate over language has been raging in African literary circles since 1963, when critic Obi Wali published an article in which he wrote: " . . . until these writers and their Western midwives accept the fact that any true African literature must be written in African languages, they will merely be pursuing a dead end which can only lead to sterility, uncreativity, and frustration." On the other side are those who argue that literature written in English reaches a far wider readership. In any case, writers of Osundare's calibre add considerably to the richness of the English language.

GRACE PALEY has established herself as a writer almost entirely through her books of short stories. She was born in New York in 1922, the daughter of Russian immigrants. Encouraged by her parents, she began writing poetry at five. She eventually married, began teaching at universities, and published her first book, *The Little Disturbances of Man,* in 1959. All the material for her stories is gleaned from her surroundings in the Bronx and the people she knew there. An ardent feminist and active pacifist, Paley says she is often distracted from writing by political causes. "Art is too long and life is too short. There is a lot more to do in life than just writing," she explains.

Critics point out that Paley relies on conversation, rather than action, to establish character, and that she expertly reproduces Jewish, Black, Irish, and other dialects. Another trademark is her part serious, part comic tone, as can be seen in "Anxiety." This story, published in *Later the Same Day* in 1985, also reveals her objections to American involvement in the war in Vietnam.

MARGE PIERCY, a committed feminist, was born in Detroit in 1936, and was the first member of her family to go to university. After graduation, she worked for ten years to get her writing published. Her first six novels, each with feminist protagonists, were rejected by every publisher who read them as being too shrill. During this time she was active in the Civil Rights movement and the radical Students for a Democratic Society. Success as a writer came eventually, and she is now the author of twelve collections of poetry, including her selected poems, *Circles on the Water.* She has also published eleven novels, including *Gone to Soldiers, Summer People,* and *He, She and It,* a science-fiction novel. Her work has been translated into fourteen languages. Piercy lives with her husband in Cape Cod.

"Bite into the Onion" comes from her 1992 poetry collection, *Mars and Her Children.*

VASCO PRATOLINI is known for his realistic portrayals of Italian life. He was born in Florence in 1913, and that city is often the setting for his fiction. His stories usually portray the struggle of working-class lives with honesty and sympathy. During the Second World War, he was involved in the resistance, an experience which found its way into several of his novels. In 1957 he won the Premio Feltrenelli, an important Italian literary prize, for his whole body of work.

Pratolini is also known for his portraits of women, as in "Vanda." This story of a gentle, uncertain love, with its sudden descent into tragedy, reveals how political realities (in this case anti-Semitism) can intrude on personal lives.

RU ZHIJUAN, a Chinese writer, tells her own story: "I was born in Shanghai in 1925, and from a very early age helped my grandmother eke out a living by taking in handwork. In 1943 I taught school for six months, then followed my elder brother in joining the New Fourth Army, and became an actress with the Modern Drama Troupe of the Battle Front. My first short story was published in 1950. In 1955 I left the army and became a literary editor. In 1957 my novel *Story Before Dawn* was published, and in 1958 my short story "Lilies," which extolled the flesh-and-blood ties between the people and the army. Most of my stories since then have been about the lives of women during various different periods, and the changes in their ways of thinking and feeling."

NAWAL EL SAADAWI is a psychiatrist, feminist, novelist, and author. Born in Egypt in 1931, her outspoken support of political and sexual rights for women has resulted in her arrest on more than one occasion. Her books have been banned in Egypt and elsewhere, but they continue to be best-sellers in most Arab countries. The first of her books to be available in English was *The Hidden Face of Eve: Women in the Arab World,* a work which is part autobiography, part history, and part sociology. El Saadawi has also written several novels and numerous short stories.

About the importance of writing, El Saadawi says: "Writing to me is like breathing. I cannot live without it. Expression of one's self is an essential part of a process of knowing and fighting for liberation." In "Essay", she expresses her belief that the oppression of women is not restricted to Arab or Third World countries.

HANAN AL SHAYKH was born and educated as a Muslim in Lebanon. She worked as a journalist on a leading Arab newspaper there until the civil war forced her to move to England. She now lives in London but continues to write in Arabic. Her fiction has been widely translated into English and other languages. Two of her works of fiction are *The Story of Zahra* (1987) and *Women of Sand and Myrrh* (1989).

"The Women's Swimming Pool" gives a richly textured picture of everyday life in Lebanon, especially the contrast between rural and urban perspectives. It also offers considerable insight into the links—and the differences—among three generations of Arabic women.

ISAAC BASHEVIS SINGER was born in Poland in 1904, immigrated to the United States in 1935, and lived there until his death in 1991. Singer wrote all of his books in Yiddish, the Jewish language that originated in eastern Europe. He is regarded as one of the world's great storytellers, one particularly attuned to the oral tradition. Over fourteen volumes of his stories have been published, including novels, plays, autobiographies, and books for children. He was awarded the Nobel Prize for Literature in 1978.

Singer has said, "I never thought that my fiction—my kind of writing—had any other purpose than to be read and enjoyed by the reader." "Fire" was taken from *Gimpel the Fool and Other Stories* (1957).

ROBERTA SOSA was born in Honduras in 1930, where he has become a noted writer and cultural leader. At times his work has been banned by the Honduran government. Sosa says that the death of his father was an important turning point in his writing career: "It helped me better identify myself with the social marginality from which I come." He feels that poetry, and art in general, has an important role to play. "It's possible, I think, that a poem or a story could help civilize those who govern; that's why we need governors who read."

"The Poor" comes from *The Difficult Days*, a collection of his poems translated into English by Jim Lindsey in 1983.

GARY SOTO comes from a working-class Mexican-American background. Born in California in 1952, his childhood experiences of poverty and racial tension helped to make him a social critic. In his books of poetry and in his prose memoirs (*Living Up the Street and Small Faces*), he paints a grim portrait of the hard labour of rural life and the violence of urban life. Besides being an active writer, Soto teaches Chicano Studies and English at the University of California in Berkeley.

After the birth of his daughter, Soto's poetry seemed to take a new turn. In an interview he said: "There are a lot of mixed emotions involved in raising a kid. It's another life. It's like falling in love. *That*, for me, was a great inspiration and actually a turning point in my poetry." "Evening Walk," from his collection *Who Will Know Us?*, reflects these feelings.

MAY SWENSON has been called a "verbal magician" who "speaks for animals and birds, for astronauts and trees, for statues and cities." Born in Utah in 1919, she now lives in New York. She travels frequently, giving poetry readings and writing workshops. Much of her poetry can be enjoyed by young readers as well as adults, including the intriguing book *Poems to Solve*, in which the poems are actually solvable riddles. She has received many honours and awards.

Swenson writes that the experience of poetry is "based in a craving to get through the curtains of things as they *appear*, to things as they are, and then into the larger, wilder space of things as they *are becoming*." Perhaps this quotation offers a clue to the interpretation of "How to Be Old."

RABINDRANATH TAGORE is India's classic poet, and the winner of the Nobel Prize for Literature in 1913. He was born in Bengal in 1861. He studied law in England, then returned to India at twenty-four to manage his father's huge estate and pursue interests in writing, painting, and music. He founded a school built upon "the idea of the spiritual unity of all races" which has since become an international institute. Tagore was knighted in 1915, but he renounced the title in 1919 following the Amritsar Massacre, in which British troops suppressed an Indian demonstration. He died in 1941.

Tagore writes with ironic humour, gently criticizing both those who are too tied to tradition, and those who are too greedy for wealth and power. Claiming that the modern age is in too much of a hurry, he advises people to take the time to consider "whether life is in harmony with the intellect."

SHUNTARŌ TANIKAWA is one of Japan's most popular poets. Born in Tokyo in 1931, he was profoundly influenced by the devastation caused by the Second World War. He felt that "after the defeat, all the values that the Japanese believed in were totally destroyed." He then set about exploring Western culture. While listening to Beethoven's music, he once said, he realized that life and writing were still possible in the postwar age. Since then he has published numerous volumes of poetry, and many books for children. He has translated both *Mother Goose* and the comic strip "Peanuts" into Japanese.

"Growing Up," a poem about how we view time at different ages, reflects his interest in children.

EDLA VAN STEEN, like other Latin American writers, works in the tradition of "magic realism." While the situations in her fiction may seem absurd, the stories illuminate psychological truths. Born in Brazil in 1936, van Steen has worked in film and theatre, has directed an art gallery, and has won a number of prizes for her writing.

She says that the idea for "Mr. and Mrs. Martins" came to her "at the funeral of an architect friend, in the middle of the cemetery, as I waited for the coffin to be lowered into the grave." Her translator, Daphne Patai, was intrigued with the story's central idea of rehearsing for death. "The simple and apparently transparent writing, the banal dialogue, leave the reader at the story's end with a sense of shock—as if everyday life had slipped away while our attention was elsewhere, and all that is left is the abyss."

ALICE WALKER is an important African-American poet, novelist, short story writer, and essayist. She was born in Georgia into a family of share-croppers. While at university, she participated in civil-rights demonstrations. She has been a professor of literature and creative writing at a number of colleges, and in 1974 became a contributing editor for the feminist magazine, *Ms*. She is especially concerned about black women's struggle for self-fulfillment in an environment where both race and gender are major obstacles to be overcome. Her novel *The Color Purple*, which deals with this theme, became a popular movie in 1985.

Walker's writing, like the short and sassy "The Kiss," often reflects her own experiences, including her travels to Europe and Africa.

YEVGENY YEVTUSHENKO was one of the few voices speaking to the West from behind the Iron Curtain during the Cold War. He was born near the town of Zima, Siberia, in 1933, when it was part of the Union of Soviet Socialist Republics. He always insisted he was a loyal Soviet citizen, but he frequently took political stands for which he was censured. In 1968, for example, he wrote a letter condemning the Soviet Union's occupation of Czechoslovakia. In response, the government cancelled one of his performances. Although known chiefly as a poet, in the 1980s he also wrote a novel and made a feature film, "The Kindergarten."

Many of Yevtushenko's poems, like "Siberian Wooing," tell stories with plots drawn from his own experiences. His rediscovery of folk rhymes and deliberate use of conversational language make his verse immediately comprehensible to readers.

YU KWANG-CHUNG is a young Chinese poet now living abroad. His poetry, like that of many of his contemporaries, is Western in style, but contains a poignant rebellion of its own. Following the Cultural Revolution (1966-69), tensions grew among the youth who had been forced to abandon their education and work in the countryside. After Mao's death, Deng Xiaoping allowed them to return to the cities, but in 1979 there was another crackdown. Growing resentment finally led to a huge demonstration by students in favour of democracy in Tienanmen Square, Beijing.

"Mother, I'm Hungry" is a tribute to the protesters who were crushed by the army on June 4, 1989. An unknown number of people were killed. In the poem, the soul of a dead student begs his mother to let him rest by remembering him and keeping the struggle for freedom alive.

Countries of Origin
and Prize-Winning Authors

	AFRICA
Nigeria	The Sacrificial Egg, Chinua Achebe
	The Novelist as Teacher, Chinua Achebe
	You Walked Gently Towards Me, Ben Okri (B)
	Our Earth Will Not Die, Niyi Osundare
Uganda	The Winner, Barbara Kimenye
Zimbabwe	No Witchcraft for Sale, Doris Lessing

	ASIA
China	The River-Merchant's Wife: A Letter, Li Po
	The Long March, Mao Tse-tung
	Tienanmen Square: A Soldier's Story, Nie Jian-guo
	Lilies, Ru Zhijuan
	Mother, I'm Hungry, Yu Kwang-chung
India	A Horse and Two Goats, R.K. Narayan
	The Man Had No Useful Work, Rabindranath Tagore (N)
Japan	Immortality, Yasunari Kawabata (N)
	Swallowtails, Shiina Makoto
	Growing Up, Shuntarō Tanikawa
Pakistan	Decomposition, Zulfikar Ghose
Russia	"Everything Is Plundered . . .", Anna Akhmatova
	Siberian Wooing, Yevgeny Yevtushenko
Singapore	The Chosen One, Catherine Lim
Sri Lanka	Roots, Rienzi Crusz

	AUSTRALASIA
Australia	American Dreams, Peter Carey (B)
New Zealand	Two Sheep, Janet Frame
	At the River, Patricia Grace

(B) - Booker Prize for Literature winner
(G) - Governor General's Award winner
(N) - Nobel Prize for Literature winner

CARIBBEAN

Antigua	Girl, Jamaica Kincaid
Barbados	Dives, Edward Kamau Brathwaite
Guyana	Limbo Dancer at Immigration, John Agard
	Flowers, Dennis Craig
Trinidad	The Duel in Mercy Ward, Ian McDonald

CENTRAL AND SOUTH AMERICA

Argentina	The Meeting, Jorge Luis Borges
Brazil	Mr. and Mrs. Martins, Edla van Steen
Colombia	A Very Old Man with Enormous Wings, Gabriel García Márquez (N)
Guatemala	The Natural World, Rigoberta Menchú
Honduras	The Poor, Roberto Sosa
Peru	From a Mother, Antonio Cisneros

EUROPE

Croatia	Watching Death, Live on Cable, Slavenka Drakulíc
England	Mother, John Berger (B)
	The Vanishing Princess or The Origins of Cubism, Jenny Diski
Germany	*from* Return to Frankfurt, Marie Luise Kaschnitz
Italy	Last Comes the Raven, Italo Calvino
	Vanda, Vasco Pratolini
Northern Ireland	The Wall-Reader, Fiona Barr
	Secrets, Bernard MacLaverty
Poland	In Music, Czeslaw Milosz (N)
	Fire, Isaac Bashevis Singer (N)
Romania	A Man, Nina Cassian
Scotland	The Prisoner, William McIlvanney
Spain	The Ghost, Rafael Alberti
Sweden	The Experimental World, Pär Lagerkvist (N)

MIDDLE EAST

Egypt	Half a Day, Naguib Mahfouz
	Essay, Nawal El Saadawi
Lebanon	The Women's Swimming Pool, Hanan Al Shaykh

NORTH AMERICA

Canada	A Girl's Story, David Arnason
	Epaulettes, Margaret Atwood (G)
	O What Venerable and Reverend Creatures,
	Sharon Butala
	War, Timothy Findley (G)
	Trap Lines, Thomas King
	Obasan, Joy Kogawa
	Where the World Began, Margaret Laurence (G)
Mexico	Iguana Hunting, Hernán Lara Zavala
United States	Notes of a Native Son, James Baldwin
	Bears Discover Fire, Terry Bisson
	A Wedge of Shade, Louise Erdrich
	Deportation at Breakfast, Larry Fondation
	What's a Bum, Mom? Kathleen Rockwell Lawrence
	Anxiety, Grace Paley
	Bite into the Onion, Marge Piercy
	Evening Walk, Gary Soto
	How to Be Old, May Swenson
	The Kiss, Alice Walker

Passport to Themes

A closer look at the broad themes in the Table of Contents.

CONVERSATIONS: childhood, adolescence, parents and children
PROMISES: love, marriage, old age and death
RUMOURS: inequalities between races, sexes, rich and poor
ROOTS: cultural identity, cross-cultural encounters, relationships to nature
CLASHES: violence and war
VISIONS: meaning and miracles, experimental fiction

The following groupings are more detailed suggestions for thematic study.
As might be expected, many selections appear in more than one theme.

Children growing up

Growing Up, Shuntarō Tanikawa
Half a Day, Naguib Mahfouz
Girl, Jamaica Kincaid
Iguana Hunting, Hernán Lara Zavala
Dives, Edward Kamau Brathwaite
The Women's Swimming Pool, Hanan Al Shaykh
Where the World Began, Margaret Laurence

Between the generations

Evening Walk, Gary Soto
Anxiety, Grace Paley
O What Venerable and Reverend Creatures, Sharon Butala
Swallowtails, Shiina Makoto
Trap Lines, Thomas King
Mother, John Berger
Secrets, Bernard MacLaverty
Notes of a Native Son, James Baldwin
Obasan, Joy Kogawa
What's a Bum, Mom?, Kathleen Rockwell Lawrence
War, Timothy Findley

Love and marriage

from Return to Frankfurt, Marie Luise Kaschnitz
You Walked Gently Towards Me, Ben Okri
Vanda, Vasco Pratolini
Siberian Wooing, Yevgeny Yevtushenko
In Music, Czeslaw Milosz
A Wedge of Shade, Louise Erdrich
The River-Merchant's Wife: A Letter, Li Po
The Winner, Barbara Kimenye
The Sacrificial Egg, Chinua Achebe
Immortality, Yasunari Kawabata

Aging and dying

How to Be Old, May Swenson
Mr. and Mrs. Martins, Edla van Steen
Mother, John Berger
Secrets, Bernard MacLaverty
The Duel in Mercy Ward, Ian McDonald
At the River, Patricia Grace
Obasan, Joy Kogawa
The Chosen One, Catherine Lim
Bears Discover Fire, Terry Bisson

Inter-racial tensions

The Kiss, Alice Walker
Limbo Dancer at Immigration, John Agard
Notes of a Native Son, James Baldwin
Obasan, Joy Kogawa
Essay, Nawal El Saadawi
No Witchcraft for Sale, Doris Lessing

Inequalities

The Prisoner, William McIlvanney
The Poor, Roberto Sosa
Decomposition, Zulfikar Ghose
What's a Bum, Mom?, Kathleen Rockwell Lawrence
Dives, Edward Kamau Brathwaite
Flowers, Dennis Craig

Identity and culture

Roots, Rienzi Crusz
A Horse and Two Goats, R.K. Narayan
American Dreams, Peter Carey
The Chosen One, Catherine Lim
The Sacrificial Egg, Chinua Achebe
The Novelist as Teacher, Chinua Achebe
The Women's Swimming Pool, Hanan Al Shaykh
Where the World Began, Margaret Laurence

The natural environment

Flowers, Dennis Craig
Where the World Began, Margaret Laurence
The Natural World, Rigoberta Menchú
Our Earth Will Not Die, Niyi Osundare

Battlefronts

The Meeting, Jorge Luis Borges
The Long March, Mao Tse-tung
Lilies, Ru Zhijuan
Last Comes the Raven, Italo Calvino
The Wall-Reader, Fiona Barr
War, Timothy Findley

Reflections on war

"Everything Is Plundered . . .", Anna Akhmatova
Mother, I'm Hungry, Yu Kwang-chung
Tienanmen Square: A Soldier's Story, Nie Jian-guo
From A Mother, Antonio Cisneros
Watching Death, Live on Cable, Slavenka Drakulic
Epaulettes, Margaret Atwood
A Man, Nina Cassian

Parables of the human condition

Half a Day, Naguib Mahfouz
The Prisoner, William McIlvanney
The Meeting, Jorge Luis Borges
The Experimental World, Pär Lagerkvist
The Vanishing Princess or The Origins of Cubism, Jenny Diski
Two Sheep, Janet Frame
Fire, Isaac Bashevis Singer

Glimpses of paradise

The Man Had No Useful Work, Rabindranath Tagore
A Very Old Man with Enormous Wings, Gabriel García Márquez
Bite into the Onion, Marge Piercy
The Ghost, Rafael Alberti
Immortality, Yasunari Kawabata
Bears Discover Fire, Terry Bisson

Writers on creativity

The Novelist as Teacher, Chinua Achebe
Deportation at Breakfast, Larry Fondation
A Girl's Story, David Arnason
The Vanishing Princess or The Origins of Cubism, Jenny Diski

Credits

355